3302188901

CW00926526

To renew this book, phone 0845 1202811 or visit
our website at www.libcat.oxfordshire.gov.uk
You will need your library PIN number
(available from your library)

OXFORDSHIRE
COUNTY COUNCIL
SOCIAL & COMMUNITY SERVICES
www.oxfordshire.gov.uk

THE MARCH TO KANDAHAR

THE MARCH TO KANDAHAR

KANDAHAR

ROBERTS IN AFGHANISTAN

Rodney Atwood

Pen & Sword
MILITARY

First published in Great Britain in 2008 by
Pen & Sword Military
an imprint of
Pen & Sword Books Ltd
47 Church Street
Barnsley
South Yorkshire
S70 2AS

ISBN 978-1-84415-848-5

A CIP catalogue record for this book is
available from the British Library

Typeset in 11/13pt Palatino
by Concept, Huddersfield

Printed and bound in England by
CPI UK

For a complete list of Pen & Sword titles please contact

PEN & SWORD BOOKS LIMITED
47 Church Street, Barnsley, South Yorkshire, S70 2AS, England
e-mail: enquiries@pen-and-sword.co.uk
Website: www.pen-and-sword.co.uk

Contents

Maps

Acknowledgements

In picking a way through a tangle of conflicting accounts and views, a historian new to the late nineteenth century finds much help. A number of historians have written extensively on the late nineteenth century Victorian Army. Brian Robson wrote a comprehensive modern history of the 2nd Afghan War. He also edited a selection of Roberts's papers for the Army Records Society, and published articles on Maiwand, Kandahar and the Eden Commission established to reform the Indian Army (Roberts was a leading member). Tony Heathcote, historian of both Afghan Wars and the Indian Army of the Raj, led me to the translation of Major General Soboleff's interesting account from a Russian perspective, based largely on newspapers in India and England. Dr Jacqueline Beaumont made suggestions about Roberts and the press. Professors André Wessels and Stephen Miller gave advice about later aspects of Roberts's life. No one could venture into this field without acknowledging the work of Professors Ian Beckett and Edward Spiers, both of whom answered email questions and gave pointers based on their extensive knowledge. Professor Beckett kindly allowed me to present a paper on Roberts at a military history conference. Dr Stephen Badsey gave advice at that conference. Dr David Washbrook and Charles Allen answered questions about Lord Lytton's viceroyalty. Borrowing on the work of many, my book is also based on primary sources at the National Army Museum, Chelsea, the India Office Library at the British Library, especially the letters of Field Marshal Sir George White, those of Sir Mortimer Durand at the library of the School of Oriental and

Asian Studies, Lady Roberts's letters to the later Lord Minto at the National Library of Scotland and papers dealing with Roberts at the National Archives. The staff of these libraries have been courteous and helpful throughout, particularly at the National Army Museum, where Dr Simon Moody among others has answered innumerable questions and enabled me to lay my hands on many documents.

Lieutenant Colonel Will Townend, Luci Gosling, Garen Ewing and Szilvia Szabo were most helpful in finding illustrations and giving information about them. I formally acknowledge copyright permission for illustrations from the Royal Artillery Institute, the British Library, the Mary Evans Picture Library and the National Army Museum.

I owe a particular thanks to the two who kindly read my draft: Peter Boyden and Keith Surridge, who answered many questions, gave encouragement and made wise suggestions; and to John Schofield and Nicholas Griffin who read these pages in a different form as a larger book. These four saved me from many errors of fact and judgement, and numerous faults of style and language. The faults and errors that remain are entirely my own.

My special thanks go to Brigadier Henry Wilson, the publishers of Pen & Sword and the book's editor, Bobby Gainher; to my daughter for drawing the maps; and to my wife for her forbearance and understanding in sharing her husband's waking thoughts with a diminutive Victorian hero and a cast of thousands.

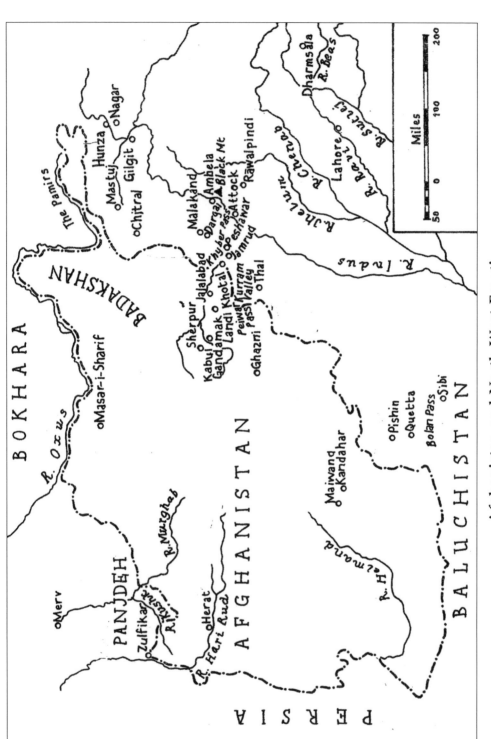

Afghanistan and North-West Frontier

Introduction:
Disaster and Triumph in Afghanistan

The news could not have been worse. The new Viceroy of India, the Marquess of Ripon, had expected something of the sort. For several days in late July 1880, he and his military advisors at Simla in the foothills of the Himalayas had watched with increasing concern and divided councils the advance of the Afghan Sirdar Ayub Khan and his soldiers towards the Anglo-Indian garrison of Kandahar. The year 1880 was the third in which the Indian Army had been at war in the harsh mountains and green valleys of Afghanistan. It was not a war of Ripon's making and he was keen to negotiate peace, settle the government of the country and withdraw. The Indian Army and British regiments deployed in Afghanistan were fully stretched. The best were stationed at Kabul and elsewhere, and only a division of less than five thousand men was at Kandahar. Their commander, Major General Primrose, and his chief brigadier, Burrows, were not thought to be men of resolution or firm action and both had occupied desk jobs before the war. Ayub Khan had marched from Herat some months before, hoping to seize the Amirship, thus making himself ruler of Afghanistan. As he neared Kandahar the local ruler or Wali, a British nominee, had led out his force, but they had gone over to Ayub. Primrose had then dispatched Burrows with over 2,000 men. Ayub was known to be in much greater strength and increasing his numbers as he advanced. Local Afghan levies were untrustworthy. Ripon, the Indian Army Commander-in-Chief,

1

Sir Frederick Haines, the Viceroy's personal military advisor, Colonel Allen Johnson, and other senior soldiers had met to deliberate. On the morning of the 22nd, Ripon had advocated sending instructions to Primrose to risk all and advance with nearly his whole force from Kandahar to reinforce Burrows, leaving only a small garrison in the citadel. The Adjutant General, Greaves, and Colonel Allen Johnson had supported him. Haines however firmly opposed the plan, as had Sir Edwin Johnson, the Military Member, as advisor to the Viceroy senior to Allen Johnson. Ripon, relatively new to India, would not override the objections of these two powerful and experienced figures. Instead, it was agreed that Haines would send a telegram to Primrose giving him full liberty to advance and attack Ayub if he considered himself strong enough. 'Government consider it of the greatest political importance that [Ayub's] force should be dispersed and prevented from passing on to Ghazni.' The vital fortress of Ghazni lay on the route to Kabul; its possession would give Ayub the strategic key. Primrose and Burrows must appreciate the importance of swift action. The men on the spot would decide.[1]

There was for a moment relief. A letter arrived about that time saying that Ayub's force was very small. Subsequent despatches showed his numbers were greater than advised, but no further uneasiness was felt. Then came the news of disaster.

On 27 July, Burrows had advanced his 2,600 men and been confronted by at least 10,000 Afghans, both regular troops and irregulars including numbers of the fanatical ghazis, who would give their lives fighting the unbelievers. The battle against overwhelming odds in intense heat lasted four hours. Vastly outnumbered, Burrows' men had also been outgunned by superior Afghan artillery. As young Indian soldiers of Jacob's Rifles and the Bombay Grenadiers huddled together under a withering artillery fire, the enemy's superior numbers lapped round their flanks. A host of ghazis made use of a sunken ravine to advance close to Burrows' brigade and then burst out with their knives and swords onto the rear of the Indians and British. The defeat was catastrophic, many of the Indian soldiers simply standing in a huddled mass and being annihilated; others, both British and Indian, breaking up into small bodies and trying to escape. One hundred men of the 66th Regiment made a gallant but forlorn stand in an orchard, the last eleven dying in a sortie. Others plagued by thirst and by villagers who came out to harass and kill the stragglers made their desperate way towards Kandahar.

'Then came the most awful part,' recorded the Reverend Alfred Cane, accompanying the force. 'Wounded men lying down & giving all up. Others getting off their ponies or camels & lying down to die. All begging for water.' Some gathered in vain round an old well which proved to be empty.[2]

At last succour came from Kandahar. On receipt of news of the defeat, Brigadier Henry Brooke led out infantry, cavalry and guns, drove off the harrying Afghans and brought the survivors safely back into the mud-walled citadel. The confusion in the citadel was intense, the feeling of defeat overwhelming and a telegram was sent to Bombay rather than Simla, as most of the defeated brigade came from Bombay, describing the defeat as 'the total annihilation of Gen. Burrows' Brigade'. It was sent on to London unedited and read by the Marquess of Hartington, the Indian Secretary, to the assembled House of Commons. The 'gloomy telegram', as Haines described it to Ripon, was reported, not just round the Empire, but all over the world.

The Duke of Cambridge, Commander-in-Chief of the British Army, Queen Victoria's cousin, wrote to Lieutenant General Warre, commanding at Bombay, that the defeat had 'filled us with grief & anxiety', wondering why so small a force had been sent with so few British troops. 'God only knows what effect it may produce all over India & in Afghanistan.' Warre was angry that a copy of the exaggerated telegram had been posted in the Poona Club and published in the Bombay newspapers. In England some editors demanded that England's 'only general', Sir Garnet Wolseley, victor of the brilliant African campaign against the bloodthirsty Ashanti, be sent out. He alone, they asserted, was certain to redeem British honour and success. Cambridge prepared to despatch British regiments.[3]

Ripon had been a radical, an anti-imperialist, opposed to the 2nd Afghan War which had led to this defeat. His appointment as Viceroy was intended by the Prime Minister, Gladstone, to get the Liberal Government out of the Afghan imbroglio in which Beaconsfieldism, the policy of Disraeli, now elevated to the Lords as Beaconsfield, had landed them. He was aware, however, that British prestige everywhere, most of all in India and Afghanistan, demanded that the defeat be avenged, and he acted resolutely. He and the soldiers on his council were equally determined that forces should be sent promptly to Kandahar, both from Quetta, the obvious route, and from Kabul.[4]

Lieutenant General Donald Stewart, commanding Anglo-Indian forces at the Afghan capital, had been negotiating with another sirdar, Abdur Rahman, a former Russian pensioner, to assume the Amirship and thus give Britain a chance to conclude the costly war on a favourable note. He agreed with Ripon that Primrose should have taken his whole force. On 31 July, he told his wife he was still uncertain whether a force, fine as it would be, composed of the pick of the troops, should be sent, although two days before he had advised Ripon he was preparing one. 'I know it would beat Ayub into a cocked hat,' he told her, 'but there are objections to sending a force away by itself through a country which is sure to be hostile, and we should rouse animosities, which would bring about further complications, and, perhaps, prevent our withdrawal from Kabul.'[5] But Stewart's second, his friend for nearly three decades, Major General Frederick Roberts,* shared Ripon's certainty rather than Stewart's doubts. The day before, 30 July, he had sent a 'personal and secret' telegram to the Adjutant General, strongly recommending that a force be sent to Kandahar. Rather ahead of his friend, Roberts told Greaves that 'Stewart has organized a very complete one ... He proposes sending me in command.' The 2nd Afghan War had seemed to the troops involved endless and difficult, and Indian soldiers were longing to be home, but Roberts said he would answer for the loyalty and good feeling of the men, promising to tell them that they would go straight back home as soon as Ayub Khan had been beaten.

In England Ripon had been an outspoken critic of Roberts's conduct of affairs at Kabul at the end of the previous year, 1879, but he knew a fighting general when he saw one. On 31 July he called his chief military advisors to a conference at Simla, and the following day Haines confirmed arrangements in a telegram: Roberts was to command a force of 10,000 men to march from Kabul to Kandahar. 'Than this no better arrangement can be made,' wrote Haines. Stewart had unselfishly but willingly stood

* Local rank of Lieutenant General.

4

down, allowing his good friend Roberts the opportunity to retrieve British fortunes and win life-long fame.[6]

That indeed was to be the result. The march was so famous that it made Roberts a national hero almost overnight, the rival of Sir Garnet Wolseley as late Victorian Britain's leading general, 'our only t'other general', as *Punch* was to dub him. A special medal, the Kandahar Star, was awarded to those who took part in the march, including Roberts's grey charger, Vonolel, the only horse of thousands of animals which accompanied the march so honoured. Such was the enduring fame of the march that it was debated in memoirs and in *The Times* at least as late as 1929. Maud Diver, novelist, born in India, a soldier's daughter, an officer's wife, dedicated her *Kabul to Kandahar* published in 1935 'To the abiding memory of Field-Marshal Earl Roberts of Kandahar'. In 1944, in the midst of a much greater war, a brief book on the British Army reiterated the fame of Roberts and Kabul to Kandahar. When Britain sent troops to Afghanistan in alliance with the United States in 2001, Prime Minister Tony Blair was seen boarding an aircraft for Kabul with Roberts's auto-biography *Forty-One Years in India* under his arm, and he told the *Daily Telegraph* he was much enjoying the book. Roberts was remembered at the start of the twenty-first century, although admittedly faintly, as 'the only general to have emerged with flying colours from an expedition into Afghanistan in the last 200 years'.[7]

Ripon, who had taken sole responsibility for the despatch of Roberts, despite fears that cutting the 10,000 men adrift of a firm base would lead to disaster, proudly wrote to Roberts after the victory:

> In my last letter to you I ventured in anticipation to say that your march would be famous in military history. It has more than fulfilled my expectations, and it seems to me to be one of the most remarkable exploits of the kind upon record. The criticisms upon the despatch of your force from Kabul have been noisy and confident, both in India and in England, but you have utterly refuted them and have confounded the prophets of evil.

Nothing is as straightforward as it seems. Roberts was a controversial figure at the time, like his rival Wolseley and that most famous of desert generals, Bernard Montgomery, a true media star. Both before and after Kandahar he was to be embroiled in all the major questions of the Indian Army – 'forward' school on the North-West Frontier versus 'masterly inactivity', recruitment of the martial races, relations with the press, accelerated promotion for his young protégés, a favouritism dubbed by his enemies 'Bobs and Jobs', and excessive brutality in dealing with the Afghans. Had he not redeemed his reputation by a brilliant march and victory, he would have ended the 2nd Afghan War under a cloud, perhaps his career in abeyance. If so, the history of the Indian Army of the late nineteenth century would have been completely different. Personal rivalries were strong among senior British officers, and when Roberts set a cracking pace on his march to Kandahar there were sarcastic remarks about a 'race for the peerage'. His chief rival to redeem the situation, Major General Phayre of the Bombay Army, was widely mistrusted at Simla, otherwise he, not Primrose might have commanded at Kandahar and the whole story would have been different.[8]

It was Roberts's misfortune to be intensely disliked by the historian of the 2nd Afghan War, Colonel Henry Hanna, partly because Roberts refused to promote him, partly because they were on opposite sides in the debate on policy on the North-West Frontier, and partly perhaps because he saw Roberts at his worst at Kabul in 1879, trying to untangle the Gordian knot of Afghan politics, somewhat ineptly it must be admitted. One of Roberts's leading subordinates, his Chief of Staff in 1879, brigade commander in 1880, fellow advocate of the 'forward school', Charles Metcalfe MacGregor, wrote a personal diary savagely critical of Roberts (and just about everybody else), and in 1985 the hitherto suppressed parts of this were published in a learned, but in my view misleading, edition by an American professor. Other modern professional historians, increasingly aware of the role of the press in forming Victorians' views of their soldier heroes, have emphasized Roberts's press contacts at the expense of his military exploits, thus endeavouring to cut down to size a man whose deeds, like Wolseley's, were exaggerated by admirers, press and public in late Victorian England and were hymned by the Empire's greatest poet, Rudyard Kipling.[9]

This is not an account of the now mostly forgotten 2nd Afghan War, but of the part in it played by the future Field Marshal Earl Roberts. It is always difficult to catch the drama and excitement of events which have passed from popular memory, or to judge the importance of historical characters whose ideas and beliefs are so unlike our own, and in many cases antipathetic to them. Roberts was an unabashed imperialist who believed, with Curzon, that British greatness depended on holding the Indian Empire. He accepted the racial and class prejudices of his age, and concealed the mixed origins of his family, which today would carry no stigma. He married a forceful woman whose role in furthering his career had to be concealed at a time when women's aspirations were frustrated or sublimated into acceptable channels; today she would be a Virago heroine. This book is based largely on research for a biography of Roberts which I hope one day to publish. His fame firstly rested on the special achievement of Kabul to Kandahar. Subsequently he wielded great influence as a famous general, as an imperial symbol and as a man who quickly came to understand the importance of the press. This influence was not sufficient for him to convert a Liberal Government and a British people to accept compulsory military service in the years before 1914, but the outbreak of the First World War was held by Roberts's many admirers to vindicate his position.

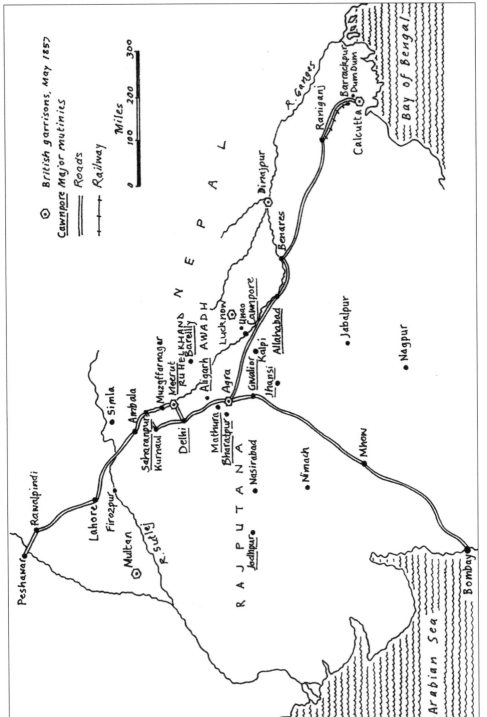

The Mutiny

Chapter 1

Background:
Afghanistan and Roberts

We have men, and we have rocks in plenty, but we have nothing else.

Amir Dost Mohammed of Kabul

The country ... is a very wild one ... the houses are towers built as little Fortifications ... The people are robbers and cut-throats, and are only kept in awe by their great fear of our reprisals.

Major George White

There was something of immense strength, talent and resolution in his whole frame and manner, and a power of ruling men on high occasions which no one could escape noticing. His imperial air never left him.

Description of Brigadier John Nicholson

You have no idea what nasty fighting we have. No quarter is given on either side. We bayonet all their wounded, and they cut up ours with their tulwars [swords].

Lieutenant Thomas Cadell writing from Delhi, 1857

It was Ahmed Shah who had welded Afghanistan out of a host of petty states, some of them the nominal vassals of the Great Mogul in Delhi, others owning a vague allegiance to the Shah of Persia. A soldier of genius, he styled himself 'Durr-i-Durran', the pearl of the age, and renamed his tribe the Durani. Ahmed's

9

boundaries ranged beyond those of modern Afghanistan, over Scinde, Baluchistan, Kashmir and Peshawar. To north and east his empire was bounded by immense mountain ranges, to south and west by vast sandy deserts, a country for the most part wild and forbidding, of rock-strewn passes and lonely valleys. Savage was the landscape and fierce could be the people, 'a nation of tigers' when invaded, which was often. For a time Ahmed Shah's genius held together his kingdom and an army which was based on a feudal levy, the Duranis, Ahmed Shah's own tribe, for example, contributing a horseman for each parcel of land requiring a single plough. The tribal system was strong, each one led by a sirdar, equivalent to a European duke or count. The support of the sirdars was vital to a successful Amir. A weak one could fall to their intrigue and rivalry.

In 1773 Ahmed Shah died. His son Timur who succeeded had a famous name but lacked his father's genius, and outlying provinces seethed with revolt. Scinde was lost. When he died he left behind twenty-three sons, who entered with ferocious zest upon a struggle for the succession. A period of intrigue and struggle followed. Eventually Dost Mohammed emerged as ruler over a much-reduced kingdom; his brothers had Kandahar, the outer territories were independent, and the Sikhs held Peshawar and Kashmir. His main rival, Shah Sujah, went into exile under British protection in India.

Afghanistan occupied an unenviable position between rival great powers: Persia to the east, Ranjit Singh and the Sikhs in the Punjab to the south, the British successors of the Moguls in Delhi and Russia to the north. To the British the Russians seemed an ever-growing threat as they advanced eastward. The Indian government endeavoured to prevent a possible war between Dost Mohammed and Ranjit Singh, leader of the Sikhs, for Peshawar. Russia, meanwhile, took advantage of the tense situation to fish in troubled waters. At the very end of 1837, Captain Vitkievitch, a young Cossack officer from the staff of the Governor of Orenburg, arrived in Kabul with messages of goodwill from the Tsar to Dost Mohammed. In spring 1838, Shah Mohammed of Persia, at the urgings of Count Ivan Simonich, laid siege to Herat, one of the keys to western Afghanistan. He had the assistance of a Polish officer and a battalion of Russian deserters, but an attempt to storm the city walls on 24 June was badly mauled. British diplomatic pressure caused the Tsar's government to repudiate Simonich and recall Vitkievitch to St Petersburg. By then, however, the Governor-General of India, Lord Auckland, had taken a fateful step. He launched the Army of the Indus of 9,500 men with a vast baggage train and 38,000 camp followers to restore British influence by deposing Dost Mohammed and replacing him with Shah Sujah as Amir, which led to the 1st Afghan War of 1838–1842.

After initial success and the occupation of Kabul, a series of incredible blunders by the British commander Elphinstone and the political agent Macnaghten undid all that had been achieved. Macnaghten was murdered at a conference with the Afghans and on 2 January 1842, Elphinstone signed a treaty of evacuation. The Anglo-Indian army attempted to return to India through the snowy passes to Jalalabad; everywhere Afghans lay in ambush and every hut poured forth its inhabitants to slay and plunder; at Gandamak the last remnant of the 44th Regiment made its final stand, Captain Souter wrapping the regimental standard round his waist; the bones of those killed remained a grisly reminder of Afghan prowess. A week after the army left Kabul the sole survivor, Dr Brydon, arrived on a sorely wounded pony, narrowly escaping the knives and treachery which had claimed nearly all the remainder; a handful of prisoners remained in Afghan captivity. The British appearance of invincibility was destroyed. Auckland resigned, and his martial successor as Governor-General, Ellenborough, sent invading columns to avenge the defeat, destroying villages, slaughtering stock, burning crops, razing Ghazni to the ground, freeing the few prisoners and demolishing the bazaar at Kabul. The Afghans remembered the British invasion with deep hostility. It was an inauspicious warning in the Great Game, the struggle between Britain and Russia to secure dominance in central Asia. Shah Sujah, unable to sustain his rule without British support, was murdered by a nephew in April 1842 and Dost Mohammed returned. He reasserted his authority, ruling until 1863, but always having to deal with potential rivals. At the age of eighty he had just recovered the city of Herat from one of these, when he died. His ablest son, Sher Ali, succeeded, but three brothers rose successively in revolt and threw the country into disorder. By 1868 Sher Ali had secured his rule and recognition by the Indian government.

By this time, too, the Russian advance into Asia had been revived. In 1844, Russia had agreed with Britain that the central Asian Khanates would be a neutral zone between the two empires, enabling Britain to reach out diplomatically to Dost Mohammed. Russia's ambitions lay south-west towards Constantinople and the Mediterranean, but the Crimean War checked that advance. At the same time the understanding over the Khanates was broken when Russia began her Asian advance again; the Muslim princedoms, poor and depopulated, were too weak to resist, and in 1868 Bokhara became Russia's subordinate and ally. Further Russian strides in the late 1860s and 1870s would lead again to British fears of Russian encroachment and intervention in Afghanistan.

Despite the defeat of the 1st Afghan War, British India continued to expand. The conquest of Sind to the north-west in 1843 and the annexation of the Punjab in 1849 after two fierce wars with the Sikhs added 80,000 square miles to Britain's dominions and advanced their borders to the mountains of Afghanistan and Kashmir.[1]

Expansion was paralleled by reform, carried out in a high-handed and autocratic manner. After 1818, the old policy of allowing Indian ways to continue was changed under the influence of Radicals and Evangelicals to one of westernization. Bentinck, Governor-General from 1828 to 1835, introduced Western learning and education in the English language, English replacing Persian as the official state language and in the higher law courts and Western medicine in the teaching of the Calcutta Medical College; the law was codified; *sati*, the burning of widows on the funeral pyres of their husbands, and thuggee, ritual murder and robbery in the name of the goddess Kali, were suppressed; missionaries were encouraged to proselytize.

Dalhousie, most ambitious, energetic and westernizing of British Governors-General, ruled India from 1848 to 1856, believing profoundly in Western moral superiority. He reformed many aspects of Indian life, as he saw it, for the good of the people he governed. In the Punjab, administered by the young men of the famous Punjab school under the direction of John and Henry Lawrence, roads, bridges, schools and courthouses sprang up. In time, irrigation made it prosperous. Under the controversial policy of 'lapse', Indian princedoms which lacked a male heir were annexed. So too were those like the great Muslim state of Oudh, allegedly corrupt and ill governed. Dalhousie told the aged Mogul Emperor Bahadur Shah that his title would lapse at his death. The continued introduction of Western education and the preaching of Christian ministers seemed to attack Hindu orthodoxy. The arrogance and certainty of the British and the activities of the evangelical missionaries aroused Indian fears that their way of life would be destroyed or remade in a Western image. White officers and bureaucrats segregated themselves from their former social equals among the Indians.

Frederick Roberts, future hero of the 2nd Afghan War, arrived in 1852 to a land in which Western innovations threatened traditional ways, or brought progress, depending upon one's viewpoint. Dalhousie introduced the civil engineer to India – military engineers had already been present – created a Public Works Department; introduced the telegraph speeding communications, some 4,000 miles of telegraph lines being built; and completed the Grand Trunk Road from Calcutta to Peshawar. But his greatest innovation was the railway. Railways would bring famine relief, develop trade and profitable crops, and improve the condition of the people. In April 1853, the first train of fourteen carriages with 400 guests set off on the Great Indian Peninsula Railway from Bombay to loud applause and a field-gun salute. In a society as complex and traditional as India, these striking changes spread dismay and fear.[2]

Roberts's birth and family background placed him firmly in early nineteenth-century British India. He was born at Cawnpore, on 30 September 1832, the son of General Abraham Roberts, a long-serving officer of the East India Company who came from an established family of Huguenot descent in County Waterford, Ireland. Between them, Abraham Roberts and his son Frederick served nearly a century in the armies of India, from 1805 to 1893. Abraham Roberts was not wealthy, although he enjoyed a wide range of contacts in the Indian Army. The difference between father and son illustrates how British attitudes changed in India. Abraham Roberts's first three children were all born to an Indian woman, either wife or mistress. William became a colonel in the army of the native ruler of Oudh. His brother John, a devout Muslim known as Chote Sahib, manufactured gun-carriages there. Eleven years after William's birth Abraham Roberts married

Frances Isabella Ricketts. She died after seven years of marriage, and Frederick Roberts's mother was Abraham's second English wife, Isabella, widow of Major Hamilton Maxwell. According to Geoffrey Moorhouse, Isabella's mother was a Rajput. There were thus mixed relations on both sides, not unusual for those days. Roberts said nothing of these later in his autobiography – in race-obsessed late Victorian India, being dubbed a Eurasian could damn a man's career. Isabella Roberts had two children from her first marriage. Frederick Roberts was the eldest child of the new marriage, with two others rapidly following. In contrast to his father, Frederick was to be married to one woman, an archetypal memsahib, for fifty-five years.[3]

Isabella Roberts and her children were settled in 1834 into a modest establishment at Clifton in Bristol while her husband fought on the frontiers of British India and narrowly avoided the disasters of the 1st Afghan War. Abraham served on the Quartermaster General's staff and then commanded the Bengal European Regiment in the East India Company's army. He saw much action, and his greatest feat was to lead his brigade in the storming of Ghazni on 23 July 1839. Frederick was nearly seven at the time. Many years later he told his own family of the children crowding round their mother to hear father's letters read, and of how stories of Afghans and fighting were woven into his early memories. Throughout his life close family was a constant theme. Life for young children born in India in the nineteenth century was harsh, Victorian families in India knew separation and early death; Roberts himself lost brothers and sisters in infancy, and three of his six children. There is no reason to doubt the genuine affection of the young Frederick for his mother and father. He was small and delicate, nearly died from an attack of brain fever (presumably meningitis), and although he survived, the illness deprived him of the sight of his right eye. He was never more than 5' 4" and would have failed a physical examination for today's army. His mother was determined to provide the best education, sending him to a small school at Hampton and then at the age of thirteen to Eton. His father knew the low pay and uncertain prospects of an army career, and wrote, 'If Freddy is clever I hope he will not think of the army.' His mother wanted him to go to Oxford or Cambridge and enter the Church. Roberts by contrast wrote later: 'I had quite made up my mind to be a soldier, I had never thought of any other profession.' He left Eton after a year and was sent to Sandhurst at the age of fourteen, coming second in the entrance examination. Cost was to change things and his father decided he must enter, not the Queen's Army, but that of the East India Company. The course for East India Company cadets at Addiscombe was briefer and cheaper than that at Sandhurst, officers in the Company's army could live off their pay and a commission in the Indian service would allow young Fred to be self-supporting within a year. In a dutiful letter to his father of October 1848, he admitted the disadvantages of a soldier's career, but told his father that he would not like the Church or Law. He finished respectfully: 'If you and Mamma wish me to go to Addiscombe, I will go there willingly, and after all the advantages you have given me by the best education I should be ashamed of myself were I not to get the Engineers.'[4]

Roberts left Sandhurst for Stoton's Preparatory Military Academy at Wimbledon, and then, once a space was available, on 1 February 1850, he entered Addiscombe near Croydon, the East India Company's academy. After two years of a Spartan regime he passed out ninth of a class of forty, with marks insufficient to gain a place as an engineer, but good enough to be a gunner, received £50 and a gold watch from his proud father, and was commissioned on 12 December 1851 in the Bengal Artillery. He was poor, ambitious, affected a dapper appearance and loathed cats; his reports were good, but not outstanding. He embarked at Southampton for Calcutta in February 1852. As he later noted, in those days leave could only be taken by a young officer after ten years spent in India. 'Small wonder, then, that I felt that I were bidding England farewell for ever.' Of the forty young men commissioned from Addiscombe, only a handful survived fever and battle to the age of thirty.[5]

He landed in April 1852, and after four months of unspeakably dull service at Dum Dum, persuaded his father to take him as an ADC and battery officer at Peshawar on the North-West Frontier. Despite the beginning of transformation wrought by Dalhousie, the journey to Peshawar was long and slow, by barge, by dak-tonga, a horse-drawn mail vehicle, and finally in a palanquin. The three months it took would be reduced to a couple of days by the building of the railways.

In Peshawar he held a privileged position as ADC to his father who commanded a division, but entered into garrison life and became popular as a vigorous rider and sportsman. Throughout his life he remained an outstanding horseman. After two years' service, he was accepted into the elite Bengal Horse Artillery, whose jacket was the coveted prize of many young officers. On duty with the Peshawar Mountain Train raised in 1853 he saw action on the North-West Frontier between Peshawar and Kohat against border tribes in three successive campaigns, in 1854 and twice in 1855. Roberts served thirteen months as a lieutenant in the Mountain Train, and the introduction to the North-West Frontier was the beginning of a long and adventurous association. On the Frontier infantry adopted loose, flexible formations and took the inconspicuous khaki for their dress; mountain guns broken down into small loads could be carried by pack mules. Frontier troops enjoyed greater mobility, dispensing with cumbersome supply trains, and camps were fortified against snipers.[6]

Equally important was the offer from the Quartermaster General, Colonel Becher, an Anglo-Irishman, to serve as his deputy. To secure the position he had to learn Hindustani. Roberts always attributed his rapid rise in the Army to his position in the Quartermaster General's Department. The QMG's department did not deal only with boots and socks in India, but was the operational staff of the East India Company's army.[7] At the start of 1857 Roberts was at Peshawar for the colourful visit of the Afghan Amir, Dost Mahomed, to sign a treaty of friendship between Afghanistan and British India.

The year 1857 was a fateful one for both Roberts and British India, being the year of the sepoy mutiny. British power rested on the loyalty of their Indian soldiers – sepoys (foot soldiers) and sowars (cavalry troopers) – trained and equipped as Europeans. Of the army of 278,000 which held India, all but 45,500 were Indians. The westernizing of Governors-General like Bentinck and Dalhousie, the suppression of traditional customs, the arrogance and certainty of the British aroused Indian fears that their way of life was threatened. When Dalhousie's successor Canning arrived in 1856, rumours abounded among sepoy battalions that he had been sent by Queen Victoria to convert all her Indian subjects to Christianity. The sepoys of the Bengal army were more susceptible to such stories than those on the frontier, whose officers lived alongside their men and endured a Spartan, active life. Bengal officers were too often aloof and treated their men, including native officers, with contempt. The high-caste Brahmin sepoys were sensitive to any threat to distinctions of caste, diet and religion. The immediate cause of the revolt was the adoption of the new Lee-Enfield rifle: its paper cartridge, ripped open with the teeth before loading, was rumoured to be greased with animal fat, both from cows, sacred to Hindus, and swine, anathema to Muslims. The high-caste sepoys were convinced they would be defiled. The authorities were caught by surprise with British forces, denuded for the recent Crimean War, outnumbered eight to one. In May 1857, clumsy attempts to introduce the new rounds at Meerut, a garrison in northern India between the Ganges and the Jumna near the Grand Trunk Road, lit the touchpaper of revolt. On 9 May, Colonel Carmichael-Smyth, the tactless and short-tempered commander of the 3rd Bengal Light Cavalry, held a punishment parade for eighty-five of his sowars before the entire garrison. They had refused an order to take the cartridges. The men's sentences to ten years' imprisonment with hard labour were read out, and iron fetters were hammered onto their feet. The evening of the next day, a Sunday, as some Englishmen and their wives were preparing to attend Evensong, mutiny broke out among the native regiments and the badmashes ('bad hats') of the bazaar. Scenes of arson, looting and murder followed, among the victims being women and children. The gaols were broken open and prisoners released, including the eighty-five whose fetters were knocked off. The mutineers left Meerut during the dark hours of that night and made their way to the old Mogul capital, Delhi. A feeble attempt to pursue them was unsuccessful. At Delhi the same scenes of arson, murder and looting occurred. By evening the British survivors had fled and the mutineers had secured the Mogul Emperor, Bahadur Shah II, aged eighty-two, who was powerless but a figurehead of resistance.[8]

Roberts was still serving at Peshawar in the Punjab when news of the outbreak reached them; the spread of insurrection was aided by the incompetence of senior British officers and officials. Outside the Punjab, where the best men were in charge, he told his family, India was at the mercy of 'idiot after idiot', the government at Calcutta were 'quite imbecile', some of the officers were 'perfect children – quite unable to take care of themselves'. He wrote: 'Oh, my dear Mother, you would not believe Englishmen could ever have been guilty of such imbecility as has almost inevitably been displayed during this crisis ... We have a most dilatory, undecided Commander-in-Chief.' This was Anson, who moved slowly to gather men and munitions, but others such as General Hewitt at Meerut – 'a dreadful old fool, a sad stumbling block', in the words of Brigadier Archdale Wilson – were equally bad. Only 'the most strenuous measures and decided exertions will save India now,' thought Roberts.[9]

The early stages of the Mutiny impressed on Roberts the need for quick and decisive action, as taken by those in command at Peshawar in contrast to indecision and slowness elsewhere. Other than his father, the first man to influence Roberts profoundly in his pre-Afghan career was the redoubtable Deputy Commissioner of Peshawar, Lieutenant Colonel John Nicholson. Nicholson was a legend on the North-West Frontier for marches of extraordinary speed and endurance, and feats of incredible boldness. They began just before the 2nd Sikh War in the spring of 1848: although laid low with fever, he rose from his sick bed and led a force of mounted and unmounted irregulars on an all-night ride to seize Attock Fort on the Indus from superior forces. By sheer bluff, by the authority of his voice and by wrenching the musket from the hands of a sentry who was about to resist, he mastered the entire fort without a shot being fired. The Punjab, British India's new province, was administered by the brothers Sir Henry and Sir John Lawrence, and the former's band of young men, later celebrated by Kipling, among them Nicholson. Roberts wrote years later: 'Nicholson impressed me more profoundly than any man I had ever met before or have ever met since. I have never seen anyone like him. He was the beau-ideal of a soldier and gentleman.' In early letters he referred to him as 'about the best man in India'.

Roberts's view must be tempered, however: Nicholson was a ruthless and determined soldier who readily dealt with his foes. He had been captured in the 1st Afghan War and seen the Afghans ignore the promise to treat their prisoners honourably by assaulting the Hindu sepoys with him and hacking to death all those Hindus – but not the English captives – who refused to convert to Islam on the spot. Thus he especially loathed Afghans

18

as 'the most vicious and bloodthirsty race in existence, who fight merely for the love of bloodshed and plunder'. In a withdrawal in the closing stages of the 1st Afghan War, riding through the Khyber Pass, he had come across the body of his brother Alexander, an officer serving with the British rearguard, killed in an Afghan ambush in a rocky defile at Ali Masjid – stripped, hacked to pieces, and his genitalia stuffed into his mouth. Did Nicholson tell Roberts the story? He certainly impressed him with many of his views, and the British Army of Retribution in which Nicholson served had, in the autumn of 1842, more than evened the score for the destruction of the Anglo-Indian army in the retreat from Kabul. In villages, no man above the age of fourteen was spared, the Afghan capital looted, the bazaar burnt amidst dreadful scenes of plunder.[10]

When news of the revolt at Meerut, Delhi and elsewhere reached Peshawar, Nicholson and the Commissioner, Sir Herbert Edwardes, said that the only chance of keeping the Punjab and the frontier quiet lay in trusting the chiefs and the people, and in endeavouring to induce them to side with the British, out-numbered by sepoys four to one. Six days which Roberts spent at Rawalpindi later in May 1857, in the Chief Commissioner's office, drafting or copying confidential letters and telegrams, made him aware of the magnitude of the crisis through which they were passing. Determined measures by Edwardes and Nicholson were equal to it. At Peshawar four native regiments were forcibly disarmed. The Subadar-Major of the 51st Bengal Native Infantry, whose letters called on the men of another regiment to join him in mutiny, had been intercepted by Nicholson's police, was found guilty by a brief drumhead court martial, marched in front of each regiment on parade and hanged before the entire garrison. Until then, there had been very few recruits to the British from the men of the Punjab, whom Nicholson hoped would join them. By the time the parade was over, wrote Commissioner Edwardes, 'the air was cleared, as if by the thunderstorm. We breathed freely again ... Hundreds of Khans and Urbabs [landowners] who stood aloof the day before, appeared as thick as flies and were profuse in offers of service.'[11]

Among the decisions taken by a speedy conference at Peshawar was one to form a 'Movable Column', which Roberts accompanied

19

as a staff officer. Further measures included the blowing of two sepoys of the 35th Native Infantry from the mouths of cannon before the eyes of their comrades following court martial, a measure commonly used by the Moguls. It was, wrote Roberts, the 'death that seems to have the most effect ... It is rather a horrible sight, but in these times we cannot be particular. Drumhead courts martial are the order of the day in every station, and had they begun this regime a little earlier, one half of the destruction and mutiny would have been saved.' On 20 June, Nicholson joined the Movable Column to take command, accompanied by a 'motley crew' of frontier horsemen, following their leader without pay, but from personal devotion. Among them, Nicholson's young orderly or frontier squire, Muhammed Hayat Khan, was intensely loyal to his chief, who had been a friend of his father, and was later to accompany Roberts to Kabul in fateful circumstances. On the road between Jullundur and Phillour Nicholson ordered the British 52nd Regiment and artillery to press on to a place selected by him and Roberts at an earlier reconnaissance. The guns were unlimbered and made ready. As the 35th and 33rd Bengal Native Infantry approached, they were successively covered by the gunners and their weapons taken. The disarming complete, an old Sikh colonel watching from the side rose to his feet and remarked that Nicholson had drawn the fangs of fifteen hundred serpents.[12]

British hold on the Punjab was mirrored elsewhere. The south gave little trouble; many native princes were loyal. In Sind 'the people remembered with gratitude how they were rescued by the British government from the grinding tyranny of the Amirs.'[13] The revolt covered about a sixth of India and about a tenth of the population. In this area military mutiny was complemented by civil revolt and for a time the British lost control. The Mutiny in the Ganges plain resolved itself into the British siege of the capital Delhi and sepoy sieges of Cawnpore and Lucknow, and British attempts to relieve these garrisons. In late June, Roberts joined the staff of the force on Delhi ridge, and during the last stage of the siege did double duty as staff and battery officer. The outnumbered British with their Indian, Sikh and Gurkha allies were tested to the utmost. Roughly a third died lingering and painful deaths from illness or wounds. Intense heat and scorching sun without a vestige of shade tested the besiegers, assailed by the numerous enemy sallies from Delhi's Kabul Gate barely half a mile distant, using the cover of a tangled mass of bazaars and garden walls. Roberts had several narrow escapes, culminating in a wound which would have been fatal had the round not struck an ammunition pouch which had twisted round accidentally and protected the base of his spine. He wrote home: 'Am I not a lucky fellow, my own Mother, and has not God been merciful to me, I can never be sufficiently thankful.'[14]

He commanded a section of two guns in the bombardment of Delhi's defences, preparatory for an assault by five columns, planned by Nicholson. At dawn on 14 September 1857, the attackers hurled themselves at the breaches in the walls, the first column led by Nicholson. Roberts was a spectator as the columns penetrated the outer defences and hoisted British colours on the Kabul Gate. In the city the assault columns were brought to a halt by vicious street fighting. Roberts, sent to investigate the truth of a report that Nicholson had been wounded, found his hero abandoned by bearers in a doolie, a two-wheeled cart for wounded, stricken by a chest wound. Nicholson was lying inside the doolie 'with death all over his face', but he gave no sign of the agony he was suffering. Roberts said he hoped that he was not seriously wounded. Came the reply, 'I am dying; there is no chance for me.' The sight was almost too much for the young Roberts. To lose Nicholson, he later wrote, seemed at that moment to lose everything. With difficulty he collected a party and ordered them to take his hero direct to the field hospital. That was the last he saw of him. On 16 September, Roberts wrote to his mother: 'General Nicholson is, I am afraid, mortally wounded. He led his Column like no other man could, and in him we lose our best Officer.'[15]

By the time Nicholson died on 23 September, Delhi had been taken, Roberts, Lieutenant Arthur Lang and a party of fifty capturing the Burn Bastion on the 19th. The confused street fighting at Delhi was a memory that forever prejudiced Roberts against fighting in cities. Delhi had to be recaptured street by street, but its fall was a turning point, a tremendous blow to the mutineers' morale, beaten by a force scarcely one-third their strength. Nicholson was buried on 24 September in a new cemetery between the Kashmir Gate and the Ridge, mourned by the men of the Delhi Field Force.[16]

Roberts was not present. He was attached as DAQMG (Deputy Assistant Quartermaster General) to the force of 2,800 men detailed for the relief of Cawnpore. 'Our way from the Lahore Gate by the Chandi Chauk led through a veritable city of the dead,' he wrote. 'Not a sound to be heard but the falling of our own footsteps; not a living creature to be seen. Dead bodies were strewn in all directions.' The desolate city was littered with the debris of war, among them a portmanteau with the name 'Miss Jennings' on it, 'an extremely pretty girl,' wrote Roberts to his mother, '... murdered coming out of church on the 11 May.' The scenes remained with Roberts all his life. Both sides in the Mutiny behaved mercilessly: the ambush and killing of most of the Cawnpore garrison who had surrendered under terms, and the subsequent slaughter of women and children on the approach of a relief column, provoked an explosion of anguished rage among the hardened soldiers and incited the avenging British to deeds of cruel retribution. Cawnpore remained a potent symbol in British Indian memories.

Sir Henry Havelock's small force had already marched to relieve Lucknow, penetrated to the Residency, but then were besieged there with the original garrison. Sir Colin Campbell, the new Commander-in-Chief, took charge of a stronger force for Lucknow's relief on 9 November 1857, with Roberts serving on his staff. The heroic resistance of the garrison in a siege lasting from 30 June to 22 November exercised a mystique in British India equal to the massacre of Cawnpore. The 65-year old veteran Campbell coaxed the best from his men, especially the Scots of the Highland Regiments who vied with Sikhs, Punjabis and Pathans to be first in action. Approaching Lucknow Roberts led the column part of the way, was frequently in action, detached for dangerous missions, fired upon and was in hand-to-hand conflict. He was fortunate to survive in the lottery of death. Corporal William Forbes-Mitchell of the 93rd (Sutherland) Highlanders recorded how two companies halted in a field of carrots before advancing into a park swarming with deer and enemy. When Roberts, who had been associated with the 93rd in several skirmishes and was familiarly known to the Highlanders as 'Plucky wee Bobs', galloped to the front to reconnoitre, an enemy masked battery opened fire from behind the Dilkusha Palace. One shot struck Roberts's charger just behind him, cutting the horse in two, both horse and rider falling in a confused heap. Roberts, unwounded, got clear of his mount, struggled to his feet amidst the rousing cheers of the 93rd, found another horse and was soon in action again, bringing forward artillery. The shot that had killed his horse ricocheted at almost a right angle and took off the top of the skull of a young Highlander, Kenneth Mackenzie, killing him instantly. Moments before Mackenzie had been eating tasty carrots with his colour sergeant, whom he had begged to write to his mother if anything happened to him. 'Poor lad! How can I tell his poor mother?' the distraught Colour Sergeant asked Forbes-Mitchell. 'He was her favourite laddie.'[17]

At the storming of the Sikandarbagh, a low-walled enclosure of great strength with loopholes for defence, the garrison of 2,000 fought to the death, leaving bodies in piles, dead and dying inextricably tangled. Campbell then made an appeal to the 93rd, his favourite regiment, for a final effort. The last advance captured the Shah Najaf Mosque, a great white building whose dome, surrounded by thick jungle, stood out half a mile away, heavily garrisoned by desperate men. After its capture, Roberts lay down to sleep after almost sixty hours in the saddle. The following morning, 17 November, he hoisted regimental colours to show the Residency how close stood relief. As Campbell's men continued to advance, the commanders of the besieged rushed out to meet them. Campbell with Roberts and another subaltern, Henry Norman, later a distinguished field marshal, went forward through a breach to meet them. At the same time another fire-eating young officer, Captain Garnet Wolseley of the 90th, led his company in an attack on the Moti Mahal, a palace surrounded by orange and lemon trees and a high brick wall. In his thirst for glory he had exceeded orders, enraging Campbell momentarily, but the success of the relief march restored his good humour. On 19 November, he withdrew the women and children from the city, the guns and stores over the next three days, and on 22nd-23rd the garrison.

Campbell next turned his force towards Cawnpore where General Windham, who had been left in the city by Campbell, had been forced to withdraw by rebel forces. On 6 December, Campbell's attack, surprising the enemy, routed them. Cavalry and horse artillery, Roberts with them, pursued them for 14 miles. 'The sepoys scattered over the country, throwing away their arms

23

and divesting themselves of their uniforms,' he wrote. 'Nineteen guns, some of them of large calibre, were left in our hands.'[18] Next, Campbell's column marched towards Fatehgarh, northwest of Cawnpore and Lucknow, scene of an infamous massacre of Christians in July 1857. The capture of Fatehgarh would open communications between the Punjab and Bengal. Roberts was attached to the cavalry force under Brigadier Sir James Hope Grant, and with them he won the Victoria Cross in a cavalry charge at the village of Khudaganj, for saving the life of a loyal sowar and capturing one of the enemy's standards. He had already been mentioned in despatches for his services and thirsted for glory, as did many other young officers, writing to his mother that he wanted to win the V C 'more than any other'. Recommending Roberts for the award, Hope Grant reported: 'Lieutenant Roberts's gallantry has on every occasion been most marked. On following up the retreating enemy on the 2 January, 1858, at Khadagunge [sic], he saw in the distance two Sepoys going away with a Standard. Lieutenant Roberts put spurs to his horse and overtook them just as they were about to enter a village. They immediately turned round and presented their muskets at him, and one of the men pulled the trigger, but fortunately the cap snapped [i.e. the weapon misfired] and the Standard Bearer was cut down by this gallant young Officer, and the Standard taken possession off by him. He also on the same day cut down another Sepoy, who was standing at bay, with musket and bayonet, keeping off a sowar. Lieutenant Roberts rode to the assistance of the horseman, and rushing at the Sepoy, with one blow of his sword cut him across the face, killing him on the spot.' Many years later a neighbour of Rudyard Kipling's at Bateman's, Colonel Wemyss Feilden, formerly of the Black Watch, recounted how 'he heard one morning as they were all shaving that "a little fellow called Roberts" had captured single-handed a rebel Standard and was coming through the Camp. "We all turned out. The boy was on horseback looking rather pleased with himself, and his mounted Orderly carried the Colour behind him. We cheered him with the lather on our faces."'[18]

Roberts's service in 1857 was drawing to a close. The recapture of Delhi and relief of Lucknow broke the back of the Mutiny, but Sir Hugh Rose still faced a difficult campaign in central India

24

against Tatya Topi and the Rani of Jhansi, the ablest of rebel leaders. The British enjoyed better leadership, the superiority of Enfield rifles against the sepoys' muskets, reinforcements brought by steamer, the loyalty of the Madras and Bombay armies and of many princes, and useful intelligence from the banking Seth family and other important Indian merchants. Divisions among the mutineers at Delhi were equally vital to their defeat; while clashes between the Hindu sepoys and Muslim jihadis, looting of the Delhi-wallahs who had originally welcomed the rebellion, and the aged emperor's failure to provide leadership weakened their cause. Had the Mutiny been a truly national uprising, British rule would have been overthrown. The Raj had been shaken to its core and the effects were to be long felt.

Heat and disease took a heavier toll of casualties than battle and Roberts did not escape. The doctors put him on the sick list for a rest from exhaustion and the affects of the climate, and insisted on leave in England. On 1 April 1858, the sixth anniversary of his arrival in India, his post passed to Garnet Wolseley, although the two officers did not meet for many years. Towards the middle of the month he left Lucknow for Calcutta, but his trials were not quite over: travelling with Captain William Peel who was recovering from a wound, he soon found Peel in a high fever and with strange-looking spots on his face. He had contracted smallpox and died on the 27th. Roberts embarked alone at Calcutta on P & O steamer *Nubia*. He had won the Victoria Cross and £500 of prize money, and been mentioned in dispatches seven times, several times narrowly escaping death. He had gained a reputation, and not just for courage and luck. Captain Oliver Jones of the Naval Division wrote: '[Roberts] is one of those men who to uncommon daring and bravery in the field and unflinching hard-working discharge of duty in camp, adds the charm of cheering and unaffected kindness and hospitality in the tent, and his acquaintance and friendship are high prizes to those who obtain them.'[19]

Chapter 2

Marriage, Friends and Frontier

Campaigning on the Indian frontier is an experience by itself. Neither the landscape nor the people find their counterparts in any other portion of the globe.

Winston Churchill, *My Early Life*

Luck, the attribute Napoleon always demanded in his generals. The Indian subcontinent – and the Frontier in particular – is littered with half-forgotten graveyards filled with the bones of the unlucky, their lives extinguished before they had a chance to shine.

Charles Allen, *Soldier Sahibs*

The Mutiny had a profound influence on Roberts's thinking and his future. For most of his life his closest friends were those who had served with him in 1857. With many others he knew that British rule in India hung by a thread, and in his memoirs forty years later he included a special chapter on how to avoid a second Mutiny. Even without Nicholson's teaching, he must have learnt that harsh and determined action paid rewards. Blowing mutinous sepoys from the mouths of cannon and hanging traitors proved decisive in the Punjab: securing Sikh loyalty was as essential as Gurkha recruitment to British victory. While British vengeance in the mutiny is now thought by historians to have been excessive – more perceptive Englishmen like Governor-General Canning and the journalist W.H. Russell saw it as such at the time – the threat to their rule and to British womanhood had been deemed so great that at home as well as in India Englishmen applauded brutal methods. But Roberts had another side. Early in his career, he records, he had hated watching, for the only time in his career, a flogging parade in which two soldiers were punished. 'They were fine, handsome young Horse Artillerymen, and it was hateful to see them thus treated. Besides, one felt it was productive of harm rather than good, for it tended to destroy the men's self-respect.' Roberts relates how they had committed the same crime again, but when about to be punished in the same way with a further fifty lashes, the Battery Major promised to remit the flogging if they gave their word to behave in the future. They appreciated the act of clemency and they kept their word. Roberts followed their careers in which their conduct was uniformly satisfactory, and they became good, steady soldiers.[1] His mercy extended further, at a time when few granted it. Captain Oliver Jones tells how as Assistant Quartermaster General Roberts was ordered by Brigadier Hope Grant to see about burning part of a town that had been stormed.

> An old, infirm man, who was sitting at the door of a house, entreated him to spare it saying 'that yesterday morning he was the happy father of five sons; three of them lie there, pointing to three corpses; where the other two are God only knows; that he was old, and a cripple, and that if his house was burned he would have nothing left but to lie down and die.' Roberts, who is as good as he is brave, gave directions for sparing the old man's house; and I hope the two missing sons have escaped, and have returned to comfort his few remaining days.[2]

En route to Ireland Roberts bought new clothes in London before proceeding to Waterford on leave, writing to his sister, 'Major Fred Roberts V.C. must cut a dash you know, Harriet.' He was still a captain, but keen on promotion. He had written the previous year: 'your brother Fred, Harriet darling, has no end of ambition ... It will be doubly sweet going home when all is over. You must look out for some nice girl with "blue eyes and yellow hair" ... for me, Harriet dearest, who will console me for having to return to the gorgeous East.'[3]

The girl with 'blue eyes and yellow hair' whom Roberts wooed at Waterford in Ireland was Nora Henrietta Bews, the tenth and youngest child of John Bews, retired Black Watch officer. The town at that time was a regimental headquarters, and the playing of the band made the drill ground a fashionable promenade for chaperoned young men and women. In such circumstances, Roberts first met his future wife, who was then living with a married sister not far from the home of Roberts's parents. They were married at Waterford Church on 17 May 1859; she was twenty, he was twenty-six, and they were to be together for fifty-five years. Their honeymoon was in Scotland. Among Nora's proud early moments of her marriage was when she was called to Buckingham Palace on 18 June where Roberts received his VC. Three weeks later they sailed to India together. If he took three months' extension of leave, he would lose his post in the Quartermaster General's department, so he and Nora agreed that they would return, despite this being the hottest time of the year. It was not exceptional for Victorian soldiers' wives to sacrifice their wishes and comfort to their husbands' careers, but in supporting and advancing her Fred, Nora Roberts was to be exceptional. From the start of their marriage she was conscious of her husband's prospects, and prepared to subordinate her own desires to his ambition. Almost their first visits in India were to the battlegrounds of the Indian Mutiny where Roberts had fought, Nora showing a keen interest. Roberts had hoped to accompany Hope Grant on the Anglo-French China expedition launched by Palmerston when Chinese officials seized the *Arrow*, a ship technically British because it was based on Hong Kong. In deference to Roberts's new bride, Colin Campbell, now Commander-in-Chief as Lord Clyde, kept him back from the expedition and told Mrs Roberts that he had earned her gratitude by not sending her husband away as he was a newly married man. The outspoken future Lady Roberts said she could not be grateful as she felt she was ruining his career. 'Well, I'll be hanged if I can understand you women!' exclaimed the astonished Campbell. 'I have done the very thing I thought you would like, and have only succeeded in making you angry.'[4]

Although later the pain of childbearing, the loss of children in infancy, the climate of India, and supporting her husband through thick and thin took the flush of youth from her cheeks, early photographs of Nora Roberts show a comely enough young woman. In the winter of 1862–3, Owen Burne on the Viceroy's staff wrote of her as 'a charming bride ... not only handsome, but full of goodness and brightness'. He described Roberts as 'a slim, active fellow, full of life, quick of thought, and an exceptional organizer'.[5]

In his autobiography *Forty-One Years in India* Roberts recounts how some of the early bloom of youth may first have gone from his young bride's cheeks. In October 1866, he took her from Calcutta to Allahabad, her first experience of a hot season in the plains. Cholera was rife and the garrison had to be sent away into camps, all to be visited by Roberts and other staff officers once or twice daily. People seen alive and well one day were dead and buried the next, and in the midst the officers:

> had constantly to get up entertainments, penny readings and the like to amuse the men and keep their minds occupied. My wife usually accompanied me to the cholera camps, preferring to do this rather than be left alone at home, on one occasion just got into a carriage after going round a hospital when a young officer ran after us to tell me a corporal in whom I was much interested was dead. The poor fellow's face was blue, and he had the cholera panic. 'He will be dead the next,' I said to my wife. I had no sooner reached home than I received a report of his having been seized.

In an age of evangelism – although less encouraged after the Mutiny than before – Roberts's Christian faith sustained him, strengthened by the example of the garrison chaplain, later Bishop of Lahore. The Revd Matthews and his wife, only lately come to India, never wearied, Roberts wrote, in doing all that was possible for the soldiers. Three of the Roberts's six children did not survive infancy. Their first, a baby girl, died at Simla within one week of her first birthday – 'our first great sorrow'. In the first two-thirds of the nineteenth century it was estimated only one white child in five born in India lived to the age of six.[6]

Roberts and his new bride had returned to India at a time of momentous change. Widespread and savage reprisals by the British were ended, fortunately, by the wisdom of Governor-

General Canning – damned in the eyes of the diehards as 'Clemency Canning' – and the strength of men like Sir John Lawrence. An amnesty was declared, to extend to 1 January 1859, for rebels who surrendered, except the leaders and those involved in the worst crimes. Tatya Topi, held responsible for the tragic events at Cawnpore, was betrayed by the Rajah of Narwar and hanged; Nana Sahib disappeared; the Rani of Jhansi was killed in battle. After a trial of doubtful legality, the Emperor Bahadur Shah was exiled to Rangoon where he died in 1862.

Among those who benefited from the amnesty was Roberts's half-brother, John Roberts, known as Chote Sahib, a devout Muslim who wore Indian dress having adopted Indian habits and had worked in the state of Oudh manufacturing gun-carriages, which were used against the British in the Mutiny. In 1860 his father Abraham Roberts wrote an angry letter to John, who had asked him for money, but did not cut him out of his will, confirming that his part in the Mutiny was at most peripheral. John Roberts continued to draw an annual pension from the old General's estate until his own death in 1892.[7]

On 2 August 1858, Queen Victoria signed the Government of India Act abolishing East India Company rule, replacing the President of the Company's Board of Control with a Secretary of State for India who sat in the cabinet and was advised by a Council of India. The Governor-General continued to rule, aided by an Executive Council, its members now holding 'portfolios' of responsibility. To him was added the honorific title Viceroy as the personal representative of the Crown. The Indian government's finances, running at a deficit of £7 million per annum, were reorganized: reforms included a uniform tariff of 10 per cent, a convertible paper currency and additions to the salt duty. By 1864 the deficit disappeared. One of the poor Indian's complaints was that improved farm production was taken by the *zamindars*, the tax collectors, and in 1859 an attempt was made to remedy this with the Bengal Rent Act, which applied to the whole of north-west India as well as Bengal itself. In an effort to keep in touch with Indian opinion, aristocratic Indians were added to the existing Legislative Council, set up in 1853. The British wooed by conciliation and rewarded the princes and landed classes. The Queen's Proclamation of 1 November 1858 promised to respect the 'rights, dignity and honour of the native princes'. Instead of being seen as anachronistic, they became an integral part of the British Empire, props of imperialism. The thrusting, reforming style of Bentinck and Dalhousie was abandoned for respect for 'ancient rights and customs'. Missionary proselytizing was replaced by religious toleration, all faiths alike enjoying 'the equal and impartial protection of the law'. India was thought to be slow in responding to change – if it was not transformed quickly, British trusteeship might be expected to continue almost indefinitely. This vision of a changeless India of princes, peasants, castes and temples led the British rulers to neglect to their cost the new rising westernized middle class. India with its teeming millions was run by an elite of 1,000 senior men of the Indian Civil Service (ICS), renowned for being impartial, high-minded, conscientious and incorruptible. District officers were in charge of a million people and 4,000 square miles. In their districts they were omnipotent, responsible for everything from administering justice to sanitary conditions, dealing with the plague of snakes that killed 10,000 people in Bengal in 1878 and with that recurrent disaster, famine.

While some aspects of Indian life remained, it seemed time-less. British engineers, amongst whom the Scots took the lead, transformed communications. The railway system planned in 1853 was virtually complete by 1900, giving India the best system in Asia. Irrigation, begun by repairing Mogul canals, pushed forward by Dalhousie and continued under succeeding viceroys, reached its apogee in the Punjab and Sind. By 1947 one-fifth of the cultivable area was under irrigation and so immune from monsoon fluctuations. Steamships via the Suez Canal shortened the journey to England, and they and new harbours encouraged the rise of industries: jute and cotton, coal and iron. They also brought Englishmen's wives and enabled them to travel home more frequently; relations with Indians, once close, changed to stand-offishness and a belief in racial and moral superiority. The work of the ICS became more bureaucratic, less in touch with the people, the British creating the mountain of paperwork by which India is still governed.[8]

The key reform was reorganization of the Army. The Queen's proclamation of November 1858 converted former Company troops into servants of the Crown. European soldiers were to join the Queen's regiments, while sepoys were to form the Indian

Army under the Crown. Many British soldiers objected that they should not be switched from one to another without prior consultation, and asserted that they should have been discharged and offered a bounty to re-enlist. During May and June 1859, rumours of discontent spread and became so serious that the Government permitted NCOs and men to take their discharge and return to Britain at government expense. Re-enlistment was not permitted. As the soldiers eagerly claimed their discharge, the protests known as the 'White Mutiny' petered out and died. The only serious incident, the refusal of the 5th European Regiment at Barrackpore 'to do any duty' was promptly crushed without bloodshed by the despatch of 500 men. Of the 15,000 men of the old Company regiments, 10,116 claimed their discharges and returned to Britain. Henceforth, British regiments stationed in India would belong to the British Army. Their strength was 60,000, roughly three times that pre-Mutiny.

The newly created Indian Army remained separated in the three forces of Bengal, Bombay and Madras, each with its own Commander-in-Chief and its own traditions; their distinctness had prevented the spread of the Mutiny from Bengal. This division and potential rivalry was reflected at the top – the Commander-in-Chief was an 'extraordinary member' of the Viceroy's Council, but his proposals could be disputed by the Military Member, a senior officer on the Council, who advised the Governor-General. The latter's military and political secretaries, usually serving officers, also had an influence. Of the Bengal Army, 120,000 out of 128,000 sepoys had mutinied and most had been scattered or killed. Only eleven loyal regiments and some fragments remained. The proportion of Indian troops was reduced to about double the English. Throughout the sub-continent Indian troops were to total about 190,000: 45,000 in each of Bombay and Madras, which had remained loyal, and 100,000 in Bengal. Indian artillery was transferred to British hands, except for a few mountain batteries. Everywhere two Indian battalions were brigaded with one European so that no important station would be without its European contingent. Regiments were either 'class' regiments (Sikhs or Gurkhas), or were divided into companies of different 'class' to lessen the threat of mutiny. The number of Gurkhas, Sikhs and Punjabis was increased, and these 'martial races' of the north came to predominate.[9]

When Roberts returned to India in mid-1859, he served under Sir Robert Napier, then a brigadier general at Gwalior. He was known to successive commanders-in-chief: Campbell (Lord Clyde), Sir Hugh Rose (Lord Strathnairn) and Sir William Mansfield. His first major task on return was to organize logistics for Lord Canning's and Lord Clyde's tour of Oudh, Punjab and the northern provinces to heal the wounds of the Mutiny. On Clyde's retirement he became private secretary to Rose and he was to remain in the Quartermaster General's department, a shrewd career move, suggested by his father because this was in effect the operational staff of the Army. He was to be at the centre of planning throughout the 1860s and 1870s, and able to catch the eye of men in power.[10]

In 1863 he was promoted Assistant Quartermaster General and at the end of the year saw active service on the North-West Frontier against the Bunerwals. At one point Roberts and six other British officers found themselves surrounded by hundreds of potentially hostile Buner warriors, and could easily have been murdered, had it not been for the intervention of an old chief with one arm and a grey beard who protected them, saying that his word had been pledged.[11] In 1867 an expedition to Abyssinia was mounted from India under Lieutenant General Sir Robert Napier, now Commander-in-Chief at Bombay, including a brigade from Bengal under Roberts's good friend Donald Stewart. The Commander-in-Chief, Mansfield, recommended Stewart take as his quartermaster, Roberts, 'eminently qualified for the appointment by his activity and well-known military qualities, as well as by his experience in the Quartermaster General's Department in peace and war for nearly ten years'. Napier was to rescue sixty British and other European captives held by 'mad' King Tewodros ('Theodore') of Abyssinia, in the prisons of his capital, Magdala, diplomacy having failed.

The friendship of Roberts and Stewart, and their wives, had begun in August 1852 when the then Lieutenant Frederick Roberts, coming up-country to join his father on the North-West Frontier, was able to help a cavalcade of ladies and children in distress, among them Mrs Donald Stewart, en route to her husband at Lahore after a summer at Simla. Stewart and Roberts served together on the staff at Delhi during the Indian Mutiny. Stewart's letters record his pleasure at having Roberts with him on the Abyssinian Expedition and at Roberts's appointment to serve with him on the Lushai expedition in Assam. Their wives shared hospitality and on the death of relations gave one another emotional comfort. The friendship was strengthened when the couples stayed together in the Commander-in-Chief's quarters at Fort William in Calcutta, as the Abyssinia expedition loaded and prepared to sail. On the evening of 1 November, as a fierce wind rose, they abandoned plans to go to the opera. The wind reached cyclone force, the opera house was unroofed and Calcutta half flooded. The Stewarts and Robertses were woken by the terrific storm, the windows burst open and rain poured in. As the two officers struggled in vain to shut the windows, they were driven with their wives by wind and rain out of each room in turn, ending up in a little box room about 10 feet wide in the middle of the house. On land, there was great destruction, but less so in the harbour. As morning came, the storm subsided and loading continued; Roberts's suggestion of using a novel system of stowage was effected, whereby every unit embarking had its own equipment and transport complete.[12]

In Abyssinia Napier had to organize supplies and transport for an immensely difficult march of 420 miles rising to an altitude of 9,000 feet in a harsh tropical climate. Two piers 900 feet long were constructed and a railway laid to the camp 12 miles inland. Reservoirs were constructed for water supplies and stores, and transport animals assembled. Roberts's system of loading up of transports for the Division of which he was Staff Officer enabled the units to disembark complete with ammunition, equipment, rations, stores and transport, ready to march straight away from the beach., and as the troops set forth he remained as beach-master, ensuring smooth movement of stores to construct a road and keep the force supplied with necessities. Napier reached Magdala well before the rainy season, the King committed suicide and the prisoners were freed. The expedition re-embarked with the loss of only thirty-four men out of 12,000. Napier was sufficiently impressed with Roberts's services to choose him to take home the dispatches, a mark of particular distinction.

Napier, raised to the peerage as Baron Napier of Magdala and appointed Commander-in-Chief of the Indian Army in succession to Mansfield in 1870, was the first of Roberts's important patrons

34

and henceforth followed his career with interest. Roberts's next service was in late 1871, organizing a punitive expedition against the Lushai people of Assam. He had his first experience of command in action, leading his troops by a turning movement against an enemy stockade and then using his guns to drop a couple of shells into their village. The hostage was recovered and the troops returned before the onset of the rains. Recognized as the most promising officer in his department, in 1873 and 1874 he was acting Quartermaster General. On 1 January 1875, aged forty-two, he was promoted substantive colonel and became Quartermaster General, India, with the temporary rank of major general. To Napier, he wrote appreciatively: 'I have always hoped to be at the head of the Quartermaster General's Department, but I never anticipated getting the appointment so soon, and I feel that my advancement is entirely owing to your Excellency's great indulgence and kind assistance.' Napier had written to the Duke of Cambridge that the post 'could not be better filled', and remained a lasting influence on Roberts. It was Napier's tireless efforts on behalf of the ordinary soldier, both Indian and British, which Roberts wished to emulate. He noted that no commander-in-chief carried out inspections with more thoroughness, that on the hottest day he would toil through barrack after barrack and satisfy himself that soldiers were properly cared for. Napier pioneered temperance against alcohol to improve soldiers' behaviour. After Roberts's success in the opening stages of the 2nd Afghan War, Napier sent congratulations from Gibraltar where he was military governor: 'I always tell everyone that you are not a bit lucky but that your success is the natural result of good ability, good courage and an unfailing determination to see everything that was possible and to study everything that could fit you for your present position.'[13]

In the year of the Lushai Expedition the Roberts-Stewart connection was strengthened when the latter fell ill and was nursed back to health at Simla by the Robertses. He told his wife that he had recovered to enjoy 'much better health than he had been in for many years' and bought Nora Roberts a beautiful Trichinopoly bracelet. 'It is a very small return for all their kindness and attention to me since I came here,' he wrote to Mrs Stewart. 'I attribute my recovery almost entirely to their watchfulness and care of me, and I am very sure that no one else except yourself would have taken such trouble with a sick friend.'[14] Later Stewart was to repay Roberts with more than a bracelet.

These were years in which, despite busy military service, Roberts was also a happy family man. He and his wife purchased a new home at Simla, 'Snowdon', which was to be theirs until 1892, when it was bought by the British government as the Commander-in-Chief's residence, and was later enlarged by Kitchener. Their three surviving children, Aileen, Freddie and Edwina, were born in 1870, 1872 and 1875 respectively. Roberts recorded that his wife had had much trouble in his absence in Assam, having been at death's door herself, and nearly losing their son at Umballa three weeks after his birth. In early January 1874, he received by telegram the sad news of his father's death within a few months of his ninetieth birthday.

Political developments in the 1870s were to bring Roberts and the British Empire into violent contact with the North-West Frontier and Afghanistan. Lord Mayo, a man of great charm and personal qualities, was appointed Viceroy in 1869 and had invited the Afghan Amir Sher Ali to Amballa, treated him well and afterwards assisted him in helping to secure Russian recognition of the Oxus as the northern Afghan frontier. In the 1870s this settlement was threatened by international events and Mayo's rule was cut short by a seven-inch kitchen knife wielded by a Pathan fanatic on a visit to the Andaman Islands in February 1872. Roberts's friend Stewart was horrified and mortified, as he was in charge of military arrangements on the island, but no blame attached to him as he had warned Mayo not to visit Mount Harriet amidst the convicts at night.[15] Mayo's successor was Northbrook, an astute businessman, head of the banking family, Baring, who, although less colourful than his predecessor, followed his policies. When there was the threat of famine in Bihar, Northbrook sent Sir Richard Temple who commenced relief works and improvised transport for the distribution of huge quantities of rice, working chiefly by using military and police officers. Many lives were saved, but the cost to the state was enormous: £6½ million.

Northbrook was less successful in his handling of Afghan relations. He proposed to the Amir to send a British mission to announce the results of British arbitration between the Afghans and the Shah of Iran over a disputed border. Sher Ali said he did not want British officers to enter his country and sent a trusted and experienced minister, Said Nur Mohammed, to meet Northbrook at Simla in July 1873. There Northbrook suggested that the Anglo-Russian agreement meant Sher Ali could spend less on defence. Nur Mohammed replied that his master had no faith in Russian promises nor in British assurances of support, for if they would not stand up for him in the border dispute against Iran, a country which was weak, how would they stand up for him against the much stronger Russia. Sher Ali's exasperation at the British increased when Northbrook attempted to intercede on behalf of his difficult eldest son, Sirdar Yakub Khan, whom the Amir had arrested in early 1874. Northbrook's major failure was not signing an offensive–defensive alliance with Sher Ali, a step which put India on the road to the 2nd Afghan War.

For advocates of a more active policy, Sir Henry Rawlinson, a friend of Roberts, Sir Bartle Frere, Governor of Bombay, and Sir Robert Napier advocated a more active approach. Northbrook's 'master inactivity', as they deemed his policy, would in their view lead to disaster. Without diplomatic agents at Kabul and Herat, and a reliable source of intelligence on events in central Asia, British India might be caught by surprise by Russian infiltration. 'Masterly inactivity' meant that British officers did not enter Afghanistan, none were stationed there, and ignorance and prejudice prevailed among British policy-makers in India who lacked knowledge of the country and understanding of its people.

It was another of Roberts's Indian Army acquaintances, Colonel Charles Metcalfe MacGregor, soldier-explorer and Deputy Quartermaster General, who argued most strongly. MacGregor, who had extensive knowledge of mountain warfare and of the topography of the North-West Frontier and states beyond, saw that Russian military reforms after the Crimean War and taking strategic Khiva in 1873 threatened India. To prevent Russia seizing key strategic points such as Merv and Herat, and stirring up revolt in India – a second Mutiny – should be aims of British policy in India. Roberts joined MacGregor in the mid-1870s in urging upon the Indian government a more forward-looking policy towards Afghanistan. The best defence of India was well forward of her borders.[16] This advocacy coincided with the election of a British government sympathetic to these views and the arrival at Bombay of an active new Viceroy, a handsome, flamboyant diplomat and poet who was to be Roberts's next patron.

Chapter 3

War in Afghanistan

Nearly every invasion of India has come from Kandahar.

Major Waller Ashe

The critical state of affairs in Central Asia demands a statesman. I believe, if you will accept this high post, you will have an opportunity not only of serving your country, but of obtaining an enduring fame.

Disraeli to Lord Lytton

The ground was laid for the 2nd Afghan War and Roberts's rise to fame by a change of government in London. In 1874 Disraeli and the Conservatives took office. A brilliant opportunist with little detailed knowledge of foreign or imperial matters, Disraeli sensed that England was 'really more of an Asiatic Power than a European', and conferred the title of Empress on Queen Victoria in 1876. When the Khedive of Egypt sold his shares in the Suez Canal Company, Disraeli arranged their purchase against the opposition of cabinet colleagues; the French-built Suez Canal was a life-line of empire, four-fifths of ships passing through it being British. He identified the Conservatives with patriotism and imperialism, feelings which reached a high point in the Eastern Crisis of 1878. His policy reflected a growing English interest in empire and the cultivation of ties with overseas people of British stock. Sir Charles Dilke in his book *Greater Britain* published in 1868, and the historian J.A. Froude, were early advocates of this 'new imperialism'. Disraeli wished to assert British interests and the security of British possessions overseas; he did not necessarily want wars. The conflicts with the Zulus in Natal and with the Afghans were brought about by his imperial pro-consuls, undeterred by telegraphic communication with a reluctant cabinet.[1]

The Liberal Viceroy Northbrook could not agree with the new Secretary of State for India, Lord Salisbury, over tariff reductions and over Salisbury's plan to send an envoy to Kabul, and resigned a year early in 1876. His successor, after a number of possible candidates refused, was Lord Lytton, son of the novelist Bulwer Lytton. He had no Indian background, was a diplomat and man of letters, handsome, witty of speech and bohemian in habit, with a talent for flamboyance and powers of expression like Disraeli's. He was without racial prejudice, a quality bound to appeal to moderns, but his apparent nonchalance, hiding his serious aims, could be mistaken for frivolity. Calcutta society was to be horrified by his endless smoking of cigarettes, his inveterate flirting, his demonstrative affection for Indians. Conversely Lady Lytton with her diplomatic experience supported her husband with style, transforming the 'dull and coarse' viceregal court and becoming a benefactress of female education, especially the zenanas of Indian princes. Salisbury approved the choice with reservations, writing to Disraeli: 'Lytton – with an occasional bilious fit – will be better than any other candidate you have at your disposal.' Disraeli told Salisbury, 'We wanted a man of ambition, imagination, some vanity and much will – and we have got him.' The consequences were to be greater than either Disraeli or Salisbury imagined.[2]

Disraeli's arrival at 10 Downing Street and Lytton's at Bombay led to Roberts's meteoric rise in the nine years following 1876. In that year he was a substantive colonel and local or temporary major general, but virtually unknown outside the Bengal Army, and had only commanded troops briefly. By 1885 he was the Indian Army Commander-in-Chief and Sir Garnet Wolseley's rival as the most famous late Victorian general. When Lytton arrived, Roberts had travelled to Bombay to say goodbye to Napier. Roberts was not the man to let a patron depart without thanks, but the visit to Bombay gave him a chance to meet the new Viceroy, who had arrived on the steamer *Orontes,* having read on the voyage out a paper on Afghanistan which Roberts had written for Napier.

> His Excellency received me very kindly, telling me he felt that I was not altogether a stranger, as he had been reading during the voyage a paper I had written for Lord Napier, a year or two before, on our military position in India, and the arrangements that would be necessary in the event of Russia attempting to continue her advance south of the Oxus. Lord Napier had sent a copy of this memorandum to Lord Beaconsfield [Disraeli], by whom it had been given to Lord Lytton.

Thus Roberts caught the eye of the new Viceroy, who may also have heard Napier's high opinion of him. 'From that moment,' wrote Roberts, 'Lord Lytton was my friend. The "Forward Policy" which I advocated was the policy that appealed to him.'[3] Roberts benefited greatly from Lytton's favourable first impression, was included in his small entourage of favourites and given a series of important tasks. The first of these was as one of the organizers of the Imperial Durbar to proclaim the Queen Empress of India on New Year's Day, 1877. Sixty-three ruling princes and 100,000 people heard the proclamation. General Sir Bindon Blood in his autobiography recorded the care taken by Roberts as Quartermaster General in preparing for the event. He held a meeting of the Bengal Sappers and Miners in early October beforehand to co-ordinate arrangements. A few days before the Durbar there was an extraordinary storm which lasted twenty-four hours, about 17 inches of rain fell, the roads were badly cut up and in places destroyed, mud walls in houses and elsewhere fell down, and the whole scene of the event looked as if there had been an earthquake. Blood adds: 'However, needless to say, under Colonel Roberts' direction everything was spick and span when the date arrived for the commencement of the imperial Assemblage!' Roberts's skilful organization further impressed Lytton.

The key feature of the Durbar was the ceremonial display of loyalty and fealty to the Queen-Empress by India's princes and maharajahs, who still held a third of the sub-continent and whose loyalty was to be a pillar of the Raj. The series of events went well, except that the firing of the *feu de joie* stampeded the elephants. Luckily no one was hurt. The march past of the native contingents a day or two after the inspection of Indian Army troops was the most picturesque procession Blood had ever seen: horsemen in chain armour with inordinately long lances, others with cuirasses of leather and long straight swords, uniforms of all sorts and colours, and over 1,000 elephants. Within a few years, recorded Blood wistfully, change replaced these romantic figures by more efficient but far less picturesque arrangements. The celebrations across India for the proclamation were huge, comprising military reviews, medal investitures, a 101-gun salute, fireworks, speeches, a massive state banquet, pension increases, restoration of decommissioned mosques to religious use, amnesties to release thousands of prisoners, and the cancellation of all debts of under 100 rupees. Schools were renamed, statues erected and large sums donated to famine relief. Lytton's spectacle satisfied Salisbury's two criteria: 'gaudy enough to impress the orientals, yet not enough to give hold for ridicule here, and furthermore the pageant hid "the nakedness of the sword on which we really rely"'. It also won over the princes, the Maharaja of Indore praising the Durbar as a symbol of national cohesion: 'India has been until now a vast heap of stones,' he told Lytton. 'Now the house is built and from the roof to the basement each stone of it is in its right place.'[4]

Unfortunately the Durbar coincided with the failure of rains over half of the Madras Presidency – 200,000 square miles with a population of thirty-six million – and the beginning of the worst famine in nineteenth-century India. The Durbar's glitter and lavishness shone in ironic contrast to the suffering of many. Lytton claimed that having imperial governors at hand enabled him to concert measures. He responded with energy, rushing emergency stocks, sending Sir Richard Temple who had experience of famine to deal with the crisis, and touring Madras himself. But the fall of rain in May and June 1877 did not help matters, the railways and irrigation had not extended sufficiently to have an effect, foodstuffs gathered could not be transported quickly, and the prolonged famine took the lives of over five million people. If such a tragedy could be said to have a good side, it was that measures including the implementation of a Famine Insurance Fund, laying aside cash each year for emergency measures, were imposed. Lytton believed that in the long run railways and irrigation schemes would overcome famine, but the event cast a shadow over his Viceroyalty.[5]

At the same time as a new Viceroy there was a new Commander-in-Chief, General Sir Frederick Haines, 'a good honest fellow... but not of the modern school'. In his fifty-sixth year, Haines had served against the Sikhs and in the Crimea, but in the Mutiny was at Madras and saw no action. He had risen largely through staff jobs. A cautious man, standing on seniority, he shared the views of the Duke of Cambridge, Commander-in-Chief at Whitehall, suspicious of Wolseley and the reformers. He was the antithesis of the younger, ambitious, less conventional Roberts, but at first pleased with his services, writing to Cambridge: 'He [Roberts] is thoroughly master of his work, and in every way acceptable to me.'[6] Differences between the two subsequently emerged over military policy on the North-West Frontier and in Afghanistan.

Lytton proposed that British India west of the Indus, including Sind, should form a new province under a Chief Commissioner, responsible directly to the Government of India and charged also with relations with Kabul; as part of the plan the Punjab and Sind Frontier Forces would be amalgamated. For the post Lytton wanted the victor of the famous Ashanti campaign in Africa, General Sir Garnet Wolseley, then Adjutant General in London. This was hardly surprising, for Lytton had brought to India as his Military Secretary and then Political Secretary the most brilliant of Wolseley's 'Ashanti ring': Colonel Sir George Pomeroy Colley, former professor of military administration and law at the Staff College, and the man who had organized Wolseley's transport in his African campaign. Wolseley accepted and then withdrew, the efforts of Lytton and Colley to prepare the way for him frustrated by an implacable alliance of the Duke of Cambridge, Army conservatives including Haines, and Indian bureaucrats. 'The Ring' in the person of Colley still inspired Lytton's policy: Colley's 'Memorandum on the Military Aspects of the Central Asian Question' remained with modifications the essential foundation of Lytton's war programme.[7]

Lytton then offered the post to Roberts who accepted in early 1878. Lytton proposed he take command of the Punjab Frontier Force in order to familiarize himself with the geography and problems of the frontier. Although this would mean coming down in rank from Major General to Brigadier General, Roberts accepted, supported by his wife, and took up his new command in March 1878, embarking immediately upon an extended tour of all stations and their garrisons, returning to Simla in May, when Lytton conferred with him regarding details of the Commissionership.[8]

From a contemporary English perspective, the 2nd Afghan War had its origins in Disraeli's foreign policy, a robust defence of British interests overseas, or dangerous adventurism, depending upon your politics. The 'Forward School' viewed it as stemming from the failure of the Liberal Viceroy Northbrook to grasp the hand of friendship advanced by Sher Ali, which was subsequently withdrawn and held out towards Russia. From the point of view of the Indian government, it was a consequence of Russia's relentless advance across the Asian wastes. Following her defeat in the Crimean War, Russia had pacified the Caucasus with great brutality, and then advanced steadily into Asia in the third quarter of the nineteenth century. Tashkent in 1865, Khojent in 1866, Bokhara in 1867, Samarkand in 1868, Khiva in 1873 and Khokand in 1875 had fallen successively to Russian force. Russian Army reforms emphasized the increased employment of irregular cavalry and techniques of insurrectionary warfare, foreshadowing twentieth-century 'wars of liberation'. Possible Russian ascendancy among the Afghans, border raids on the North-West Frontier, an Afghan attack supported by Russian detachments, and arms and money, followed by penetration into the Punjab – this was the danger to British India. Russian encroachment was regarded with alarm and some dismay in India. Roberts himself wrote: 'Thus, in a little more than twenty years, Russia had made a stride of 600 miles towards India, leaving but 400 miles between her outposts and those of Great Britain.'[9]

From the point of view of Frederick Roberts, Quartermaster General and now commander-designate of the Punjab Frontier Force, the war was a logical continuation of family business. His father had served in the 1st Afghan War (1838–1842), his wise advice had been disregarded and disaster had followed: the destruction of a British army in the snowy retreat from Kabul. Roberts long remembered his father's letters, written from the Afghan campaign and read to him as a small boy, and he shared a lively and intelligent concern for India's North-West Frontier with other imperial soldiers and administrators. The Indian government could adopt either of two possible approaches to Russia and the Asian buffer states like Afghanistan: the appeasement-like policy of 'masterly inactivity' officially enunciated by Sir John Lawrence as Viceroy in 1868, refusing to intervene in Afghan wars of succession, and largely applied by his successors Mayo and Northbrook; or the 'forward policy', which argued that disengagement deprived India of agents in these states who could provide intelligence of Russian movements and of possible help in the form of native forces, and in addition threw the rulers of these states of necessity into the arms of Russia. Salisbury, taking over the India Office in Disraeli's government, found no agents, secret or otherwise, at Herat or Kabul providing vital information. Northbrook, then Viceroy, had refused to send them. Roberts shared an advocacy of the 'forward school' with two influential writers he knew well: Sir Henry Rawlinson and Colonel Charles MacGregor. Rawlinson's *England and Russia in the East* published in 1875 formed one basis of Lytton's Central Asian policy. MacGregor, who had served in the Mutiny, China, Abyssinia, and with Roberts in the Quartermaster's Department at Army headquarters, worked hard to obtain topographical and military intelligence about potential border enemies, laid the foundations for the Indian Army's Intelligence Department, and in 1868 published the *Gazetteer of Central Asia*, a huge six-volume collection of statistics about the North-West Frontier and the border states. The eye-catching adventures of soldier-explorers like MacGregor and Colonel Fred Burnaby had a serious purpose: to gather intelligence and make contacts for future use in anticipation of Russian advances beyond the Khivan Desert. MacGregor feared Russian threats to Herat, commanding all important roads to India from Central Asia and the strongest fortress between the Caspian and the Indus.[10]

The Russian threat to India was complicated by her advances to the south-west as 'protector of the Slavs', exploiting a possible collapse of the Ottoman Empire in the Balkans. A Russian attack on Constantinople threatened the eastern Mediterranean and the lifeline to the Empire. The tensions leading to the 2nd Afghan War coincided with the Eastern Crisis beginning in spring 1877. Russian armies invaded Ottoman territory to help the Turk's Christian subject people, the Bulgarians, who had risen in revolt. Disraeli, with the backing of Queen and cabinet, ordered the British fleet to Constantinople and Indian troops under Napier to Malta. Against this background, the Russians hoped a threat to India's North-West Frontier through Afghanistan would give a lever for negotiation. Forgotten was the assurance given to Britain in 1869 by the Russian minister Gorchakoff that Afghanistan lay 'completely outside the sphere within which Russia might be called upon to exercise influence'. In May, General Kaufman, Governor-General of Russian Turkestan, mobilized his entire force of 20,000 men and declared he was ready to establish a Russian sphere of influence over Afghanistan. One of his more indiscreet officers boasted, 'Now we march to India and drive out the English.' Kaufman despatched a diplomatic mission to Kabul. Leaving Tashkent, General Leonid Stolietov with six officers and twenty-two Cossacks rode to the Afghan capital, arriving on 22 July 1878, brushing aside Afghan protests, and delivered a letter of introduction from Kaufman to the Amir. It was reported that Sher Ali received the Russian mission with all honour, sent out elephants to meet them, and, mounted on these and attended by Afghan ministers and nobles, Stolietov and his officers had ridden in state through Kabul to the Bala Hissar, the ancient citadel containing the royal palace of Afghanistan's rulers. The purpose of the Mission was to ascertain Afghan military resources and persuade or frighten the Amir to place them at Russia's disposal.[11]

Lytton came to India with clear views based on the ideas of the forward school: build up the Afghan Amir Sher Ali and his country into a strong, stable and peaceful power favourable to Britain as the best defence against Russian expansion. He believed, from a meeting with Shouvaloff, Russian Ambassador in London that the Russian government had direct communication with Sher Ali, that the Russian General Kaufman had acquired such influence at Kabul that he could not only communicate with the Amir, but reckoned on his obedience to Russian instructions, and that Britain carried so little weight there that Sher Ali refused to receive a diplomatic agent from the Viceroy or allow the passage of a British officer through his territories. The departing Commander-in-Chief, Napier, had strengthened Lytton's resolve to reverse this by writing that Britain's position towards Afghanistan was 'unsafe and humiliating', and measures ought no longer to be delayed for improving it. Napier had adopted this stance following Russian military and diplomatic advances – previously a supporter of 'Masterly Inactivity', he now pointed out that the Russian encroachment in Central Asia had rendered that policy obsolete and dangerous.[12]

The official Indian Army history of the war blamed mutual tension on the unstable and suspicious character of Sher Ali, who fought his way to power, defeated three brothers successively in power struggles, experienced every vicissitude of an 'asiatic' ruler, was 'always of a morbid temperament . . . suffering extremes of elation and depression . . . the violent death of his eldest son giving rise to popular belief in his insanity'.[13] He wished to remain balanced between Russia and British India, offending neither; but worried by British advances into Baluchistan and towards Quetta, he declined to accept a British embassy. His reply reached Lytton at the time that the Eastern Crisis had taken a dangerous turn with the despatch of the British fleet and with British occupation of Quetta. This British gain at the end of 1876 by a treaty with the Khan of Khelat roused Sher Ali's suspicions – a strategical position of great natural strength, the city commanded the Bolan Pass, one of the gates to Afghanistan. Sher Ali could scarce forget that Quetta was the base from which a British army had marched to conquer his country in the 1st Afghan War.[14]

Disraeli's strong action in the eastern Mediterranean was successful. The Russian-imposed Treaty of San Stefano, by which Russia gained Bessarabia from Rumania and Armenia from Turkey, and created a large Bulgarian state reaching the Mediterranean, was overturned by the Berlin Conference of June–July 1878, hosted by Bismarck. War and Russian aggrandisement were averted, the 'big Bulgaria' was broken into three parts, one of them to be returned to Turkey, Russia was excluded from the Mediterranean and Disraeli acquired Cyprus as a base. He returned to London in triumph claiming 'Peace with honour'. In deference to British protests Stolietov was recalled, returning to

Tashkent in just over three weeks, although the staff of his mission stayed on at Kabul.[15]

The lapse of time before news of 'Peace with honour' reached Kabul and before India learnt of events in the Afghan capital proved fatal. Lytton's continued suspicion of Sher Ali was confirmed and strengthened by abortive negotiations with an Afghan envoy, who inconveniently died. Only a fortnight after the Treaty of Berlin, the news reached Calcutta that the Amir had welcomed Stolietev's Russian mission, whilst continuing to refuse a British one. The Amir in fact had not wanted the Russians, but was angry with British approaches, and received Lytton's request at a bad moment, when he was mourning the death of his favourite son and heir, Abdulla Jan, in August 1878. When the British emissary Ghulam Hasan Khan reached Kabul to present letters requesting that he accept a mission, Sher Ali was very angry, and announced:

> I do not agree to the Mission coming in this manner, and until my officers have received orders from me how can the Mission come? It is as if they wished to disgrace me. It is not proper to put pressure in this way. It will tend to a complete rupture and breach of friendship. I am a friend as before, and entertain no ill-will. The Russian envoy has come and has come with my permission. I am afflicted with grief at the loss of my son, and have had no time to think over the matter. If I get time, whatever I consider advisable will be acted upon. Under these circumstances they can do as they like.[16]

His bitter reaction was also partly suspicion of a large escort which accompanied Lieutenant General Sir Neville Chamberlain, formerly commander of the Movable Column in the Mutiny and now British envoy; and partly the bribing of the Afridis of the Khyber Pass to allow the envoy and escort to pass, although they owed allegiance to the Amir. The cabinet was divided, but Salisbury did not wish Lytton to send a mission. When Salisbury moved to the Foreign Office, his successor at the India Office, Lord Cranbrook, ordered Lytton to do nothing and await orders. Lytton delayed Chamberlain's mission at Peshawar until mid-September, and then despatched it with demands that British agents should be posted at Herat and Balkh with free access to Kabul for special envoys, in return for a subsidy, recognition of the Amir's chosen heir and defence of his territories. Chamberlain advanced to the Khyber Pass with his staff and an escort of 250 sabres. Fearing these numbers were unduly provocative, he decided to send forward a small party to test the state of things and reduce to a minimum any indignity of an Afghan refusal to allow the British to pass. On 21 September, Major Louis Cavagnari, with Chamberlain's advanced party of only twenty-four men of the Corps of Guides, reached the mountain fortress Ali Masjid just inside the Khyber Pass. The Afghan commander Faiz Mohammed Khan had received the stiffening of the Afghan Master of the Horse, and he made clear, in the absence of orders from Kabul to allow the mission to enter Afghanistan, that he would open fire if necessary. The exchange was as follows:

Cavagnari: 'I only came to get a straight answer from you. Will you oppose the passage of the Mission by force?'
Faiz Mohammed: 'Yes, I will; and you may take it as kindness and because I remember friendship, that I do not fire upon you for what you have done already.'
The two sides shook hands and remounted, and Faiz Mohammed said, 'You have had a straight answer.'

Rebuffed, Chamberlain withdrew to Peshawar, and wrote to the Viceroy:

Nothing could have been more distinct. Nothing more humiliating to the dignity of the British crown and Nation ... After what has taken place the status quo cannot, I think, continue without loss of dignity, if not loss of prestige, and I hope that such steps as are within our reach may at once be taken to prove to the Ameer [sic], and to the border tribes, and to our own native chiefs and people, that the British government loses no time in resenting a gross and unprovoked insult.

Chamberlain had earlier written: 'Our *great end is a peaceable solution*, any other would be a great misfortune forced on us,' but he now believed British prestige demanded a full apology. In

49

England Lytton's report that a British envoy had been 'forcibly repulsed' on his way to Kabul was widely publicized and there was an outcry, the public imagining that a friendly mission had been insulted and not appreciating that the real object of the mission was to coerce Sher Ali into subservience. Salisbury thought Lytton had blundered, but active measures had become inevitable, the cabinet after a long meeting supporting an ultimatum followed by military action if no adequate reply was received.[17]

On 2 November the Government of India sent a demand for an apology and for a permanent British mission at Kabul. A belated reply reached the Viceroy on 30 November, dated the 19th, and although promising Sher Ali's acceptance of a mission, was declared to be inadequate as containing no apology. Lytton sent orders to his troops to commence hostilities by advancing along the Khyber, Kurram and Kandahar passes.

The responsibility for the war rested primarily with Lytton.[18] Neglect of Sher Ali by previous viceroys, the Amir's state of mind after his son's death, the Russian failure to control Kaufman, the views of the Forward School and delays in communication – these all contributed, but were not main causes. Not until 20 December did Salisbury hear from Schouvaloff in London that the Russians had withdrawn Stolietov. By then it was too late. During the war, the Amir's friendly correspondence with the Russians fell into British hands, the forty-eight letters between Sher Ali and General Kaufman seeming to confirm Russian influence, but when the Amir wrote to Kaufman for help, he was told to make peace. Russian influence, real or suspected, at Kabul, did not make war necessary.

Opposition in Britain to the war was widespread. Former Viceroy Lord Northbrook said that with patience it could have been avoided. In a powerful speech, Gladstone denounced the war as repeating the errors of the previous invasion of Afghanistan. 'May heaven avert a repetition of the calamity which befell our army in 1841!' Disraeli's cabinet was divided and Disraeli wrote angrily. 'When V[ice]roys and Comms-in-Chief disobey orders, they ought to be sure of success in their mutiny. Lytton by disobeying orders had only secured insult and failure.' The Prime Minister's own vague reference in a speech, however, to India's north-west 'as a haphazard and not a scientific frontier', hinting that steps would be taken to correct it, gave the opposition ammunition for criticism.[19] In India, three members of the Viceroy's own council strongly dissented from the policy towards Sher Ali. Lytton, however, viewed senior officials and soldiers such as Haines as unimaginative and obstructionist, and found support for his ideas among younger men, including Roberts. His key advisor was Colonel Sir George Colley, whose 'Memorandum on the Military Aspects of the Central Asian Question' was derived from MacGregor's appreciation of the situation, but contained a major change since it regarded Kabul rather than Herat as the true key to India. Lieutenant General Neville Chamberlain, when acting Military Member on the Viceroy's council, wrote in November 1878 how Colley was always present at crucial meetings as the crisis developed, sitting alone and saying nothing, but giving the Viceroy 'the key to the discourse, and is his real military mentor ... and one cannot help admiring his reticence and apparent indifference to all that is said, and his being content to be a nobody'.[20] Besides being a brilliant and dedicated career soldier, Colley had looks and charm, was intellectual, musical and artistic, all qualities which Lytton valued. Hanna blamed Colley, Roberts, Cavagnari, the Adjutant General, Lumsden, and the Viceroy's Private Secretary, Owen Burne, for 'fostering the Viceroy's ignorant contempt for the danger he was preparing to run'. This ignores the limited aim of the opening campaign. There was to be no subjugation of Afghanistan, but rather a restoration of British prestige and influence. Hanna shows that MacGregor's *Central Asian Gazetteer* was not made available to operational staff for the war, and he blames Roberts as Quartermaster General. The blame must surely rest with the former Viceroy, Northbrook, and his advisors, wedded to 'Masterly Inactivity' and against posting intelligence-gathering envoys in central Asia, and with the Indian Army's lack of an intelligence branch, which MacGregor was forming but was still incomplete on the outbreak of hostilities.[21]

The driving force was Lytton, even if Colley was his chief advisor. A few months into the war, a young officer from England, Lord Melgund, later as Lord Minto to be Viceroy, wrote:

The entire plan of the campaign, and the carrying out of it, comes from the Viceroy, he is in fact Commander-in-Chief,

51

of course guided by his military advisers, amongst whom Colonel Colley and Colonel Baker [Military Secretary] must have of course great influence. I fancy Sir F. Haines has very little to do with the management of the campaign, and that [Government House] is actually the Head Quarters Office, and that any important change of operations would come from here.[22]

When the war broke out, Roberts, as Chief Commissioner-designate of the new Frontier Province, had already undertaken a tour of frontier stations, returning to Simla in May 1878. At the end of September, with the British massing their forces, and against the wishes of the Indian Commander-in-Chief, Haines, Lytton secured Roberts's appointment as commander of the Kurram Column, the smallest of the three forces to invade Afghanistan. Roberts's diary in August shows him closely in touch with Lytton, dining at the Viceroy's house, playing whist with the Lyttons, and meeting Colley to discuss negotiations with the Afghans. On 9 September 1878, when Roberts was told by Lytton he was to command the Kurram Column, he wrote in his journal: 'It is all too splendid.'[23] That Lytton, not Roberts, originated this line and educated his subordinate is all too clear from a letter of the Viceroy's: 'he [Roberts] was my own particular selection, and I had been personally coaching him in my own notions about that line of advance ... for more than a year before he got his command there.'[24]

Roberts, a happy husband and father, recorded on 13 September the children's health, on the 26th he sadly bade 'the dear children' farewell, and the next day 'Parted from my own darling wife at 8 am.' He had already had a farewell lunch with the Viceroy and the Commander-in-Chief and said goodbye to his many army friends. In October he was very busy preparing the column, but found time on 5 November to drink a bottle of champagne with Brigadier Hugh Gough 'to our wives' health', and then, as he saw Gough again on the 6th, they consumed a second. All three columns were having trouble gathering supplies and transport, so perhaps it was as well that the operations were postponed until 20 November, giving Sher Ali every chance of making an apology. Roberts had his hands full assembling stores and transport animals, and obtaining an additional three battalions to strengthen his force. This was his first independent command, a proud but anxious moment, conscious as he was of the weaknesses of his column, with Muslim soldiers not keen to march against fellow Muslims, his English regiment young and sickly.[25]

Chapter 4

Into Battle:
the Peiwar Kotal

You'll be cut to pieces before you're fifty miles across the border. You have to travel through Afghanistan ... It's one mass of mountains and peaks and glaciers, and no Englishman has been through it. The people are utter brutes.

Rudyard Kipling, *The Man Who Would be King*

Roberts had no experience of command, and his constitutional daring and his contempt for an uncivilized foe predisposed him to rash resolves and hasty action.

Colonel Henry Hanna

The strategy of advancing in three columns was a compromise between Lytton and Haines, following violent disagreement; at Haines's insistence the Kandahar and Peshawar forces were strengthened. Lytton and Colley wished to launch only a small offensive, relying on speed, superior firepower and the element of surprise, attacking in winter. They had planned two columns, a southern force under Major General Donald Stewart operating towards Kandahar through the Bolan Pass, and a northern force under Roberts threatening Kabul by way of the little-known Kurram Valley. Haines warned the Viceroy that the Kandahar column could run into 15,000 Afghan regulars armed with good artillery, and prevailed on Lytton to form a second column in the north under Lieutenant General Sam Browne, inventor of the famous belt, to advance up the Khyber Pass. The Khyber route was the only one that could be kept open all year. The three columns totalled 36,000 men and 148 guns, and was not a force to conquer Afghanistan – it was one, as Stewart told his wife in a letter of 31 October, to ensure that the Amir did not make friends with people who could threaten British India.[1]

Sir George Colley's studies led him to place enormous confidence in the firepower of modern breach-loading weapons. Lytton, relying on his advice, wisely chose a war of limited objectives, occupying Kandahar and the Kurram Valley to bring the Amir to heel. He had no intention of embarking on a full-scale invasion or even seizing Kabul; indeed it was unlikely the Indian Army's transport and supply arrangements could cope with such an effort. The Indian famine had had disastrous effects on the country's ability to support a war, although not on the Army directly. British and Indian troops generally enjoyed high morale, especially in Sikh, Gurkha and Highland battalions. The British infantry's breach-loading, single-shot Martini-Henry rifle was reliable and hard hitting, reasonably accurate to 1,000 yards; the Indians' Snider was not as good but better than earlier weapons. The cavalry carried a sword, lance and carbine. The artillery's rifled cannon fired out to 5,000 yards; the screw guns carried on mule-back to 4,000. Telegraph and heliograph provided improved communications. Chief weaknesses were organizational and logistical. The division of the Indian Army into three Presidency armies – Bengal, Bombay and Madras – and with the Commander-in-Chief and the Military Member advising the Viceroy at the top made for slowness, inefficiency and rivalry, especially when the Viceroy and the Commander-in-Chief Haines did not trust one another. The introduction of short-service enlistments brought young soldiers to India who were not yet acclimatized. Medical care was improving, but conditions were still harsh, with many dying from cholera, pneumonia and typhoid. There were no proper ambulances; the sick had to be transported in two-wheeled carts (doolies). Indian Army commanders, promoted by seniority rather than merit, were mostly conventional and unimaginative, and several called from desk jobs did not have the flexibility of mind to cope with a quickly changing situation.

Against an enemy hiding in rugged mountains and armed with the accurate, long-range jezail, regiments dispensed with traditional scarlet tunics and followed the dress of the elite Corps of Guides. A 14th Bengal Lancers officer noted: 'blue, scarlet and gold [were discarded], and all were dressed from top to toe in *Khakee*, or mud colour.' 'The uniform is decidedly irregular,' wrote Major Le Mesurier of the Royal Engineers, 'a suit of brown cloth and brown boots with canvas tops.' Major George White of the Gordon Highlanders told his wife, 'We are all fitted out in khaki, and won't look in the least like the old 92nd; however, the men stick to their kilts ... We have discarded all our white belts and steel scabbards, and have our swords sharp and in leather scabbards ... I am fitted more as if going on a shooting excursion than on a campaign.' Tea was often used to dye uniform serge.

The Army's dispersed cantonments meant that regiments had to be assembled at railheads at short notice. Once beyond the railways, the men marched on foot and horse, supported by bullock carts, mules and camels. An enormous number of animals had to be hired, and every column was accompanied by a host of camp followers responsible for watering and feeding the troops. Religious restrictions on certain foods complicated logistics. As war approached, both Roberts as Quartermaster General, and Haines as Commander-in-Chief, had submitted memoranda to Lytton pointing out the need for improvement in organization, transport and equipment before war started. Virtually nothing had been done. MacGregor's gazetteer and its maps were not made available, and what little intelligence there was came from Indian police service reports. In a harsh and mountainous country, most supplies would come from India by pack train, mule and camel; the routes were long and passed through defiles which could be easily attacked. There were no metalled roads and wheeled transport was often unusable.[2]

The Afghans were known to be 'a race of Tigers' who had already shown their teeth in 1838–42, a hard, warlike people toughened by a harsh, dry, mountainous country, passionately nursing their independence, family loyalty, courage, and a highly developed sense of personal honour and hospitality, but conversely regarded by unwelcome visitors as 'robbers and cut-throats', 'very interested in fire-arms'. A Russian estimate placed Afghan strength at nearly 50,000 regulars and 140,000 irregulars.

The Amir depended upon force of personality and personal prestige to persuade and cajole the sirdars – local lords with political and military power – to lead out their local levies. To supplement the traditional long-barrelled jezail they had Enfield and Snider rifles, mostly given to the Amir by the British, and plenty of ammunition. Indeed, some British officers expected Afghans to enjoy an unlimited supply of rounds stolen from the Indian Army factory at Dum Dum. Uniform was the same as the Indian Army's and drill was taught by Indian deserters. Afghan artillery was particularly good, one estimate giving the Afghans 379 guns, including thirty-four siege weapons, their fire so effective that British observers thought Russians must be manning them. After a first encounter, Roberts reported that there could be no comparison with the Afghan army of the previous war. 'The men are now armed with excellent rifles, and provided with abundant ammunition ... Their shooting is good; their men are of large stature and great physical strength and courage, and are well clothed. The Afghan artillery is also well served and efficiently equipped.' His report proved remarkably accurate, except that it ignored the ghazis, fanatical irregulars armed only with swords, who made up in religious fanaticism what they lacked in discipline.

Afghans enjoyed great mobility, and could assemble and disperse with remarkable rapidity, making excellent use of the ground they knew. The countryside was wild and rugged, the valleys narrow, the defiles perfectly made for ambush, commanded by high rocky hills and mountains. Most of the country was thinly populated and in many places the houses were towers built as little fortifications, the doors being 10 to 15 feet above the ground and approached by means of a rope ladder which could be pulled up at a moment's notice. A Russian observer thought every settlement was fortified to some degree. The climate was harsh, dry and hot in summer, bitterly cold in winter, and only in the valleys around places like Kandahar did green fields introduce a gentler element to the landscape.[3]

The first action was a bungled attack by Lieutenant General Sir Sam Browne as he tried to seize the stronghold of Ali Masjid at the mouth of the Khyber Pass. More by luck than judgement, the encircling columns under Brigadiers MacPherson and Tytler seized the fortress from behind after a night's freezing march in the wrong direction. Sher Ali, however, in an imaginative reversal of reality wrote to the Governor of Herat: 'By the grace of God, a series of victories have been won by our lion-devouring warriors.' Browne's force went on to take Dakka at the west end of the Khyber and then Jalalabad, capital of the region, a dirty town, where the troops settled down to improve drainage and roads, and the 10th Hussars sent back for the regimental band and a supply of tennis balls. The southern column under Major General Donald Stewart, Roberts's friend and a highly respected officer, made the advance through the Bolan Pass to Kandahar almost without serious opposition and with scarcely any human casualties. Among the baggage animals 12,000 camels died in the intense cold and biting winds. Captain Hoskyns of the Royal Engineers, with the column, felt that his chief's achievement was afterwards neglected by public and press: 'The English public, who know but little of military matters ... took but scant notice of the General who marched an army rapidly for hundreds of miles through bitter cold and dismal waste, and through his rapidity of movement alone, paralysed the enemy and won his goal without a fight.' Many generals, thought Hoskyns, would not have reached Kandahar.[4]

Of the three columns, Roberts's saw the most action. He had worked strenuously from the time of his arrival at Kohat in early November to make good deficiencies in transport and equipment, and took particular care with medical arrangements, providing a static base hospital, a small hospital with each regiment for treatment of slight wounds and mild cases of sickness, and a divisional hospital for the reception of more serious cases. Roberts's harshest critic, Colonel Hanna, praised his 'energy, clear-headedness and practical knowledge displayed ... during those busy weeks of preparation.'[5] It was typical of Hanna in his history to blame Roberts for the poor state of transport; in fact, Sam Browne, head of the Military Department before taking command of a column, had sold off 'surplus transport' in the summer of 1878. Roberts's able staff and senior officers included Colonel Hugh Gough, whom he had met in the Mutiny, commanding the cavalry, Colonel Aenas Perkins, a classmate at Addiscombe as Chief Engineer, and the Revd J.W. Adams, chaplain, a veritable muscular Christian of remarkable courage and quick instincts in action. His reinforced column now had the

58

72nd and 92nd Highlanders, both seasoned regiments, and as native infantry Sikhs, Punjabis and Gurkhas, 'the martial races' of the north and veterans of the Frontier. Less good was the young 2nd Battalion of the 8th King's Regiment, composed of soldiers who were 'very sickly, very young, and scarcely fit for service'. And would his Muslims prove loyal to the British or favour their Afghan co-religionists? He had 5,500 fighting men, eighteen guns, 3,000 native followers and 2,000 transport animals. Roberts's friendship with both Lytton and Colley ensured that he had full political powers and as few detailed instructions as possible.[6]

Ahead lay the Kurram Valley, 60 miles long, the road a rough track with magnificent wooded mountains on all sides. Of the local people, Major Collett of the Royal Engineers recorded that the Turis 'were glad to see us, and that, smarting as they were then, under Sher Ali's late exactions, they regarded General Roberts's troops as deliverers from an oppressive government'.[7] Less welcoming were the Managals and Wazirs, both exceptionally independent and aggressive, and the Zaimukhts and Ghilzais, notorious for their raids. His two chief difficulties were guarding lines of communication and maintaining transport 170 miles from his base.

Promptly at 5.00 a.m. on 21 November, Roberts's advanced guard at the head of his force crossed a trestle bridge, and moved forward to occupy Kurram fort on 25 November. Local inhabitants said that Afghan forces, numbering some 1,800 men and twelve guns, were withdrawing over a high wooded pass, the Peiwar Kotal. Early on the 28th, Roberts concentrated his main force and advanced. Receiving reports that the Afghans were retreating in disorder, abandoning their guns, he pushed on along the narrow and rocky track climbing steeply up the massive stone face of the ridge to the Kotal, a narrow depression or saddle, his men in single file. Contrary to reports, enemy troops and guns were strongly positioned, and the advancing infantry came under intense rifle and artillery fire from front and flanks. Roberts pulled his men back and encamped, but the Afghans brought forward mountain guns and succeeded in dropping shells into the British camp. Little damage was done, but the weary troops had to shift their tents a mile further back.

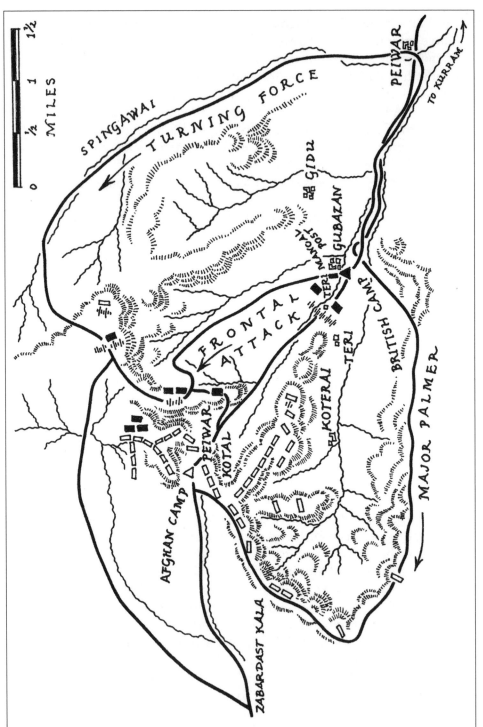

Peiwar Kotal – 2 December 1878

Wisely Roberts spent two days reconnoitring, sending forward Colonel Perkins and Major Collett. The position they scouted was an extraordinarily strong one. A later observer commented: 'The Paiwar[sic] is a magnificent position, if properly held; no troops in the world could carry it. The approach is hemmed in by commanding spurs and the road to the Pass itself winds up the almost perpendicular hill-side.'[8] It was strongly occupied by regular troops and artillery behind a breastwork of stones and pine logs. Collett proposed a night flank march round to the Spingawai, east of the enemy's extreme left, from where successive ridges could be commanded by fire. Roberts adopted the idea, fixing on tactics that repeatedly served him well: feinting at the enemy's front or one flank while striking round the other. To disguise his intentions, he arranged for gun positions to be laid out in full view of the Afghans and for reconnaissance parties to examine ostentatiously both sides of the main valley. He then marched with a flanking force of about 2,300 men at 10.00 p.m. on the night of 12/13 December, leaving his camp fires burning. The frontal diversion was carried out by Brigadier General Cobbe with 870 men, while Major Palmer with Turi levies would make a wide sweep round the right flank of the Afghans as a further diversion.

The march up the Spingawi valley was extremely arduous, the troops scrambling over ridge upon ridge of loose rocks. As the sun rose, they could see the route lay over a pass 9,400 feet high surrounded by mountainous forests. Roberts's suspicion that the march was being deliberately slowed down by Pathan sepoys of the 29th Bengal Native Infantry leading the column was confirmed when two shots were fired from their ranks to alert their Afghan fellow Muslims. It was a critical moment, for the majority of his force was Muslim. Roberts showed imperturbable sang-froid despite being isolated with a partly disloyal regiment. Fortunately his ADCs and the Revd Adams brought on the rest of the column, and he replaced the 29th with the 5th Gurkhas and pressed forward. He abandoned a plan to halt for an hour's rest, because of the delay, and just before 6.00 a.m. the Gurkhas in the lead reached the foot of the Spingawi Kotal just below the Afghan defenders entrenched above them. Undetected until within 50 yards of the first barricade, the Gurkhas aided by the 72nd Highlanders charged forward in the face of heavy fire and seized the defences, and a heliograph signal was flashed back to the camp telling of success.

By 9.00 a.m. Roberts was ready to continue his advance along the main ridge, and led it himself with the 29th. A mile further on they were halted by intense fire from strong enemy forces posted on the far side of a deep ravine, with dense pine woods offering good cover for the defenders. Brigadier Cobbe meanwhile had moved out at 5.00 a.m. as planned, advancing along the northern side of the valley. In his frontal assault the 5th Punjab Infantry under Major McQueen became separated from the 8th King's. McQueen caught a glimpse of the Afghan camp through an opening in the woods and sent a messenger to Roberts, who promptly despatched two guns to the spot, their fire causing confusion and terror among the Afghan camp followers and baggage animals. The tents caught alight, terrified mules, camels and ponies, and their equally terrified drivers, fled westward. The panic spread to the troops opposing Roberts's advance. A portion of them ceased firing and withdrew, leaving the ravine in front of Roberts's force undefended. Meanwhile the 8th King's Regiment led, first by Cobbe and, after he had been wounded, by their own commander Colonel Barry-Drew, worked their way from spur to spur of the Peiwar Mountain, to a point whence they could pick off the Afghan gunners on the summit of the pass. By 12.30 p.m. the Afghans' fire was weakening and they began to fall back. Roberts took the bold decision to break off his own attack and move his force round into the valley beyond to cut off the Afghan retreat. This thrust at the enemy's escape route was decisive. Once the Afghans saw what was happening, the retreat became general, and Roberts's infantry and guns moved forward to seize the Kotal. The Afghan regulars fled down the main road pursued by the 12th Bengal Cavalry, while the irregulars dispersed into the hills. Limber boxes and abandoned guns littered the line of retreat. The victory had cost only twenty dead and seventy-two wounded, and had been achieved in the nick of time as Afghan reinforcements, both artillery and infantry, were moving up to the Kotal. The quantity of guns and stores seized by Roberts's force showed that the Afghans expected to hold the position. Their force had been larger than assumed, and in regular troops alone outnumbered

Roberts by about 3,500 to 3,200. The capture of the position made a strong impression on the Afghans and the surrounding tribes.

Roberts had boldly divided his force and led it personally on the flanking march. In his first battle he showed confident generalship, firstly by using surprise, secondly, by switching the direction of his attack when he saw he was making progress. 'From the first,' wrote Lieutenant Robertson of the King's Regiment, 'he inspired all under his command with supreme confidence in his judgement as a skilful general, as well as in his boldness as an intrepid leader.' His subordinates, Cobbe, McQueen and Barry-Drew had used their initiative in pushing forward the frontal attack. By contrast, after the British attack on Fort Ali Masjid on the Khyber, Lieutenant Eaton Travers of the Gurkhas commented: 'Sam Browne is certainly keeping up his apparently well earned reputation of being a regular old woman and quite unfit to command an army.' Haines called Roberts's victory 'an exceedingly smart affair', and the Duke of Cambridge wrote from London on 6 December to say how much officers at Whitehall were 'gratified to hear of General Roberts's glorious success on the 1st & 2nd, which seems to have been most complete & admirably done on the General's part & the troops engaged under him.' This was solid praise, as Cambridge had shared all Haines's reservations about Lytton's policy and the advance.[9]

Moreover, the timing of Roberts's success was most advantageous for his reputation and his good relations with the Conservative government. According to Colley:

> There never was such a stroke of luck for [news of the victory] was telegraphed home on the morning of the assembling of Parliament, and must have been shouted through the streets when the members were going down to the House to criticise Lord Lytton's policy. Success always carries people with it, and I have no doubt it will materially affect the division on the big debate. We were glad to see that the Queen thoroughly appreciated it also, and sent out so congratulatory a message.[10]

The force remained at the Peiwar for four days, collecting abandoned guns, equipment and stores, sending wounded back to the field hospitals at Kurram fort, bringing up supplies and improving the road on either side of the Kotal. On 6 December, they moved forward again. Roberts reconnoitred to the summit of the Shutagarden Pass, finding that it was not so formidable a route as the Peiwar Kotal, but as winter was approaching he decided against occupying it. Instead, he ordered the troops to construct winter quarters on the Peiwar Kotal and in the Kurram Valley, and to explore Khost. By then the cold had deepened, bitterest at dawn when icy winds swept down the narrow gorge, and Hugh Gough in command of the cavalry later recorded that letter writing was impossible, ink freezing in the bottles. Washing was out of the question, as sponges and water were blocks of ice.[11]

On 23 December, in keeping with his policy of providing the best care and attention for his men, Roberts visited the wounded in their hospitals. The following day he had to confirm the sentence of a court martial convened quickly because of the shot fired by a Pathan in the 29th Bengal Native Infantry to alert the Afghan defenders to their approach. During the approach march eighteen Pathans had deserted. The man who fired the first shot was executed; a younger sepoy who fired a second received two years' imprisonment; the Jemadar who failed to arrest them seven years' transportation; and the eighteen deserters terms varying from ten years to one year. It was necessary that a deterrent example be made. Roberts recorded in his diary, after the hanging: 'I am glad it is all over,' and commiserated on General Orders with the 29th, 'a gallant and distinguished regiment'. The effect of the sentences prevented further desertion for more than a year, although during that time the Muslim portion of his force were severely tried by appeals from their co-religionists.[12]

In keeping with Lytton's limited military objectives, Roberts was not to advance further towards Kabul. In the New Year he turned to exploring and dominating the adjoining Khost valley as an alternative line of communication, in view of possible further trouble. He had also been charged with ejecting the local Afghan ruler. This was to be difficult, in part because of terrain, in part because of the hostility of the inhabitants, and finally because of continued transport difficulties. Camels suffered in particular: in six months the Kurram Field Force was to lose 8,828 out of 10,861 hired camels.[13]

On Christmas Eve news reached India of the Amir Sher Ali's flight to Russia and his son Yakub's assumption of authority. Convinced that English policy aimed at destroying the independence and integrity of his kingdom, the Amir had decided on 10 December, contrary to previous thoughts, to travel to Russia to plead with the Tsar for help. This was in spite of letters from General Kaufman telling him not do so, but to make terms with the British. Although accompanied by the last officers of Stolietov's mission, he was refused entry. Abandoned by the Russians, at war with the British, without friends, he died at Balkh on 21 February 1879. The Viceroy ordered Major Cavagnari to negotiate a settlement with his eldest son and successor, Yakub, British objectives having largely been achieved.[14]

Before proceeding to Khost, where his orders obliged him to remove the headman by whom his force was being harried, Roberts invited local Turis and Jajis who had given assistance to meet him in durbar, receive rewards for their help and be assured that they would henceforth be under the protection of the Government of India. After that he set out accompanied by Colonel Waterfield, the political officer, and 2,000 men, marching through open country and narrow defiles into the rich Khost valley, with its terraced rice fields, irrigated by numerous channels drawn from the streams that flowed down from the surrounding mountains, dotted with clean, whitewashed villages, the cottages garnished with cherry trees. On 6 January 1879, they reached Matun, the name given to three villages grouped round a small fort in the valley's centre. Roberts had already been in communication with the Afghan Governor, who surrendered the fort on condition that he should be allowed to go safely to either Kabul or India. Over tea, the Governor warned Roberts that he could do nothing to prevent the attack of hillmen from adjacent districts, confident that the small invading force 'had been delivered into their hands', and coercing the local inhabitants to co-operate. Roberts pitched and entrenched a fortified camp close to a water supply, and, sending for village headmen, informed them severe punishment would be meted out if the hillmen were allowed to attack. Rifle pits were dug, cavalry stood by their horses all night and the infantry lay down with arms beside them, but the overconfident tribesmen had put off their attack until morning. As it became light Roberts and Colonel Hugh Gough led out a reconnaissance of 255 cavalry, Punjab infantry and a mountain battery, and drove back the enemy by several bold charges against superior but less disciplined numbers. They then returned at speed to the camp which had come under attack by 4,000 assailants and scattered the enemy, the cavalry taking a hundred prisoners as well as bringing in grain and 500 head of sheep and cattle. Covered by a brisk fire from the dismounted 5th Punjab Cavalry, the 10th Hussars charged uphill into the centre of the enemy's position, routed them and, rapidly dismounting, harassed them in retreat with fire from their carbines. Colonel Hugh Gough reported the charge 'as one of the most gallant episodes in cavalry warfare I have ever witnessed'.

Roberts decided to take strong action: camp followers had been murdered, local levies had watched the fight, ready to join in the attack if it appeared successful, while the enemy had used the villagers to shield their advance. He ordered the destruction of the nearest hamlets where camp followers had been murdered. But the one-sided victory, with Roberts's losses being only three killed and four wounded, did not settle things and more trouble followed that night. Some prisoners had been ransomed by agreement with the local headman, but the others held out for further payment. Soon after dark hillmen were discovered creeping up the banks of a nullah or gully at the back of the camp, where the prisoners were detained under guard. The nearest sentry fired instantly, and the piquets all round took up the firing, thinking another full-scale attack had started. The prisoners, calling out to each other in Pushtu, tried to seize the guards' rifles and the sword of the Jemadar in command. He shouted at them to stop or be shot, and when this had no effect ordered his men to open fire. Nine prisoners were killed and thirteen wounded, five mortally. Major Colquhoun with the column noted that the last were treated with painkillers by the medical staff, the remainder were attended to and sixty-three prisoners were unhurt. Roberts ordered an enquiry, appointed a commandant of Matun Fort and began exploring and surveying. In three days he had visited the whole valley. The people of Khost and the surrounding hills remained hostile to British control and Roberts decided to make use of a certain Sultan Jan as Shahzada (local governor). Sultan Jan was the ideal candidate

66

if anyone could hold Khost without British troops: he was an Indian Civil Servant of royal descent, with distinguished manners and appearance. Although Roberts summoned the local chiefs and addressed them, telling them that Sultan Jan and Turi levies would be left to maintain order, his appeal did not succeed. His force set out on its return march, but had to turn back to save Sultan Jan and his men from being overwhelmed by angry hillmen who simply waited until the Indian Army column had departed before descending like hornets. The Afghans then attacked the rearguard, but the cavalry under Gough kept them at bay. The historian, Colonel Hanna, blamed Roberts 'for the costly and unsuccessful expedition into Khost', and claimed that his force was saved from being overwhelmed only by the unusually dry conditions. Roberts would have done well to note the failure of his efforts to win over the locals and of village burning to cow them into submission. The nature of Afghan warfare and terrain made it easier to defeat than to subdue tribesmen.[15]

The Khost Valley venture brought Roberts into his first public controversy, which began with his sacking the only newspaper correspondent with his column, MacPherson of the London *Standard*. MacPherson, critical of Roberts's conduct of both reconnaissance and battle at the Peiwar Kotal, exaggerated the dangers. He made much of the deaths of the captured tribesmen and of an alleged order to the cavalry to give no quarter on 7 January. Sacking a correspondent could well be a public relations mistake, but Roberts was prepared to run the risk rather than having a man he felt he could not trust. He enlisted Colley's aid to get rid of MacPherson on the grounds that his dispatches were false and that he had added to a telegram after Roberts had approved it for despatch. He told Major General Martin Dillon at the India Office, London, that MacPherson was 'an unmitigated cad', that he had altered a dispatch after it had been passed, and that he, Roberts, had done his best to humour him, 'knowing what damage these correspondents can do'.[16] Certainly he would not have sacked him had he thought there was any alternative. The incident led to questions being raised in the House of Commons about the Khost expedition, exaggerated stories quoting that ninety prisoners had been bound hand and foot and shot. In fact, a Court of Inquiry ordered by Roberts decided that the native Jemadar in charge of the guard, a Pathan like his prisoners, had no choice and exonerated him and his men. Radical MPs asked why villages were burnt and Roberts's cavalry ordered to take no prisoners. His written reply, that the people of Khost were distinctly warned that if the Indian Army column were attacked, every village from which his troops were fired upon would be destroyed, reflects his anxious and difficult position at the head of a small force in enemy country. The cavalry who charged numbered fewer than forty sabres, facing an enemy ten times as strong; the number killed were a tenth of that alleged in Parliament. To the 'no prisoners' claim, he wrote that he had instructed Major J.C. Stewart, 5th Punjab Cavalry, who asked, 'Am I to make prisoners, Sir?' 'No, do not stay to do that, your party is too small. Disperse them as best you can.' Was this justified by operational conditions? The small force was surrounded by vastly superior numbers and bold action was necessary. What Roberts did not seem to have learnt was that the Afghans remembered harsh measures – the shooting of tribesmen, burnings and the seizure of winter stores of grain; subsequent declarations of British good intentions and humanity did not change their hostility.[17]

Roberts read one lesson carefully: in future he took pains to ensure that war correspondents who accompanied him were on his side, properly looked after and suitably flattered. Perhaps he learnt this from Lytton, Colley and Cavagnari, all aware of 'the importance which a well-instructed Press exerts', as General Luther Vaughan, former member of the Punjab Frontier Force, brother of the famous headmaster of Harrow, and by then military correspondent of *The Times*, put it.[18]

Towards the end of February, Roberts was able to take brief leave and spend a week at Kohat in north-west India with his wife, who had travelled specially to see him. Meanwhile, the new Amir Yakub entered negotiations with Lytton. He did not enjoy the support his father had had from the Afghan chiefs and was prepared to compromise, but not to renounce his authority over certain territories on the Indian border. Accordingly, Cavagnari was directed to ask for an invitation to enter more detailed negotiation. Hardly had the invitation been issued on 29 March 1879 than a proclamation by Yakub addressed to the Khagianis, a tribe particularly troublesome to the British, praising and exhorting them, was intercepted and brought to Cavagnari. Roberts told Colley when the latter visited him in Kurram that this was a piece of treachery and that the Afghans had not had a sense of defeat driven into them. But Colley convinced Lytton to continue his attempts at a settlement with Yakub, for English public feeling was against carrying on the war.[19] Britain was in the grips of a recession, trade stagnant, manufacturing crippled, agriculture – despite a good wheat harvest – depressed by un-seasonable weather and disastrous floods. Disraeli's government had become embroiled in a war against the Zulus, fomented by the expansionist policy of the Governor of the Cape, Sir Bartle Frere, and the muddled policy of Lord Carnarvon, Colonial Secretary. On 22 January 1879, just when Afghan opposition seemed overborne and negotiations were proceeding, events in Zululand took a disastrous turn. A massive Zulu impi, or army, smashed into Lord Chelmsford's camp at Isandhlwana while the main force was away, killing over 1,300 men, British and native. The subsequent heroic stand of the tiny garrison at Rorke's Drift failed to avert a public outcry, and the cloud of mismanagement worsened when Napoleon III's son, the Prince Imperial, trained and commissioned at Woolwich, was speared to death by Zulus on 1 June. Already, in the outcry following Isandhlwana, the government had decided to send Sir Garnet Wolseley as High Commissioner and Commander-in-Chief in Natal, Transvaal and Zululand with plenary powers, civil and military. He arrived too late in South Africa to snatch further honours, for on 4 July Chelmsford crushed the Zulus at Ulundi.[20]

In contrast to events in South Africa, those in Afghanistan seemed to be moving to a favourable conclusion. The inter-ception of Yakub's proclamation to the Khagianis led to fear of ambush or treachery, so he was invited to Sam Browne's camp at Gandamak. This ill-omened place was the site of the final British stand nearly forty years before in the retreat from Kabul. The bleached bones of the remnant of the 44th Regiment were still visible.[21] Tactlessly, Yakub Khan and his Commander-in-Chief arrived on 8 May in Russian uniform. His negotiations with Cavagnari as Lytton's representative were not popular with the majority of Afghans. The British could choose either Yakub or likely partition, but the latter would bring further military involvement and expense. The terms of the Treaty of Gandamak, signed on 26 May 1879 by the new Amir and Cavagnari, seemed a favourable conclusion to the war. The Amir pledged to live 'in perfect peace and friendship' with India and agreed to British control of foreign policy in return for troops, arms and money in case of foreign attack. A British Agent was to reside at Kabul, British officers were to be stationed on the frontiers, and a telegraph line would run from Kabul to Kurram. Yakub agreed to promote trade and commerce with India. In return for an annual subsidy of six lakhs (600,000 rupees), the Khyber, Kurram and Afghan enclaves around Quetta and along the Bolan Pass were 'assigned' to the British as protectorates, rather than 'annexed', suggesting a chance of their being returned.[22]

With the war apparently over, Browne's Khyber column was largely disbanded and Stewart's force was ordered to leave Kandahar in September, as soon as it was cool enough to march. Only Roberts's troops were left intact to garrison and administer the Kurram valley. The peace was to prove more apparent than real: 'Never did a state of peace bear a stronger resemblance to a state of war,' wrote Hanna. In Afghanistan there was unrest at an unpopular treaty, the Indian troops had to be kept alert, convoys were stopped from moving except under escort and supplies were at famine prices. Cavagnari was to proceed to Kabul as the first representative of Great Britain there since the murders of the British envoy Alexander Burnes and his two British companions in 1841. It was an inauspicious moment, with cholera rife in the city and the unfortunate death of Bakhtiar Khan, India's native agent, closing a valuable channel of information regarding Afghan intrigues and intentions. 'This is a great chance for you, Cavagnari,' said Haines as the envoy left Simla. 'Yes sir, it is a case of man or mouse,' replied Cavagnari.[23]

In London, Disraeli's government were pleased to claim that one of their two wars had been triumphantly concluded. Parliament passed a vote of thanks to Lytton, Haines and the troops, and approved the treaty. Salisbury wrote privately to Lytton to thank him. A round of honours followed. The Grand Cross of the Order of the Bath was given to Browne, who hardly deserved it, and knighthoods to Cavagnari, Colley, Stewart and Roberts. Some of the soldiers felt these 'gongs' were excessive. Stewart admitted to his wife that he thought he had got his KCB on false pretences.[24]

At the end of June 1879, Lytton informed Roberts that he was to be one of the military members of a Commission of Inquiry into army expenditure, with a view to achieving reorganization and savings. He was to return to Simla to join the chairman, Sir Ashley Eden, Lieutenant-Governor of Bengal, a leading Indian civil servant, and the other members including a number like Colonels Baker and MacGregor who had been serving in the war. Before then, however, he had to see Cavagnari safely on his way to Kabul.

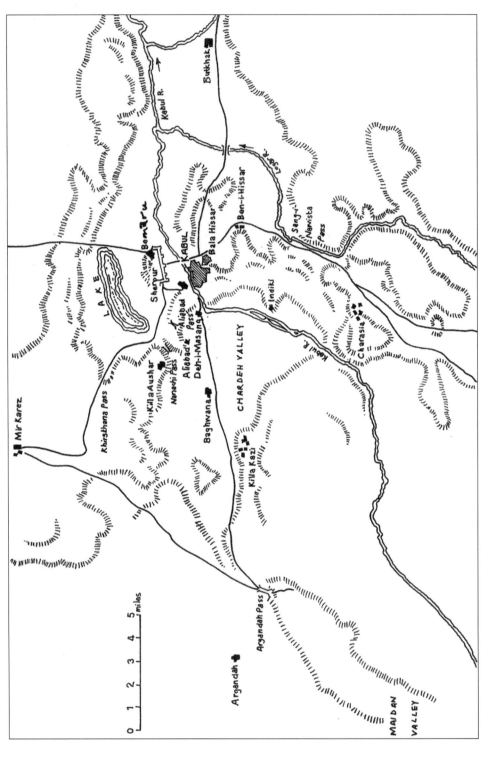

Approach to Kabul and the Chardeh Valley

Chapter 5

At Odds with Desperate Men

The web of policy so carefully and patiently woven has been rudely shattered ... All that I was most anxious to avoid in the conduct of the late war and negotiations has now been brought about by the hand of fate.

Lord Lytton

Gloomy forebodings were uttered in my presence ... It was most unadvisable that our armies should go to Kabul ... The road ran through a defile, the Afghans occupied the hills.

Colonel Luther Vaughan

In mid-July, Major Louis Cavagnari set forth as British representative to Kabul, accompanied by his secretary, a doctor, and an escort of twenty-five cavalry and fifty infantry from the Guides, the elite frontier regiment established by Colonel 'Joe' Lumsden. They were commanded by Lieutenant Walter Hamilton VC. In his autobiography, written almost two decades later, Roberts claimed to have had gloomy thoughts when he and fifty officers, anxious to do honour to the Envoy, marched with him to within 5 miles of the crest of the Shutagardan Pass and held a last formal dinner with him. There is nothing of this in his official letter to Lyall, Foreign Secretary on the Viceroy's Council, but it appears Cavagnari, Roberts and his wife all had premonitions of the worst. Lady Roberts told the young Lord Melgund that Cavagnari:

could not conceal from himself that he was going among the most treacherous people under the sun. But that he c[oul]d not believe that Yakoob for his own sake w[oul]d be such a fool as to allow any thing to happen to him. 'However,' Cavagnari told me, 'if anything *does* happen to me it will make things very easy for the Government. The course they will have to adopt will be very plain. This is a great satisfaction to me.'

Lady Roberts concluded, 'Poor little man he was full of hope when my husband left him.' That next morning, 14 July, as Roberts and his officers accompanied Cavagnari and his escort as far as the reception committee of Afghan cavalry and notables waiting by a large, tastefully decorated tent where tea was served, they both saw a solitary magpie, an unlucky omen. According to Roberts, both men separated, then spontaneously turned to shake hands in a final farewell.[1]

Outwardly at least Cavagnari was in the best of spirits. Indubitably a man of action, he was, thought Neville Chamberlain, serving on the Viceroy's Council, 'inclined to be hasty and imperious, and more likely to control those he is brought into contact with through his force of character and through fear than from any personal attachment. I should say he is more the man for facing an emergency than one to entrust with a position requiring delicacy and very calm judgement.' He feared that once at Kabul, Cavagnari would not keep out of difficulties. Lytton had chosen a man who had wanted to seize the fort at Ali Masjid by a *coup de main* before hostilities and was an object of special suspicion to the Afghans.[2]

Roberts was warmly greeted at Simla, he and his wife were honoured guests at the Viceregal Residence, Peterhof, Lytton's French chef Bonsard producing new dishes for the occasion: 'Croquettes à la Roberts and Fillets à la Koorum with bullets of truffles'. Lady Lytton recorded that Haines had not written a line to Roberts to congratulate him on his victory or his knight-hood, jealous of his junior's success.[3] Nonetheless, he was soon immersed in the discussions of the Eden Commission assembled by Lytton to consider Indian Army Reform. Throughout August telegrams and letters from Cavagnari to Foreign Secretary of the Viceroy's Council, Alfred Lyall, and to Roberts himself expressed optimism. His last telegram to the Viceroy on 3 September concluded 'All well'. Between 1 and 2 o'clock on the morning of 5 September Roberts was woken by his wife to say that a telegraph man was wandering round the house and calling. The telegram he brought was bad news from Captain Conolly, Political Officer at Alikhel, dated 4 September:

> One Jelaldin Ghilzai, who says he is in Sir Louis Cavagnari's secret service, has arrived in hot haste from Kabul, and solemnly states that yesterday morning the Residency was attacked by three regiments who had mutinied for their pay ... being joined by a portion of six other regiments. The Embassy and escort were defending themselves when he left about noon yesterday. I hope to receive further news.

For a moment Roberts was paralysed by anxiety, but was roused by his wife calling out, 'What is it? Is it bad news from Kabul?' He replied, 'Yes, very bad, if true. I hope it is not.' He woke his ADC and sent him off at once to the Viceroy with the telegram. No sooner was he dressed than Lyall arrived. They despatched a telegram to Conolly and went to Lytton. Early as it was, the Council was assembled. There were serious faces. Should the news be true, troops must be despatched. Telegrams were sent to halt the withdrawal from Afghanistan, and in the afternoon Brigadier Dunham 'Redan' Massy, in temporary command of the Kurram Field Force in Roberts's absence, was directed to move to Shutagardan and entrench, awaiting orders. The Kurram force was the only one which might reach Kabul quickly. During the day further telegrams confirmed the truth of the first report. The Mission had been overwhelmed and every member of it massacred after twelve hours' heroic resistance. Captain Conolly telegraphed that messengers had arrived from the Amir bringing two letters addressed to Roberts giving the Amir's account. These and the story of a Risaldar-Major on leave near Kabul told the tale.

When Cavagnari arrived at Kabul the situation was potentially explosive. The Afghans resented the treaty imposed by British arms, disliked the presence of a foreign embassy, especially with an escort of uniformed soldiers, and remembered the humiliating defeat inflicted upon the British in 1842. The new Amir did not enjoy widespread support. Six Afghan infantry regiments from Herat arrived in a near-mutinous state, demanding arrears of pay, jeering at Kabul regiments beaten by the British, and demanding to know why Cavagnari and his escort were allowed to remain. On the morning of 3 September soldiers from the Herat regiments rioted, demanding their back pay, and when someone shouted that they should obtain it from the English ambassador, they streamed off to the Residency in part of the old fortress of the Bala Hissar, accompanied by the 'dregs' of the city. The four Englishmen and their escort heard the rising roar of an angry crowd. Stones hurtled against the Residency walls. Cavagnari appeared on the roof as the gates were barred and refused to pay them. There was scuffling and looting, and the escort opened fire. The Afghan troops rushed to collect their rifles and gather support. Two messages to the Amir failed to bring help. Yakub feared to intervene, although he had three batteries of artillery nearby. The Heratis returned with the city *badmashes* and poured in a hail of fire from surrounding houses on three sides. The Residency was indefensible: the walls were thin and the roofs commanded by other high buildings. The seventy defenders were faced by thousands. At 1.00 p.m. two field guns were brought up to breach the walls. By then the situation was critical, the buildings were ablaze and Cavagnari was dead, having led a sortie. In a second sortie the Guides scattered the attackers 'like sheep before wolves' according to an eyewitness, but were unable to drag the guns back or disable them. The survivors fell back. Using ladders a number of the attackers clambered onto the roof of the main Residency building, in which the defenders made their last stand in savage hand-to-hand fighting. By early evening, with the four Englishmen dead and scarcely a dozen Guides still in action, the Afghans called in vain in the name of Islam to the survivors to drop their rifles and surrender, shouting that their hostility was against the British. True to their salt, the last Guides led by Jemadar Jewand Singh sallied out, striking down their foes on either side. Jewand Singh was the last to fall, having killed eight of his assailants. It was estimated later that 400 of the attackers had perished during the twelve-hour battle. The Residency lay gutted and smoking. The investigating military commission set up by Roberts when he reached Kabul wrote: 'The annals of no army and no regiment can show a brighter record of bravery than has been achieved by this small band of Guides. By their deeds they have conferred undying honour, not only on the regiment to which they belong, but on the whole British Army.' On Roberts's recommendation, the whole escort was awarded the Indian Order of Merit, the native soldier's equivalent of the Victoria Cross, and the Guides wore the battle honour 'Residency, Kabul'.[4]

The Amir did nothing to help Cavagnari and his men, except despatch his Commander-in-Chief, Daud Shah, and his son with a copy of the Koran to persuade the attackers to desist. Daud Shah was unhorsed and roughly handled by the mob. For three days Yakub remained in his palace and the shops in the city were shut. Afghan's ruler had shown himself weak and cowardly, but no evidence came to light of his being at the centre of a conspiracy. A British surgeon with the force that advanced to Kabul later wrote:

> None of the evidence goes to prove that the Amir planned the destruction of the Embassy. All evidence appears to impute the rising to the bigotry and fury of the soldiery, excited by want of pay, while much proves that the offering of only one month's pay, the taunting remarks and the general behaviour of the General present in the pay-garden, caused the rush to be made on the Residency ... [But] after the mutiny had commenced his behaviour was, to say the least of it, imbecile and useless, and he practically left the Embassy to protect themselves, and, in so doing, abandoned them to their fate.

As Donald Stewart said, if he could not protect the embassy, he was useless as an ally.[5]

There was shock and anger in both Simla and London. Edith Colley, whose husband was by now in South Africa, wrote to him: 'We had to keep up appearances, even when the look that passed over H.E.'s face when he read the telegram told us pretty well that there was little hope left ... it is all too dreadful! ... Cavagnari's face haunts me, and all our last talks, and the poor little wife at home.' The deaths of Cavagnari and his escort were a bitter blow for the Viceroy and his wife. Lady Lytton and two guests went to the theatre with his ADCs to keep up appearances as news of the massacre passed from mouth to mouth.[6]

Lytton and his colleagues were determined that Kabul should be occupied, Cavagnari avenged and British prestige restored. In this they were supported by London. The Queen wired Disraeli to urge that 'no hanging back, or fear to be found fault with, must deter us from strong and prompt measures ... Pray urge this on the Viceroy.'[7] Disraeli strongly backed Lytton and defended him in a masterly speech at the Guildhall against attacks by the Opposition. Privately he was not so sure, especially when Lytton sent to London an acid commentary in which he cut to pieces in words the principal officers in the Indian Army, Roberts apart, and said that one of them, Sir Sam Browne, deserved a court martial. Disraeli commented sarcastically: 'Except Roberts, who he believes is highly gifted, and certainly is a strategist, there seems no one much to rely on; Stewart respectable; Massy promising ... And these are the men whom, only a few weeks ago, he recommended for all these distinctions. I begin to think he ought to be tried by a court martial himself.'[8]

Perhaps, then, it was fortunate that only Roberts's Kurram Field Force was ready for action. Browne's column had been dispersed. Stewart could easily reoccupy Kandahar, but an advance from there on Kabul would take months due to the supply difficulty. Roberts's force was therefore reassembled. From the advanced base at Ali Khel, Kabul lay 80 miles away, five days' march over difficult but not impossible country. Lytton consulted Haines and his Council, and then ordered Roberts to march to Kabul to avenge Cavagnari and restore the situation. A telegram was sent to Conolly to warn the Amir that a British force was on its way. Stewart was to hold southern Afghanistan and Kandahar with his division. A division under General Bright was to assemble in the Khyber Pass, advance to Jalalabad and support Roberts. Transport would be difficult, as the first campaign had caused the deaths of many baggage animals and the rest had been dispersed. Lieutenant General Sir Michael Kennedy set to work to improvise a system, officers' baggage having already been cut. 'No more truffles and champagne,' wrote Major George White of the Gordons to his wife.[9]

As things turned out Bright was unable to reach Roberts because of transport difficulties, but as the Shutagardan Pass at

11,500 feet would be closed by snows over the winter, it was essential that he keep open communications via the Khyber Pass and Gandamak. Brigadier Charles Gough commanding one of Bright's brigades pushed forward in late November to within 20 miles of Kabul. The Kurram route along which Roberts had advanced was then abandoned.

The campaign had already stretched the Indian military machine to its limit, especially transport. There was a shortage of British officers and widespread sickness. Roberts pressed for experienced officers as senior subordinates, and was given Brigadiers Herbert MacPherson and Thomas Baker to command the infantry brigades, the latter being the Viceroy's military secretary, Brigadier Dunham 'Redan' Massy for the cavalry, and Colonel Gordon for the guns; unfortunately neither of the latter two had much experience of war, nor had Massy served with cavalry in the field. Roberts told his wife that he had wanted Hugh Gough, left in charge of communications, not Massy, but Haines had insisted against Lytton's protests. Charles Gough, Hugh's brother, also an experienced cavalryman, wrote:

> the fact is Massy never saw *any service* except when *as a lad* he marched with his Reg[iment] to the attack on the Redan [at Sevastopol in the Crimea], where he was accidentally hit, like many others, rather badly and got called by his Father 'Redan Massy'. Since which time he has never seen a shot fired. He had never in his life *seen cavalry in action* until he came up here, and was utterly without experience and untried and yet he was crammed down everybody's throat.

He was to prove a burden. Roberts kept his experienced and successful staff, adding Colonel Charles MacGregor as chief, Lieutenant Colonel E.G. Hastings as head of the 'politicals' and the young Henry Mortimer Durand as Political Secretary, and by proclamations attempted to calm the people on the route. The young Durand, whose father had distinguished himself at Ghazni in the 1st Afghan War, was delighted to be Roberts's Political Secretary. He equipped himself with an ancient Scots claymore given him by his brother-in-law MacGregor and an almost equally huge double-barrelled pistol which he thrust ostentatiously into his belt.[10]

79

Roberts visited Lytton for personal instructions. Lytton's relations with Cavagnari had been close, and he was 'in a state of deep distress and depression', grieving for his dead envoy, the collapse of the Mission and the heavy blow to his policy. Roberts asked what line he should take on future relations with Afghans. 'You can tell them we shall never again altogether withdraw from Afghanistan, and that those who help you will be befriended and protected by the British government.'[11] Lytton's written instructions, marked 'very confidential' and despatched to Roberts when he had joined his force, put much that was to follow into perspective. If the Herat regiments were dispersed Roberts should set a price on the head of every soldier and be liberal in payment of informants.

> All such persons captured and denounced by your informants, should be promptly executed in the manner most likely to impress the population ... The whole Afghan Population is *Particeps criminis* in a great national crime; and every Afghan brought to death by the avenging arm of the British Power, I shall regard as one scoundrel the less in a den of scoundrelism, which it is our present business to thoroughly purge ... You cannot stop to pick and chuse [sic] Ring-leaders. Every soldier of the Herat Regiments is *ipso facto* guilty; and so is every civilian, be he Priest or layman, Mullah or peasant, who joined the mob of assassins. To satisfy the conventions of English sentiment it will probably be necessary to inflict death only in execution of the verdict of some sort of judicial authority. But any such authority should be of the roughest and readiest kind, such as a drum-head Court Martial; and its enquiry in each case limited to the question whether the executors of retribution are satisfied that it is desirable that the alleged culprit should be put to death. For, remember that it is not *justice* in the ordinary sense, but *retribution* that you have to administer on reaching Kabul. The action of your Courts Martial should be quick, and the grounds of their decisions not recorded ... What is required is a prompt and impressive example – and do not forget that there will be more clamour at home over the fall of a single head six months hence than over a hundred heads that fall *at one*. Your objects should be to

strike terror, and to strike it swiftly and deeply; but to avoid a *'Reign of Terror'*.[12]

This was clear enough – Roberts owed his advancement to Lytton, shared his views, and was not going to contradict his patron's wishes. Moreover, his own friendship with Cavagnari and the advantages he had seen of strong action at the start of the Indian Mutiny impelled him to act as the Viceroy wished. As a young subaltern he had unflinchingly watched sepoys blown from the mouths of cannon.

Lytton also urged for the city of Kabul, as a 'great national culprit', the punishment of 'total destruction ... by fire, in order that all Afghanistan & India may plainly perceive the full flame of the candle lighted by the Kabulese as they fired the British Embassy on the evening of the 3rd of September.' The Viceroy then said that perhaps partial destruction was reasonable, considering the outcry there might be, and he would support Roberts in any efforts 'to avenge the murder of my friend – and yours', adding that 'some things I cannot order. Vengeance for precious lives will be welcomed and applauded by the public if prompt. Our immediate action is not conciliation but retribution.' In another letter which he ordered him to burn, he told him to press on, not bother about lines of communication and seize every possible strategic point 'before the political weathercock at home has shifted.'[13]

Roberts, carrying a copy of Sir Henry Durand's *History of the [1st] Afghan War*,* travelled with his wife from Simla to Umballa, where he left her and joined a train carrying his staff. He recorded in his diary: 'God help her and bless her – I am travelling as fast as I can to Kurram.' Major George White, proceeding to join the Gordons, met her 'returning slowly & sadly to Simla. I promised her that the regiment & I would look after Fred & perhaps bring him back a peer.' White, a reserved, athletic, service-hardened veteran, had been twenty-six years with the colours and had yet to have his moment of glory. He was an old friend of Roberts, and had noticed in March how he

---

*Major General Sir Henry Durand, Royal Engineers, hero of the capture of Ghazni in 1841 and father of Henry Mortimer Durand who accompanied Roberts, and edited and published the history.

had already looked 'very worn and old; all the responsibility of commanding an expedition like this, and the adverse criticism, must be very trying.' His kindness to Lady Roberts was rewarded with a Balaclava she knitted and sent to him.[14]

Roberts's force was small, 7,500 men and twenty-two guns, but they were in good spirits and included the excellent Highlanders and Gurkhas. He had also brought two of the new Gatling guns, which he thought worth giving a chance. The battery gunners had practised with the weapons, but despite much care and attention the ammunition drums could be turned only gingerly and were prone to jam.[15] Much depended upon the force's speed of movement – Roberts wished to advance before the mass of Afghan hillmen should rally to fight him on the approach to Kabul and at the city. The massacre of Cavagnari and his escort had shown that the infidels were vulnerable but would come for revenge. The Russian press observed that the destruction of the English mission demanded speedy and exemplary punishment of the murderers and their accomplices, although the march to Kabul must be undertaken by troops exhausted by recent exertions. Delay would be a sign of weakness.[16]

Everything had to be improvised. Roberts sent Baker with an advanced force to occupy Kushi, 14 miles beyond Shutagardan, protecting the entrance to the Logar valley, to collect their necessary transport and supplies for a swift move on Kabul, while trying to deceive the Afghans that no advance was to be made until spring by remaining in the vicinity of Aki Khel. He and Baker took much care over the column's organization, although the march routine appears to have been careless. Transport remained a headache, with the mules nothing but 'bare bones and sores'. MacGregor as Chief of Staff rented 500 brewery carts and issued orders to send on every beast, however sick and feeble, able to take the road. Although the 3rd Sikhs gave up ninety of their camels, the force was still short and some of the cavalry led their horses laden with grain sacks. Roberts could move only half his troops at a time which left his line of march twice as vulnerable, but it worked.[17] He reckoned his 80-mile advance to Kabul with a small force, surrounded by a hostile population, and with serious transport deficiencies, as a greater achievement than his more famous and longer advance to Kandahar.[18]

With the assistance of the former British agent at Kabul, Nawab Ghulam Hassan Khan, Roberts came to an agreement with the Ghilzai chief, Allud-ud-Din, for safe passage in return for a present of 3,000 rupees and a monthly payment of 2,000 rupees during the campaign. He issued a proclamation intended to be reassuring, saying that the purpose of the expedition was to avenge the destruction of the Embassy, but that no innocent person would be harmed. MacGregor grumbled in his journal: 'I think all this blackmail paying is very wrong in principle, but our force is so small that it requires all such help.'[19] It was Ramadan, and good Muslims were fasting during the day, a discouragement to campaigning. Passing overhead were cranes making their way towards the plains of India, one of the first signs of winter.

Food was requisitioned at gunpoint, if the villagers proved sullen and refractory. With the mood of revenge for the fate of Cavagnari and his comrades, the British and Indian troops gave little thought to whether the villagers had sufficient for the harsh winter. By 19 September, Baker was entrenched with his brigade on the Shutagardan Pass, the road was being improved, and transport and ammunition were being collected; on the 27th, Roberts marched with a small mixed forced of cavalry and infantry, intending to rendezvous with Baker. The Shutagardan defile was blocked and an ambush laid by some 2,000 tribes-men whom the flanking parties failed to detect. According to MacGregor's diary, Roberts was nearly shot when Afghans opened fire. The medical officer was wounded and five Sikhs killed. Men of the 92nd Highlanders and 3rd Sikhs, respectively under Colour Sergeant Hector Macdonald and Jemadar Sher Mahomed, a native of Kabul, drove off the enemy, the latter receiving the Order of Merit.[20]

On 30 September, amidst preparations for the final advance, Roberts managed a glass of champagne to celebrate his forty-seventh birthday. On 2 October, a hundred rifles of the 3rd Sikhs sent forward by Colonel Money routed an enemy on a strong prominence of rock. The passage of the last 35 miles to Kabul began on 3 October, a further proclamation to the people of Kabul heralding the advance: the city would be occupied, those guilty of the attack on the mission punished and anyone found armed in Kabul or nearby would be treated as an enemy. With his small force facing unknown odds, Roberts was determined to take firm and if necessary ruthless action. When the inhabitants of the village of Koti Khel fired on his men, they surrounded it at dawn on 5 October, and in a fierce reprisal two villagers were killed and five captured, of whom three were immediately shot on Roberts's orders for being in rebellion against their lawful ruler, the Amir. Roberts had already told Baker to shoot any of the Amir's troops in the field with arms, 'otherwise hanging, which does not waste ammunition'. This reflected the Viceroy's orders, Roberts's own wish to avenge Cavagnari and his belief that ruthless measures would cow opposition.[21]

The Amir was caught between the advance of the avenging British and the anger of his people. In two letters to Roberts, passed on by Captain Conolly at Alikhel, he claimed that he had done his best to prevent the tragic events at the Residency and was deeply upset. 'By this misfortunate I have lost my friend, the envoy, and also my kingdom. I am terribly grieved and perplexed.'[22] Roberts believed this pleading was a cover for the Amir's guilt. Nawab Ghulam Hussain Khan told him that although Yakub had not actually planned the massacre, he had taken no steps to prevent it and that he was now playing the British false. The Amir sent two ministers as emissaries to the British camp, but their main task appeared to be to stop the advance, and Roberts wrote to Yakub: 'After what has recently occurred, I feel that the great British nation would not rest satisfied unless a British army marched to Kabul and there assisted Your Highness to inflict such punishments as so terrible and dastardly an act deserves.'[23] Roberts was warned by Lyall that although the Amir did not seem likely to have instigated the attack on the Embassy, he and his advisers had been stirring up the tribes against the British. He told the Amir that the British Army was advancing to exact retribution on the murderers and restore the Amir's government.

At the top of the Shutagardan Pass later that evening Yakub's latest letter reached Roberts followed by the information that Yakub himself had already arrived at Baker's advanced camp, accompanied by his eight-year-old son. On 12 October, he walked into Roberts's camp accompanied by only two attendants and expressed his determination to resign. He was in very low spirits, said that he would rather be a grass-cutter in the camp of the English than ruler in Afghanistan and begged to stay until the Viceroy agreed to his being sent to India. His appearance did not impress either Roberts or the young Political Officer, Mortimer Durand: 'a weak vacillating face, pleasant enough at times, but not trustworthy or in any way impressive ... He seemed very nervous and fidgety.'[24]

Lytton warned Roberts that they must wait for cabinet instructions before accepting the abdication. He also said that General Luther Vaughan, the correspondent of *The Times*, a paper which reflected cabinet views, would soon be arriving and Roberts was to be particularly civil to him. 'General Vaughan is ready to write up any policy of which the cue is given to him by me, or by you on my behalf. His letters to *The Times* from Kabul may have a considerable effect upon public opinion at home.'[25]

Roberts regarded the Amir's presence in the camp, with a constant stream of visitors coming and going, as a security risk, and stationed a Highlander in front and a Gurkha behind his tent as sentries. He was more prisoner than honoured guest, and his plea to halt the advance because there was only one regiment to guard the ladies of his court and family, and who could tell what might happen to them, was contemptuously rejected. Roberts was more worried about street fighting and a repetition of the disaster of the 1st Afghan War. To a reassuring proclamation to the Afghan people he added one to his troops not to be guilty of 'indiscretion' with native women, a source of trouble in 1839–42, according to his father.[26]

As Roberts continued the advance across open cultivated country, parties of armed tribesmen sat watching. Early in the afternoon the vanguard reached a group of villages known as Charasia. Ahead loomed the last major obstacle before Kabul, a crescent-shaped range of defensible sandy hills running 3 miles roughly east–west, between 700 and 1,500 feet above the plain. As Roberts did not have his entire force, and reconnaissance found no serious enemy, he decided to camp nearby and bring up the rest of his troops. As dusk began to close and large parties of tribesmen were seen on the hills, Roberts had uncharacteristically made a mistake not seizing the pass ahead. At dawn on 6 October, the rising sun showed masses of regular troops with artillery deploying on the heights. The Official History recorded:

Behind these heights lay the densely crowded city of Kabul, with the scarcely less crowded suburbs of Chardeh, Deh-I-Afghan, etc., and the numerous villages which lie thickly clustered all over the Kabul valley. Each and all of these had contributed their quota of men to dispute advance of the British; and it did not require much experience of Afghans to know that the numbers already assembled would be very considerably increased, if the enemy were allowed to remain in possession of their stronghold for a single night.

About this time it was also reported that the road in rear of the column was blocked, and that the march of General MacPherson's brigade, with its long string of baggage, would be opposed; whilst on the hills on both sides of General Roberts's camp bodies of men were seen assembling and, as was afterwards learnt, only waiting for nightfall to make a general attack upon the encampment.'[27]

Any hesitation would have brought an attack in overwhelming numbers not just upon Roberts's force, but also on MacPherson encumbered with the convoys of stores and ammunition. The Afghans held a strong position with eighteen guns, several regular battalions and a host of irregulars. Their commander was Sirdar Nek Mohammed who had returned to Kabul after a long and secret interview with the Amir, ostensibly with instructions to quieten the troops, but had reappeared with a strong force to dispute Roberts's advance. He expected an attack on his left at the Sang-I-Nawishta defile. In a difficult position and greatly outnumbered, Roberts did not hesitate. He sent a message to MacPherson to join him before dark, resolved to attack the enemy's right, their weakest place, and then roll up their line from west to east. Baker was sent forward with 2,000 men and guns including the two Gatlings. The 72nd Highlanders, 5th Gurkhas and 5th Punjab infantry advanced without check and took the lower heights. Meantime a small column under Major White engaged the Afghan left with great success, drawing their attention away from Baker's flanking movement. White had spotted with his binoculars that the steep slope enabled his men to advance in dead ground, so he took advantage of this to lure the superior enemy force from their breastwork and then rout them in close fighting. A watching officer of the 5th Punjab

1. Lieutenant General Sir Frederick Roberts at the end of the 2nd Afghan War painted by W.W. Ouless. Without the help of his old friend Donald Stewart and his former critic, the Viceroy Lord Ripon, he might not have had the chance to win Victorian immortality by his march to Kandahar. (*Royal Artillery Mess, Larkhill*)

2. Earl Lytton, Viceroy of India, 1876-1880. Roberts's most important patron is usually judged a failure, despite his imagination and lack of racial prejudice. Famine and war damned his viceroyalty. (*British Library, Lee-Warner Collection*)

3. The Marquess of Ripon. Lytton's successor, a very different man, favoured Indian aspirations, but inherited a war from which he escaped with honour by sending Roberts on his most famous march. (*British Library, Lee-Warner Collection*)

4. Tribal towers of the Afridis in the Khyber Pass. 'The houses are towers built as little fortifications, the doors being 10 to 15 feet above the ground and approached by means of a rope ladder which can be pulled up at a moment's notice.'(*British Library, India Office Collection*)

5. The 8th of Foot, the King's (Liverpool) Regiment, threads its way up the Peiwar Kotal. The overwhelming setting for Roberts's first victory is well caught in a sketch by Colonel Gordon for the *Illustrated London News* of 15 February 1879. (*Mary Evans Picture Library*)

6. A rather immature watercolour by Philip Francis Durham (1852-1932) of the Battle of Futtebad, 2 April 1879, may serve for many Afghan War engagements. Indians and British in orderly lines in the valleys await the onslaught of a myriad of Afghans surging down from the heights. Here Brigadier Charles Gough was clever enough to lure the enemy out of their positions while keeping his strength hidden. (*British Library, India Office Collection*)

7. Gatling guns. British and Indians enjoyed superior military technology throughout the war, except possibly in artillery, but the Gatling guns proved a disappointment despite the efforts of armourers to put them in fighting trim. (*National Army Museum, the Roberts Collection*)

8. The Bala Hissar and burnt-out Residency. The picturesque fortress was indefensible against modern weapons. Skulls, heaps of bones, bloodstains and bullet holes were evidence of the fate of Cavagnari and his comrades, British and Indian. (*National Army Museum, the Roberts Collection*)

9. The execution of the Kotwal (Chief Constable) of Kabul, sketched from the *Illustrated London News* of 3 January 1880. The Kotwal may indeed have played a part in dishonouring the corpses of Cavagnari and his escort from the Corps of Guides, but Roberts's executions stirred up a political storm in India and England. (*Mary Evans Picture Library*)

10. Roberts's fortified camp at Sherpur. Gaps in the defences were hastily filled by improvised means, but the strong men behind them proved sufficient to withstand an all-out Afghan attack just before Christmas 1879. (*National Army Museum, Roberts papers*)

11. The Amir Abdur Rahman. Lytton's 'ram caught in a thicket', an astute but brutal ruler who helped Roberts's march to speed British departure and the defeat of his main rival. He ruled Afghanistan for thirty-nine years. (*British Library, the India Office collection*)

12. *Crossing the Zamburak Kotal on the Kabul-to-Kandahar March* by Louis William Desanges. Desanges was not in Afghanistan, but his painting, completed in 1882 for Queen Victoria, does catch the disorderly appearance of the column on the march amidst looming mountains. (*Courtesy of both Garen Ewing and the Royal Artillery Institute*)

13. The battle outside Kandahar. *Boy's Own* history come true as George White leads the Gordons to victory. For the magazine he is drawn in traditional scarlet, not the new-fangled khaki which British and Indians wore in Afghanistan. The heroism of Gurkhas, Sikhs and Scotsmen confirmed Roberts in his view of the superiority of the 'martial races'. (*Mary Evans Picture Library*)

14. Hardinge (left, Bombay), Roberts (centre, Madras) and Stewart (right, Bengal), the three Indian Army commanders-in-chief when Stewart was in overall charge, gathered for a 'camp of exercise', i.e. combined manoeuvres; although junior, Roberts seems to be giving the instructions. (*National Army Museum, Roberts Collection*)

Cavalry wrote: 'Major White led then in a most gallant & splendid way ... The hill was won. I never saw or heard of a more dashing brilliant thing.'[28]

As White then advanced to assist Baker in his attack, the Afghan right and centre broke and fled. Baker's infantry seized the main ridge, and, pivoting on their right, then swept forward against the enemy's left. With great coolness White detached two companies to assist Baker. Outflanked and enfiladed by Baker's force, the Afghans abandoned their position and retired across the river, the 92nd Highlanders ascending the height on the left and taking the enemy guns. The cavalry pursuit however was feeble, a Russian commentator observing: 'A portion of General Massy's cavalry brigade got during the day to the rear of the Afghan infantry and yet it managed to do nothing. It could have pursued the retreating enemy, but apparently it had not the heart to do so.'[29]

British casualties were eighteen killed and seventy wounded, the Afghans' upwards of 300 dead. All eighteen guns had been taken. The Gatlings had been a disappointment, one jamming after the first few rounds; the heliograph proved more effective, communicating between the wings of Roberts's scattered forces. The battle was the most critical that Roberts had yet fought – failure would probably have meant the total destruction of his force, isolated and divided as it was. While everyone on the British side displayed courage and determination, it was on Roberts that the burden of critical decision fell. Colonel Hanna censured Roberts's rashness, but acknowledged that officers and men alike had 'felt the inspiring influence of their commander's indomitable courage, and unshakeable confidence in himself and them'. On the following day at first light, Roberts rode over to White and said, 'I congratulate you, I was sure the 92nd would do well.' He told the Highlanders that no one could have surpassed them, and attributed much of the success to White's military instincts and personal gallantry, recommending him for the Victoria Cross. It was a turning point in White's career after years of undistinguished service. Likewise, Colour Sergeant Hector Macdonald, the son of a poor crofter, had shown courage and leadership at Charasia and in the action on 19 September, and was recommended for a commission.[30]

The occupation of Kabul, which lay ahead, could have been the trickiest part of the advance. The population was mostly hostile and large numbers of Afghan troops were still about. Roberts's force was too small to cope with fighting in the narrow streets and bazaars and his Mutiny experience determined him to avoid doing so, but he had to follow up his victory. On the morning after the battle, he advanced and occupied the village of Beni Hissar, 3 miles beyond the pass, intending to concentrate his force there before moving on to Kabul. At Charasia, MacPherson was threatened by large bodies of tribesmen who dispersed only after two infantry battalions were sent against them. Roberts could not concentrate his force as intended, because he was told that three regular Afghan battalions and survivors from the battle had entrenched on the Asmai hills to the north-west. He sent Massy to reconnoitre and then Baker to attack, but it was dark before the latter was ready and action was postponed. In the morning the Afghans had gone. Massy sent his squadrons down the Ghazni road, and 22 miles west of Kabul the 5th Punjab Cavalry dispersed a small enemy party, but no others could be found. Kabul merchants visited Roberts, and told him the Afghan army had dispersed, most to their homes, one group with Sirdar Mahomed Jan going off together. The enemy's camp was left standing, and guns, elephants, camels, mules and ponies were taken.

White was furious that Baker and Massy had not been more energetic. He and Captain Hay of the Gordons, with their small force tucked down for the night on the 8th, agreed that the enemy camp 'under our nose within 800 yards' should have been seized, and their prediction that by morning the Afghans would have made off was proven by intelligence received about 3.00 a.m. White told his wife that Roberts or MacPherson would have done better. 'The enemy broke up into small parties & made off. Great recrimination between Baker & Redan Massy who commands the Cavalry & who is as arrant an imposter as ever drew a sword. Self indulgent, timid, good for nothing fellow.' The men who might have included Cavagnari's murderers had escaped. Mortimer Durand, Political Secretary, echoed this assessment: 'The escape of the mutinous regiments was sheer bad management, and due to Massy. His cavalry was ample, and had he enclosed the hill as he could easily have done in a continuous chain of vedettes, the disappointment w[oul]d have been impossible ... Massy is a nice plucky fellow, but very lazy and careless.'[31] Although White censured Baker for inactivity, he had done better than the cavalry. As the moon rose soon after 11.00 p.m., he had pushed ahead with the infantry, attacked the withdrawing enemy, killed a number and taken others prisoner, occupied their camp, and at 5.30 a.m. on the 9th sent a message back to Massy, the cavalry Brigadier who should have led the pursuit. Instead of pursuing, Massy had withdrawn his eight squadrons into two walled enclosures and settled down comfortably for the night.[32]

Despite Massy's incompetence, the Afghan army was dispersed and Roberts was master of Kabul, an achievement largely due to the speed of his advance and the skill of his tactics. On the 9th, his force advanced to within one mile of the city; retribution was at hand.

Chapter 6

Martial Law at Kabul

The whole Afghan Population is Particeps criminis *in a great national crime; and every Afghan brought to death by the avenging arm of the British Power, I shall regard as one scoundrel the less in a den of scoundrelism, which it is our present business to thoroughly purge.*

Lord Lytton to Roberts

I share your anxiety about the consequences of some of Roberts' recent political and administrative proceedings. He is a splendid soldier; but his management of the political situation has not been altogether as judicious as I had hoped it would be.

Lord Lytton to Lord Cranbrook

To Scotsmen with Roberts's force, Kabul and the Bala Hissar resembled the Castle Rock and Arthur's Seat at Edinburgh, with the two squashed closer together. In place of grey massive Scots walls were crumbling irregular outlines of turrets and battlements, hot and dusty like the sun-baked heights they crowned. The city was a jumble of close-packed houses, dominated by twin citadels, the fortified walls running along the scarp of the hill known as Sher Darwaza – the Tiger's Gate. Green irrigated fields and lines of poplar and willow extended up the valleys and round the villages in every direction. Above them rose bare stony hills. The Indian and British force was dwarfed by its surroundings – thin lines of khaki and blue, tipped with steel of bayonets and cavalry sabres, followed by lines of unwieldy baggage animals, bemused by the vast assortment of cannon, ancient and modern, which they found in the Amir's arsenal.[1]

Roberts wasted no time. He examined the nearby encampment of Sherpur as winter quarters and left cavalry to guard the huge quantity of stores and equipment, including seventy-six guns left there. On 11 October, he went with a small escort to inspect the former English residency in the Bala Hissar. It was a melancholy spectacle, witness to the last desperate struggle of Cavagnari and the Guides. Walls were blackened by smoke from burning ruins, each angle where there were loopholes was pitted with bullet marks deep into the hard mud plaster, the staircase was stained with blood and whitewashed walls were bespattered with it. Ashes in the middle of one room were the remains of bodies burnt by the Afghans. Nearby were two skulls and a heap of human bones, still fetid, traces of a desperate struggle. Later Nawab Hayat Khan, one of the British agents, informed Roberts that the Kotwal or Chief Constable had ordered the bodies of the Guides 'to be treated with neglect and contumely', and thrown into a pit in the city ditch. After viewing the scene, Surgeon Duke cited the proverbial treachery and faithlessness of the Afghans, while George White would have made it much hotter for the people of Kabul. 'An Army sent to avenge the second Ambassador of ours murdered in Cabul ought to have razed it to the ground, instead of sprinkling rose water about as we are doing.'[2]

It was planned to make a formal entry to the Bala Hissar on the 12th, and on the 11th Durand persuaded Roberts to rewrite a proclamation which he proposed to read to the assembled populace. It was wrong in tone and content, thought Durand, and he went through it paragraph by paragraph persuading Roberts to change the wording. Everything was ready for the entry early on the morning of 12 October, when the Amir Yakub asked to see Roberts. His life, he said, had been a miserable one and he could bear it no longer. 'You see,' he said, 'what the people are. Who would rule over them? I have fought battles for the Amirship like my father and grandfather before me, but it is all over now. I have done with them. Let me go to India, or London, anywhere you will, so long as I leave Afghanistan for ever ... I have not one friend in the country, not one friend.'

Roberts and the politicals, Hastings and Durand, begged him to reconsider, but he would not. The Amir 'seemed utterly broken, his eyes red and swollen, his body bowed helplessly forward, with prostration in every line, and his voice tearful and quivering.' At last Roberts agreed to his not accompanying them to the Bala Hissar, and promised to send his abdication to the Viceroy, but said he must remain titular Amir until the answer came.[3]

On that day, with the Amir's son, eight-year-old Musa Khan, Roberts occupied the Bala Hissar in full-dress parade. Next day, in a deliberate show of strength, the whole Field Force marched through Kabul, mostly a tangle of dark, filthy, narrow streets and alleys, divided into quarters and sections, with no lofty minarets as earthquakes were frequent, but with bazaars well stocked with silver ornaments, iron and brass utensils, sheepskin clothing, and laden fruit stalls. Later the British observed how much more Russian than English Kabul was: Russian money, Russian crockery, Russian or Bokhara silk and Russian-cut clothes made it a mart for trade from the north. Roberts and his staff led the way, followed by the infantry regiments of his division except those forming the garrison of the citadel. The streets were densely lined with inhabitants, whose behaviour was quiet and orderly. The rich Hindu merchants welcomed the invaders heartily, and appeared delighted at the prospect of British rule, expecting order to be restored and customers with Indian rupees in their pockets to appear at their stalls. Surgeon Joshua Duke added ruefully that 'these unfortunate men will not give us the same welcome on future occasions, unless we determine to occupy Cabul permanently.' Everyone remembered the fate of the British and Indian force forty years before. The reading of the proclamation to the Afghans nearly ended in disaster with the appearance of a cat – Roberts loathed cats – which was fortunately shooed away by MacGregor, and it appears only he, Roberts and Durand saw it.[4]

The Residency was unsafe for a garrison, being commanded completely from the walls of the arsenal. Engineers and pioneers with Roberts's force dismantled half the citadel, removed much filth and cut a fine road through it, inserting loopholes and putting the defences into good repair. The extended camp at Sherpur outside Kabul was to be the British base for the winter.

Roberts's medical officers opened a 'dispensary' or medical centre on 14 November 1879 for the sick of Kabul and its neighbourhood. At first Dr Owen had only limited accommodation, two tents with a wall of mud and a fireplace for each. Then the Kotwal's house was made available, different rooms en suite served as a medical store, consulting room, waiting room for female patients, operations theatre and opthalmoscope room. On the first day there were twelve patients, and Roberts came and expressed approval. Some Afghans had a shock, as recorded by correspondent Howard Hensman: Dr Owen's superficial resemblance to Cavagnari made them think that he had risen from the dead. By 10 December, over 260 patients had been treated. It was closed when Roberts's force retreated to Sherpur and when seen again on the 25th, it had been reduced to a total wreck by some 800 insurgents who had forced their way in, appropriating furniture and wooden fittings for fuel. It was duly restored and early in 1880 became popular, some 208 patients visiting on 26 January alone. Once a lady of Kabul acted as matron, women began to attend. Soon a hundred beds were available and the daily average of patients was 220, with twenty operations being performed. Two-thirds of the patients were women. Such was Owen's success that, according to Hensman, his services were sought by well-to-do citizens in whose *zenanas* were sick wives or favourite concubines pining under mysterious ailments. He was even admitted to private homes.[5]

Roberts may have taken Kabul, but other Indian Army forces had varying success. Brigadier Charles Gough advanced to Jalalabad and sent a flying column forward to Gandamak to overawe the Ghilzais, but he had an insufficient force to extend his permanent control that far. In the Kurram Valley, Managals and Ghilzais mounted a major attack on the garrison at Shutagardan under Colonel Money who was guarding Roberts's communications. Money attacked and dispersed the besiegers, and then abandoned the Shutagardan, cutting Roberts's line of communication with the Kurram. Stewart meanwhile had reoccupied the citadel at Kandahar within twenty-four hours of receiving news of Cavagnari's death. There was a fierce action against the Ghilzais near Shahjui. Roberts's position was extraordinarily exposed. Great risks had been run in reaching Kabul, and with a less determined or able commander, there could have been disaster. MacGregor wrote on 8 October: 'We have nearly eaten all our provisions, and if we were to get worsted, not only would the whole country be up, but we should get no supplies. I hope Bobs' luck will carry him through; but we are playing a risky game.'[6] Was it necessary for the avenging expedition to be carried out so quickly when nothing could be done for Cavagnari and his comrades; why not defer action until 1880 when a stronger force could be sent? In answer Lytton and Roberts would have said that such treachery called out for immediate vengeance, and the speed of advance was justified by success. Delay would strengthen their Afghan foes and the moral effect of striking swiftly was great; no repetition of the 1842 defeat must be allowed. Rapid victory had beaten and dispersed the Afghans, and the magazines and arms, including 217 artillery pieces on which they depended, had been seized.[7]

Unfortunately Roberts was soon to dissipate the advantages won by his brilliant march, through bad political management, excessive harshness and overconfidence. Concentrating on avenging Cavagnari, he did not have the experience to recognize warning signs of impending trouble. Luckily, the quality of his force, his own leadership and the famed 'Roberts luck' averted disaster, but he still had to ensure the safety of his force, secure his communications to India, and find and deal with Cavagnari's murderers. Eschewing the city with its tangle of narrow streets and alleys, where each gateway could quickly be built up transforming the city into a nest of fortresses, he based his force at the extensive Sherpur cantonment a mile north of Kabul, bounded on two sides by a massive, loopholed wall nearly 4 miles in circumference, with towers for artillery; its east face was incomplete and its rear rested on the Bemaru heights. The wisdom of choosing Sherpur over the Bala Hissar was underlined by an accidental explosion of massive quantities of ammunition at the latter stronghold three days after occupation. Seventeen soldiers were killed and part of the buildings destroyed. Roberts interpreted the Amir's amassing arms and his construction of Sherpur as sure proof that it had been his intention to fight the British. More likely it was due to his fear of endemic rebellion. By 1 November, the filthy barracks in Sherpur had been cleaned, the accommodation was ready and the force moved there from its camp on the Siah Sang hills. Roberts did not, however, immediately begin to lay in stores for winter or clear buildings around Sherpur which obstructed fields of fire.

To secure his communications, he sent out parties to improve the route over the Lataband Pass, and by 19 November the telegraph line ran uninterrupted from Kabul to Peshawar – he abandoned as impracticable the use of carrier pigeons. He was able to send back to India all the time-expired, wounded and unfit, together with elephants, spare bullocks and sick transport animals, retaining just 8,000 men. This was a time of intense activity for Roberts, and even he with his enormous energy found himself working at full stretch, noting in his diary of 15 October: 'The days are not long enough to get into my work, and yet I am glad they are not longer, for I am ready for bed at night.'[8]

His two proclamations to the people of Kabul before he arrived stated that the object of his expedition was to take public revenge on the murderers, but made it clear that those who had nothing to do with Cavagnari's death and who abstained from opposing the British advance had nothing to fear. Two days after reaching the Afghan capital, he issued a third, harsher proclamation. 'The force under my command has now reached Kabul and occupied the Bala Hissar; but its advance has been pertinaciously opposed, and the inhabitants of the city have taken a conspicuous part in the opposition offered. They have, therefore, become rebels against the Amir, and have added to the guilt already incurred by them in abetting the murder of the British Envoy and his companions.'[9] The proclamation instituted martial law for a distance of 10 miles around Kabul, and the death penalty for anyone found carrying weapons in the city or 5 miles around it; rewards were offered for the apprehension of anyone concerned in the attack or who had fought against the British, and for the surrender of any articles belonging to members of the mission or any firearms or ammunition belonging to the regular Afghan Army.

To defeat the enemy and occupy Kabul was one thing; to produce a workable plan to govern Afghanistan was another. Roberts was not a politician, he was unskilled in compromise and negotiation, and inexperienced at drafting proclamations. Mortimer Durand, later to become a lifelong friend, but with a quicksilver mind, saw the weaknesses of Roberts's plans immediately. In the way of confident young men, he thought Roberts had 'no more idea than a schoolboy [how to carry out political plans]'. He could see that Roberts's scheme 'to disintegrate the country, creating a number of weak governorships, and to influence them by keeping forces in the Khyber & Kuyrram [sic] always ready to march … would practically hand over the northern & western provinces to Russia, who would be nearer and therefore stronger in them. I said so, and I think the little man did not quite like it.' When Roberts, with Lytton's support, accepted Yakub's abdication, Durand thought it a mistake. 'I cannot but think [Yakub's] abdication was in great measure due to the utter neglect with which he was treated by the General, and the civility shown to his enemies Wali Mohammed & the other Sirdars. He was completely set aside, never consulted in anything, and doubtless he felt it.' In this he was probably wrong: Yakub was caught between the British and his people, and had Roberts restored him, he would have appeared little more than a puppet. Roberts, Lytton and MacGregor believed in Yakub's complicity in the massacre of the Mission, but could not prove it. The British investigating commission reported the attack by the Herati regiments as spontaneous, but that the Amir and his advisers could have intervened. Lytton accepted this conclusion with reluctance. Durand sympathized with Yakub and was sorry that he was closely guarded, but admitted, 'Yakoob loose just now, and preaching a jehad, would be a most troublesome enemy.' With advice from Durand and the chief political officer, Lieutenant Colonel Hastings, Roberts issued a proclamation on 28 October announcing Yakub's abdication and British intentions:

I, General Roberts, on behalf of the British Government, hereby proclaim that the Amir, having by his own free will abdicated, has left Afghanistan without a Government … The British Government, after consultation with the principal sirdars, tribal chiefs and others representing the interests and wishes of the various provinces and cities, will declare its will as to the future permanent arrangements to be made for the good government of the people.

After Roberts had removed Yakub and most of his chief men to India, Lytton and his council wondered what Roberts was to do with Afghanistan: annex it in part or whole, break it into provinces or find a friendly Amir.[10]

Roberts set up two commissions: the first, of MacGregor, Surgeon-Major Bellew and a native member of the Indian Political Service, Mohammed Hayat Khan, to investigate the massacre and collect evidence against suspected Afghans; the second, of Massy, Major Moriarty of the Bombay Army and Captain Guinness of the 72nd Highlanders, to judge and sentence those whom MacGregor's commission sent before it. Mohammed Hayat Khan, a Persian and Pashto speaker accompanying the British force as translator, advisor and Assistant Political Officer, played a crucial role. MacGregor and Durand were both critical of him in their diaries, but Roberts had his own good reasons for trusting him: he had served as orderly – more like a mediaeval squire – to his hero John Nicholson. Hayat Khan's father had saved Nicholson's life on the Frontier and when he was killed in a border feud Nicholson insisted that his death be avenged. The son remained loyal to Nicholson, served with him throughout the Mutiny, bore his standard in the attack on Delhi, when he became separated from him in the crucial minutes before his fatal wounding, and tended him in his last illness. Any man who had fought with Nicholson in his last battle had a strong hold on Roberts's loyalty. By then Hayat Khan had 'eaten the Queen's salt', was a local commissioner in the Punjab, and at the start of the war Cavagnari's right-hand man. His idea of frontier justice and loyalty would be to avenge those whom the Afghans had killed.[11]

The only member of the Judge Advocate's Department present in Kabul was not a member, so it proved impossible to obtain reliable testimony, bribes and other inducements simply leading to the paying off of old scores. The wish for revenge strongly influenced the commissions. All who had seen the wreckage of the Residency with its nauseating remains, and heard the story of the gallant defence, were deeply angered. 'We saw the place where Hamilton charged out,' wrote MacGregor. 'Then we came home, and to listen to Morty [Mortimer Durand] talking about treating these fiends with justice of the High Court kind was sickening.' Durand recorded MacGregor as saying openly that the Amir was guilty and should be hanged for doing nothing to help Cavagnari. 'This is the general opinion,' he wrote. Lytton's instructions to Roberts told him that every soldier of the Herati regiments was *ipso facto* guilty, as was every civilian who joined 'the mob of assassins', and called, not for justice, but retribution. 'Strike terror, and strike it swiftly and deeply,' he wrote.[12]

Swift action followed. The Chief Minister, the Finance Minister, the Police Chief, the Governor of Kabul and his brother, all suspected, were arrested. Nominal rolls of some Afghan regiments were found, the surrounding villages were cordoned off by troops and every man whose name appeared on the rolls was detained for trial. To overcome the reluctance of witnesses to testify, Mohammed Hayat Khan was deputed to examine them in secret and produce at the subsequent trials their depositions rather than the witnesses themselves. Thus, contrary to the principles of British justice, the accused had no way of knowing how the evidence had been extracted, or of cross-examining witnesses. Those who denied their guilt could neither bring forward evidence for their innocence nor examine witnesses. MacGregor changed his tune once he was directly involved, and his diary is a litany of criticisms of Roberts's brutality and his own desire for justice. On 19 October, he wrote: 'I think Bobs is the most blood thirsty little beast I know.' On the 21st, he confided to his diary: 'that men were being simply murdered under name of justice and only on the word of H[a]yat [Mohammed Khan], who is himself as big a scoundrel as exists'. Durand agreed with MacGregor, writing: '[Roberts] is a most bloodthirsty little devil too – thinks no more of hanging an Afghan than of smashing a fish insect'. The Police Chief had ordered the throwing of Guides' bodies into the city ditch, was assumed to be involved in the massacre and despite the absence of direct evidence was duly hanged on 20 October. On that day five were executed, including a watchman (chowkidar) who had, according to witnesses, carried Cavagnari's head from the Embassy and thrown it into the market place, and the chief Mullah who had preached holy war and also ordered bodies of the slain thrown into the ditch. Executions went on apace. Two gallows were raised, one outside the door which the Guides had defended, one in the courtyard where they had been quartered. Those found guilty were hanged in batches of ten, while the soldiers in short sleeves and smoking their favourite short pipes looked on. The prisoners met their end impassively.[13]

Lytton's angry instructions echoed British feeling towards the Afghans. Howard Hensman, correspondent of the *Pioneer*, thought them a byword for treachery, deserving of their fate. The young Lord Melgund wrote to his mother in March 1879 that the Afghans were a terrible lot. 'Hanging is too good for them. Their game seems to be to fall on unarmed camp followers and cut them up for the fun of the thing.' Luther Vaughan of *The Times* wrote of 'the dreadful death that had befallen one of the privates of the 92nd Highlanders', who was sick, fell out and was probably enticed toward the gate of the village by the offer of milk or water. His body was afterwards found inside the gate, stripped and mutilated, his face and head being shattered and burnt by an explosion of powder forced into his mouth, recognizable as belonging to the 92nd by his only remaining item of clothing, regimental check socks. 'The sight of a cold-blooded murder like this,' wrote Joshua Duke, 'was calculated to excite feelings of horror and revenge against the perpetrators of such an outrage [and] the mild punishment of hanging was what the headman of the village richly deserved.'[14] Nonetheless, Roberts's vindictive cruelty contrasts starkly with the later image of the kindly 'Bobs, the soldier's friend', and appears to have stirred up the Afghans rather than cowing them.

The commissions officially finished on 18 November. The report sent to Simla stated that eighty-nine had been tried and forty-nine executed, although the Official History gave 163 and eighty-seven respectively. Others were executed apart from those condemned by the commission; for example, five men found by the 12th Bengal Lancers to have weapons were put to death summarily, and another five at Kabul, without trial for inciting attacks on the Shutagarden garrison. The executions fuelled Afghan hostility. 'We are thoroughly hated and not enough feared,' wrote MacGregor.' George White told his brother:

My information leads me to think that the Cabulese hate us more than ever now. We have hanged a lot, 50 within the last four or five days. Nearly all on their own showing. It was thus done. Genl. Baker surrounds a village, gets hold of the head man, asks if there are any sepoys. The Mallick replies with pride, "Yes, my son is a sepoy of the first Herati regiment." The Herati regiments were forward in attack on residency. Said son & sepoy was hanged next day with 26 others.[15]

As word reached India, questions were raised in the newspapers. In mid-November *The Times of India* reported, 'The work of vengeance was so complete as to have become somewhat indiscriminate ... a good many innocent persons should have been hanged while [Roberts] was making up his mind as to their degree of guilt.' *The Friend of India,* a Calcutta newspaper, said: 'We fear that General Roberts has done us a serious national injury, by lowering our reputation for justice in the eyes of Europe.' Lytton himself wrote on 5 December to Cranbrook, Secretary of State for India, that he was uneasy about what was going on, although his instructions were partly to blame. Again Roberts found himself the object of press criticism. Detailed reports of what had happened reached England. The radical Frederic Harrison wrote a damning account of 'Martial Law in Kabul' in the *Fortnightly Review* of December 1879, including a detailed account of Baker's brigade forming a cordon round a village and demanding grain as well as guilty men. The best that Harrison could say for Roberts was that he had not behaved as badly as Russian or Turkish generals. In both Houses of Parliament there were questions and angry words. The Afghan War had brought the Liberal Peer Lord Ripon out of political retirement; he thought it was a classic example of Disraeli's immoral statecraft. On the news of Cavagnari's death, Ripon wrote angrily in his diary: 'How swift the retribution has been – truly the Lord God omnipotent reigneth ... I fear the consequences may be very serious ... It is one of the few cases in which impeachment would be justified, because the Govt have sinned against right & the clearest warnings.' He was extremely critical of Roberts's village burning, and unimpressed by Roberts's claims, based on correspondence found between the Amir and Kaufmann, that Yakub was plotting with the Russians. Gladstone added his voice to the critics. While Roberts was hanging Afghans, Gladstone was in Edinburgh on 25 November delivering to a packed audience a sweeping condemnation of the Afghan War among other things: 'Remember that the sanctity of life in the hill villages of Afghanistan, among the winter snows, is as inviolable in the eyes of Almighty God as can be your own.' Disraeli's government was to feel the consequences of Gladstone, Zulu and Afghan the next year, 1880. Meanwhile, both Roberts and the government were in a tight spot, and with Lytton's advice he penned a brilliant reply in January 1880, which was read by Cranbrook in the Lords on 13 February. Roberts defended his force, saying martial law was necessary as the whole male population of Kabul and the surrounding area was armed and his men would have been liable to sudden attacks; he denied that prisoners taken in a fight were shot, except when they mutilated British and Indian dead; he contradicted Harrison of the *Fortnightly Review* who claimed no civilian correspondents were allowed to go with them. 'Our movements were very rapid after the order for an advance on Kabul was received. This may have prevented other correspondents joining me at the time. Had any come, they would have received every assistance. Some correspondents have arrived since we reached this. No restrictions are placed upon them.' With a straight face he went on to say the strictest discipline was maintained and there was not a single complaint against a European soldier, only a few of a trivial nature against those in Indian regiments. This was brazen indeed, but served the government well. In April 1880, George White told his brother, 'Sir F[red].R[obert]'s part in the atrocities here deserves to be forgotten from the bravery with which he has lied about them.' Roberts might not have been a politician, but he was a Napoleonic writer of dispatches.[16]

Meanwhile, he was to be faced with a military crisis. His swift arrival in Kabul gave him a month of peace, but this was the lull before the storm raised by the executions, the burning of villages and the presence of a foreign army of unbelievers. Welcome reinforcements arrived in early November, the headquarters and two squadrons of the 9th Lancers. Hugh Gough was staggered at the amount of baggage they brought, including full-dress uniform; he was even more nonplussed when he saw camels in the rear of the column toiling along with machinery which turned out to be the regimental soda-water pistol. The regiment had no carbines. These had to be issued in a rush and the men underwent a hurried course in musketry.[17] They soon put their new firearms to use.

Chapter 7

Backs to the Wall

The invader of Afghanistan may count as inevitable a national rising against him ... tribesmen and disbanded soldiers sprang to arms, the banner of the Prophet was unfurled, and the nation heaved with the impulse of fanaticism.

Archibald Forbes, *Afghan Wars*

We have entered into conflict with a race of tigers.

Colonel Charles Metcalfe MacGregor

As winter approached, the British and Indian soldiers at Kabul prepared for a severe drop in temperature. Mortimer Durand had his hair cropped too short to part, grew a six weeks' beard, and wore 'a button up shikar' and over it at night a huge and very dirty poshteen (sheepskin). His riding breaches were inserted, not into respectable boots, but into 'puttees', i.e. strips of cloth rolled round the leg down to the ankle, and finally a pair of thick ammunition boots which had not seen polish since he left Simla. He managed to keep clean with 'real English soap' and a hole in the ground with a waterproof sheet spread over it making 'a capital bath'.[1] George White told his wife he could not understand where the intense, cold wind which blew through the tents came from, for the sky was as blue as their daughter Rosey's eyes. White missed the girl and her mother, and was pleased to hear that Rosey had enjoyed seeing father's dispatches

102

in *The Times* and sketches of him leading his men in tartan trews in the *Pictorial News*. He found writing as a war correspondent for *The Times* a burden, but was angrier still that a Captain Norman, a young man cashiered from the Frontier Force for forgery, was writing articles headed 'Afghanistan'. Using MacGregor's detailed gazetteer and White's letters, Norman could dishonestly give the impression of first-hand knowledge. White was furious with such armchair generals. 'Roberts could sail round the lot of them. Our first object in the advance on Kabul was to get there as soon as possible and strike before the people and the soldiery ... unite[d] to oppose us.'[2]

Events however were soon to test White's confidence in Roberts. As ice formed on water jugs at Kabul, Afghan temperatures were rising. The executions and the Amir's deposition added fire to resentment. The necessity of laying in food, forage and fuel for the winter precipitated events, for Roberts had appropriated the government share of the crop to feed his troops. As in 1841, when the previous invasion of Afghanistan by the Indian Army took place, high prices paid by British commissaries on the open market caused inflation and shortages. An isolated fall of snow on 11 November warned Roberts that the collection of five months' supplies, the amount he calculated necessary, had to be speeded up. But the local collection met increased reluctance from villagers, and there were rumours of the assembling of large bands of armed men, inspired by the cry of Jehad or holy war raised foremost by the Mullah Mir din Mummad of Ghazni, known as Mushk-i-Alam ('Fragrance of the Universe'). He was aged about ninety, a man held in great reverence and esteem, and noted for his piety and learning. Many of the religious and legal officials in the country had been educated at his feet, and readily responded to their old teacher's call to encourage the people to take up arms. A growing combination of national and religious feeling threatened the British position. Mushk-i-Alam was so infirm he had to be carried about on a bed, and from it distributed blessings, charms and exhortations, calling on followers of the Prophet to gird on their arms against the infidel. His chief organizer was a sirdar and popular artillery officer, Mahomed Jan, who had commanded artillery against the British at Ali Masjid in 1878 and was active at Charasia. The women of

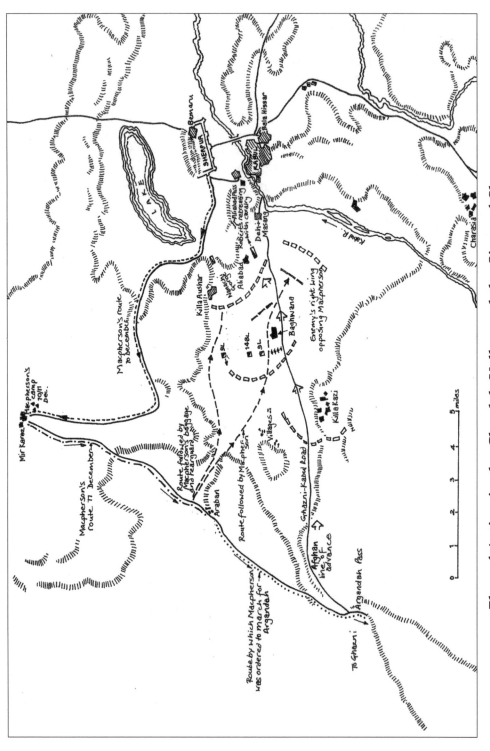

Plan of Action in the Chardeh Valley and the Siege of Sherpur

the court, including the Amir Yakub's wife and mother, did all in their power to foment rebellion.[3]

The Ghilzais launched a series of attacks on the garrison left on the Shutagardan, Roberts sent out troops in relief and the Kabul to Khyber route having been opened, the pass was abandoned and its garrison moved to Ali Khel and Kabul. On 23 November, two squadrons of cavalry sent to bring in a prominent Ghilzai chief, Bahadur Khan, who had refused to sell forage or grain, were fired on and compelled to retire. In retaliation, Roberts led out a force that smashed corn bins, seized livestock, set alight houses and stores of corn. Three days later Baker visited the village of Beni-Badam – 'Benny be-damned' to the Gordon Highlanders – with cavalry, was received with friendliness, and offered food for men and forage for horses. Suddenly two large bodies of armed men were seen hurrying to cut off his retreat, and only by hard fighting did Baker and his men escape. As November drew to a close, reports grew of opposition and insurrection, and friendly Afghans warned British officers of impending attack. The bankers and merchants of Kabul confidently asserted that a night assault upon the cantonment was imminent. Roberts was sanguine and keen to maintain the confidence and morale of his officers, giving a large picnic in early December in the Deh Mazung gorge, to which all officers were invited. After the picnic there was a paper chase which finished up near the ground over which the British and Indian cavalry were to charge so desperately a few days afterwards. General Daud Shah, former Afghan Commander-in-Chief, followed the chase and appeared thoroughly to enjoy it.[4]

Despite warnings, Roberts found great difficulty gathering intelligence, and little knew the extent of the uprising. Patrols went out, but the conditions were bitter. Bivouacking near a village where Baker and his men were almost caught, George White found his beard, 'now a long one with streaks of silver in it', covered with icicles. Roberts sent reassuring telegrams back to India, ordered the Corps of Guides from the Khyber to reinforce his men and improved the defences at Sherpur. On 7 December, he held a council of war, and set out his intelligence that there were three Afghan armies in the field, approaching from the north, west and south. He resolved on a pincer movement, MacPherson marching due west from Sherpur, Baker south from Kabul, turning through the Wardak Valley and sweeping northwards to meet MacPherson coming south-westwards; Roberts himself would remain with the rest at base. To cloak these operations a grand review of the whole garrison was to be held, ostensibly to present medals to four men of the Highlanders for gallantry at Peiwar Kotal. This went well and Roberts's Chief-of-Staff, MacGregor, thought that the impressive appearance of the force and of its commander on his famous grey, 'Vonolel', must give the Afghans pause for thought.[5] Nonetheless, dividing the small force was risky. Roberts's diary of Tuesday, 9 December records: 'a busy, anxious day, conflicting reports of the enemies movements'. He was to be so busy on the 10th that there was no entry.

MacPherson had barely started to move when he was ordered to halt, and allow insurgent forces to advance deeper into ambush and Baker to close the trap. The delay was fortunate as further intelligence reached MacPherson that there were greater numbers than reported. In fact, Roberts had much underestimated the forces facing MacPherson, not 1,500–2,000, but 10,000. When it was reported that Afghan forces from Ghazni were moving up to join those from Kohistan, north of Kabul, Roberts ordered MacPherson to leave his cavalry and horse artillery under Massy at Kila Ashar and move quickly against the Kohistanis. On the morning of the 10th, MacPherson, following orders, succeeded in breaking up a large concentration of tribesmen with little loss to his troops. Massy failed to intercept the enemy with cavalry from Kila Ashar, and the Afghans escaped into neighbouring hills and villages, or towards their allies in the direction of Arghandah.

Roberts then ordered both MacPherson, now 9 miles north-west of Sherpur, and Baker, 20 miles to the south-west, to march early on the 11th towards Arghandah, where the force from Ghazni under the leadership of Mohammed Jan was thought to be. Thus, if Mohammed Jan resumed his march on Kabul, he would find Baker in his rear, MacPherson on his left and the balance of Roberts's force in his front. If he stayed where he was, he would be attacked simultaneously from opposite directions. Massy was ordered to move his cavalry directly along the Kabul–Argandah road, keeping in communication with MacPherson, but not to join battle until MacPherson himself was engaged.

106

The Chardeh Plain, an amphitheatre surrounded by mountains, densely cultivated with orchards and market gardens, seamed with streams and watercourses fringed with willows and poplars, with scattered villages and hamlets, was bad ground for horse artillery or cavalry. Roberts and his Chief of Staff MacGregor judged Massy to be slothful and incompetent, and the former only agreed to employ him after he begged to take part. On the night of the 10th, Roberts gave him explicit instructions on the map exactly what to do, and particularly in view of the broken countryside, to stick to the road with guns and horse.

Massy instead proved Roberts's misgivings by deciding to cut several miles off the journey, leaving the road and marching across country, having weakened his small force by sending roughly a quarter of it to find MacPherson. He was 5 miles from MacPherson and closer to Arghandah than the other two columns when his scouts reported large numbers of Afghans. There was the sound of drumming and considerable commotion. Massy topped a small rise and saw, before his astounded eyes, Mohammed Jan's entire army, some 10,000 tribesmen, spread out in an arc before him, opposed to his own puny force of 300 lancers and four light field guns. The enemy came on in heavy masses covered by a line of skirmishers about 2 miles in length, the red and white standards of the mullahs dotting the line in front, and a few horsemen on rear and flanks. They had no guns, but kept up a ceaseless fire with rifles, the bullets singing over the heads of the British and Indians. Massy's force returned fire, first with the guns, and then adding the fire of thirty 9th Lancers' Martini-Henry carbines, but this had no effect on the advancing masses. Nor could he easily retreat over the broken country. Four miles away, at Sherpur, Roberts heard artillery firing and, aware that something had gone amiss with his plans, galloped out with his personal staff as fast as their horses would carry them. When he arrived at approximately 11.00 a.m. the situation was critical. He sent messages back to Sherpur for two companies of Highlanders and for Gough to hold the Nanachi Gorge towards which they were being pressed and told Massy to delay the Afghans as long as possible to give MacPherson time to arrive. Mortimer Durand, who was with Roberts, watched the 9th and the 14th Bengal Lancers wheel into line, break into a trot and disappear in a cloud of dust into the Afghan horde. Scant

107

seconds later the squadrons came back out 'in a shapeless mass', utterly broken and galloping for all they were worth. The numerous watercourses in the valley greatly impeded guns and horse. Roberts made a stand with the guns in the small village of Bhagwana, but with ammunition running low, he was obliged to retreat under cover of a cavalry charge. The villagers emerged and joined the fight, their headman attacking Roberts himself, who was only saved by the intervention of an unhorsed trooper of the 1st Bengal Lancers. 'The 9th [Lancers] were completely out of hand,' wrote Durand, 'scattered in twos and threes all over the country. The 14th Bengal Lancers rallied fairly and kept together. But it was a rapid retreat uncommonly like a rout.' Eventually the guns, which had come into action at first without Massy's knowledge and moved forward off the road which offered their best escape route, were driven into a deep ditch fringed with poplars, stuck fast and had to be spiked and abandoned. Major Smith-Windham who commanded the battery galloped straight into Sherpur and announced that the cavalry were destroyed, the guns lost and the only chance was an immediate retreat.

Among acts of gallantry, Lieutenant Hardy of the Royal Horse Artillery refused to leave a wounded fellow officer, Lieutenant Forbes of the Bengal Lancers, and they died together. The Revd J.W. Adams won the Victoria Cross pulling two men of the 9th Lancers from beneath their fallen horses and out of a ditch to safety and giving up his horse to a wounded lancer. Those who could not escape died under the Afghan knives. Roberts, with the bulk of the force, was retiring toward the Deh-I-Mazang gorge, others to the Nanachi gorge, when MacPherson and his brigade appeared, marching at top speed to the sound of the guns. He struck the rear of Mohammed Jan's force, pushing them towards the Deh-I-Mazang gorge. There, in response to Roberts's message to Gough, were 200 men of the 72nd Highlanders who got to the gorge just before the Afghans arrived and stopped them with well-timed volleys.

The arrival of Smith-Windham and Massy's survivors spread alarm at Sherpur, but the crisis was over. Mohammed Jan's forces drifted southward away from the Nanachi gorge, and this gave MacGregor the opportunity to retrieve the spiked guns, which were dragged back to Sherpur, repaired and restored to service. Roberts soon had all his troops concentrated, apart from

Baker's force, and was reinforced at midnight when the bulk of the Guides Cavalry and Infantry reached Sherpur after a forced march. Although Mohammed Jan had missed an opportunity to cut off the British and Indian force from the camp, he had outmanoeuvred Roberts. MacPherson had averted disaster by his initiative and speedy march; Roberts, with the wings of panic and terror beating about Massy's small force, had kept his head and acted quickly sending for the Highlanders. Poor intelligence and the unbroken string of victories had led him into the classic mistake of underestimating his enemy. He had lost thirty killed and forty-seven wounded, mostly from Massy's force.[6] The situation had been transformed and the British had been driven back in disorder. Roberts commented tersely in his diary for 11 December: 'Great [large] fight – enemy beat back our Cavalry and four H[orse] A[rtillery] guns [lost]. MacPherson then beat them.'[7] The Afghans had nearly repeated the annihilation of 1842. Luckily Baker arrived at 6.00 p.m. on 12 December with fresh strength, having been told by heliograph of the events of the 11th.

Roberts had tried on the 12th to recapture the initiative by sending a force under Lieutenant Colonel Money to dislodge Mohammed Jan's forces from Takht-i-Shah, but he was held up by fierce resistance, ammunition ran low and Roberts decided to await the return of Baker's Brigade before continuing the attack. On the 13th, Baker's force, with its advanced guard under Major George White, attacked the heights and gained their first objective, advancing towards Money's men. But when further parties of the enemy seized villages on the Sherpur road, cutting off Baker's line of retreat, he had to attack and clear these villages. Then an urgent heliograph from Sherpur told him the enemy were advancing on the rear of the cantonment. The city and surrounding countryside were in general insurrection and Roberts had insufficient men to dominate the area. By the end of the 13th, he withdrew all troops to Sherpur except for Money's force. The enemy had been dispersed whenever encountered, but Roberts had been unable to re-establish his dominance.

On the 14th, Baker was sent out again with a force of infantry, cavalry and guns against heights crowded with Afghans whose numbers were increasing and were so dense that when Roberts telegraphed to an outpost to know whether the enemy were in force on the plain to the west of Asmai, the answer was: 'Yes, the plain reminds me of Epsom Downs on the Derby day.'[8] Attacked in front and rear, the Afghan forces crumbled and by mid-morning the heights were in Baker's hands. The triumph was short-lived, as fresh waves of Afghans advanced and threw themselves into the attack. After a gallant defence two guns and a key hill were lost and Gough was unable to restore the situation with cavalry. Roberts bowed to Afghan pressure at about 2.00 p.m. and recalled all his troops, the withdrawal successfully carried out despite overwhelming numbers. He greeted each unit personally as it marched in in good order. Total losses since 8 December had been eighty-one killed and 213 wounded. Lieutenant Combe wrote: 'By Jove! . . . within twenty-four hours we are locked up, closely besieged, after a jolly good licking and all communications with the outer world cut off.'[9] Roberts noted in the margin of Surgeon Joshua Duke's history: 'We were overpowered and had to retire into Sherpur where everything had been prepared for such a contingency: food, forage and ammunition were there sufficient for the winter, and tho' the position was larger than our force could conveniently defend, it was scarcely possible for us to be turned out of it. Treachery alone would have effected this.' Yet had Sherpur been attacked that day by Mohammed Jan's army, it might have fallen. Luckily, the Afghans were resting on their laurels, some looting the Hindu and Qizilbash* quarters, others clearing the Bala Hissar of the powder in the magazine. The looters made for houses of those who co-operated with the invaders. Sirdar Wali Mohammed, who was known to have been on good terms with the British invaders, slipped into Sherpur, while the ladies of his harem were stripped and searched by Afghans. All citizens of Kabul were ordered to hand over stocks of grain and food, the ex-Amir's mother gave her jewels and personal fortune to the cause, and secured the nomination of Musa Khan, Yakub's young son, as Amir.[10]

Roberts confided to his diary of the 15th: 'Busy putting our defences into order. The enemy would have had a better chance if they had attacked last night.' By the next day preparations were complete. All posts were withdrawn except Lataband, a

* Those of Persian descent.

110

commanding position which served as a link between Kabul and Jugdulluk, thus keeping open the route for Brigadier Charles Gough's advance to Sherpur's relief. A telegraph line connecting the two extremities of the Sherpur camp and some intervening points was invaluable when fog made flags and heliograph ineffective. The garrison had grain for men and forage for animals, ammunition and medical supplies. 'I profited by the experience and soldierly instinct of my father, who served in the first Afghan War,' wrote Roberts. 'He repeatedly warned ... of the necessity of rendering their position at Kabul secure; of the danger of ... placing the treasure and the commissariat stores outside the British entrenchment.'[11]

The Sherpur perimeter was about 5 miles, its east wall incomplete and northern face open. The garrison filled gaps with gun carriages and barbed-wire entanglements, and built trenches and a blockhouse to dominate the gorge through the Bemaru Heights. The elite Corps of Guides held the weakest parts. Roberts had some 7,000 men dispersed around the 8,000 yards. A massive assault might break through by sheer weight of numbers, but fortunately Mohammed Jan had no siege artillery. The snowy weather was intensely cold, and the men were given hot and nourishing drinks and four blankets. Sentries in their greatcoats were white figures standing rigidly like ghosts, the snowflakes softly covering them from head to foot and freezing as they fell. By contrast, Afghan sharpshooters could retire to the warmth of Kabul and the villages. Rumours of impending night attacks added to the strain which began to take a toll of the defenders, who were barely adequate to cover the perimeter.

Roberts had his work cut out to keep up morale at this stage. Durand recorded in his diary that for some days there had been something very like panic, 'and officers bearing Her Majesty's Commission were not ashamed to talk of the "luck" of men sent down invalided a few days ago'. It was hardly surprising that Roberts himself had felt moments of depression, but for the most part he kept his usual cheerful countenance, encouraged in the hope that Charles Gough's Brigade, which had reached Lataband, would advance to his rescue.[12]

Two good auguries for the siege occurred on the first day: about noon the sun shone out through a cold leaden sky, and the besieged saw with pleasure the Lataband heliograph 21 miles away flashing; a short message was sent and received; then a lucky shot from Captain Campbell's howitzer bounced at extreme range, landing in a hollow killing eight men.[13] The defenders remained active, and a sortie mined a village obstructing their field of fire and blew it up. At Simla the Commander-in-Chief Haines had admired the calm and confident tone of Roberts's communications. 'People sleep better after Roberts' telegrams ... He is certainly doing his work most admirably,' Haines commented in October. Suddenly, in early December, he realized the situation had changed and ordered men to be pushed forward from Peshawar. In fact, they were to have no influence.[14]

On 12 December, Roberts had telegraphed Bright who was to support him that he wanted Brigadier General Charles Gough's Brigade despatched. Bright had ordered Gough not to advance until he received reinforcements but Gough moved forward to Jagdalak, gathering troops as he went. On the 20th it appeared the wings of panic were beating even around Roberts's head, for he signalled Gough to advance to his succour. Neither man knew what forces lay between them. The line was cut immediately after the message arrived and Gough's outposts were attacked, but 'in a half-hearted way', as Gough admitted. On 21 December, he set out for Kabul despite harsh conditions, snow on the ground, temperatures close to freezing, in fog and low cloud. As his column advanced they heard heavy firing from the direction of Kabul. Had Roberts's force been destroyed?

On 22 December, Roberts had been warned by the servant of one of his cavalry rissalders that an assault was planned for the early hours of the following morning, the last day of the festival of Mohurram, the signal being the lighting of a bonfire on the Asmai Heights by the Mushk-i-Alam himself. There would be a demonstration against the south wall, but main attacks would be launched against Bemaru village and the east wall. If they succeeded, the attack on the south would be renewed. The troops spent the night rolled in their waterproof sheets and blankets beside their arms. Those on duty wore thick sheepskin jackets and Roberts ordered tinned soup or cocoa issued. Sentries heard the sound of wooden scaling ladders being dragged over frozen snow. An hour before dawn the troops stood to.

A shot rang out and then a brilliant, dazzling light from the Asmai Heights gave the signal for attack. Covered by fire from the King's Garden, the Afghans rushed forward, first a decoy to the south, then the main attack along the lower eastern wall. The defenders heard the strange slapping sound of thousands of Afghan sandals on the snow and cries of 'Allah il Allah!' The attack was spearheaded by ghazis, religious fanatics prepared to sacrifice their lives. Roberts estimated their strength at 50,000, probably too many. MacGregor thought it about 15,000, but no doubt at least treble the defenders' effective strength. The guns fired star shell to illuminate the advancing masses at a thousand yards, and the cries of the attackers merged in a roar with the fire of the defenders' Martini-Henry and Snider rifles, the artillery's case shot and high explosive. The defenders' fire had awful effect and the attackers fell in scores. One large standard serving as a rallying point for the Afghans was borne along for many yards, then suddenly went down as the bearers fell under the defenders' fire. Superior numbers could not prevail against disciplined, resourceful, well-armed defenders. The fiercest attack against the eastern perimeter was met by Roberts's best troops, the Guides, the 28th Bengal Native Infantry, 67th Foot and 92nd Highlanders. At 10 o'clock the attack slackened and when resumed an hour later it was not pressed home with the same determination.

Roberts's tactical timing did not desert him and he now ordered four guns escorted by cavalry to move out through the gorge in the Bemaru heights to bring flanking fire to bear on the Afghans near the eastern end of the heights. The Afghans began to evacuate this position. Just after midday, sensing that the turning point had come, Roberts despatched the remainder of the cavalry under Massy through the gorge, followed by Baker with Sappers and Miners, Highlanders and Sikhs, and two guns. Leaving Baker to sweep through the villages and enclosures east and south-east of Sherpur, Massy sent cavalry detachments to block different roads from the immediate vicinity. By now the Afghans were in full retreat, and more infantry moved out attacking villages and strongpoints. Through the afternoon the work of dislodging the enemy was pursued with grim severity. Corpses strewed the ground for upwards of half a mile or more on the line of retreat towards Kohistan. Two or three lancers or

113

sowars were told off to each straggler, using their carbines when the Afghan had been hemmed in. Late in the afternoon the troops were recalled and manned the perimeter of the cantonment as before, but the battle was over.[15] A supreme Afghan effort had failed and the point was hammered home when Brigadier Charles Gough's force arrived unopposed next morning. He had advanced through a snowy, ominously silent, deserted country to be met a mile from Sherpur by a patrol of 12th Lancers and then Roberts himself. Gough had done well, and the Commander-in-Chief Haines recorded his 'high appreciation of the very able and satisfactory manner in which Brigadier-General Gough conducted this extremely difficult operation'. Roberts thought he was too slow, which angered Gough, who continued to think Roberts had ordered him to advance through thousands of hostile Afghans ignoring military precautions. He admitted to his wife in a letter of 2 January 1880: 'Roberts has lots of pluck and determination, and never gives way to any sort of despair,' but he felt he had carelessly failed to anticipate the Afghan rising or fortify Sherpur sufficiently in time.[16]

In the semi-official Russian account, Major General Soboleff, sometime chief of the Asiatic Department of the Russian General Staff, wrote that Mohammed Jan had used the Ghilzais or Mujaheddin to attack Sherpur and pin down Roberts's forces while he slipped away, and the manoeuvre 'enabled this clever Afghan General to carry out one of the most difficult and complex of military manoeuvres – the orderly retreat of an army without loss.'[17] This is difficult to prove, but may well be true. Nonetheless, both sides fought as if it were life and death at Sherpur, for three hours the issue hung in the balance and had the Afghans broken in, Roberts's force would have been destroyed. He estimated enemy losses at 3,000; the British and Indians suffered only five killed and twenty-eight wounded. His diary for the 23rd reads proudly: 'Grand day – beat off enemy and cleared them out of neighbouring villages.' He sent telegrams to his wife and to the Viceroy, writing of his garrison in the snow: 'All and every night in most severe weather officers and men were at their posts or sleeping with their arms in the vicinity of the trenches.' 'Hardships and exposure were cheerfully borne.'[18]

On the morning of Christmas Eve, Roberts discovered that the thousands who had opposed him had gone. Kabul and the Bala

Hissar were swiftly occupied and cavalry were despatched to harry the retreating forces. Mohammed Jan, the Mushk-i-Alam, and the young, newly proclaimed Amir, Musa Jan, made good their escape to Ghazni. Around Sherpur, Roberts's troops cleared every village and enclosure within a thousand yards, the Kabul River was bridged in three places, roads were laid out, and forts and blockhouses placed on heights and at other important points. Sherpur's extended lines were not however impregnable, and a renewed large-scale attack would have tested Roberts's force. The Hindu merchants of Kabul had had their shops and bazaars wrecked and plundered by the Afghans. They therefore took the view that 20,000 men were required to guard Sherpur and an equal force in the city, and being certain the British did not have these numbers, decamped to Peshawar.[19] Roberts was nonetheless determined to maintain the initiative and sent cavalry to burn villages where there had been trouble. The village of Bagwhana, whose inhabitants took up arms and where Roberts nearly lost his life in a nullah, was put to the torch, and four headmen were taken to Kabul and hanged for alleged complicity in the deaths of Lieutenants Forbes and Hardy.[20]

Christmas passed with six inches of snow on the ground and sombre thoughts by the garrison of comrades lost. But on Hogmanay, New Year's Eve, the Gordons celebrated in Scots style with pipers and grog, and at Roberts's quarters they cheered, calling him from his bed to partake. He obeyed despite the objections of his staff who wanted their commander to enjoy a restful night. With good humour and an eye to morale, he said, 'You have always answered when I called on you, and now I answer your call as readily.' George White, sharing in the Gordons' high spirits, sent festive greetings to his wife:

My dearest Amy,

Many happy Christmases to you and the little ones. I hope you are as jolly as I am. I was getting bored with the situation here some time ago but we are having rare times of it now … On 23rd December half an hour before day break … the cry of 'Allah, Allah' from thousands of throats told that on this, the last day of the Moharram, the full tide of the Jehad was to be hurled against the followers of the

115

Christian God, and with such fury that the 48 hours that had to elapse before their great festival should see not one of them left to hail the Natal Morn of their Prophet.

White was pleased to assure his wife that he and Fred Roberts were enjoying Christmas.[21]

Chapter 8

Kandahar to Kabul

General Stewart has displayed the qualities of a very talented general, and has understood that ultimate military success is not attained by chance military triumphs only, of whatever kind they may be, but chiefly after careful preparation.

Major General L.N. Soboleff

What designs Lytton may have harboured with respect to Kashmir, I cannot tell. It would not surprise me to find that schemes were in preparation by the late Govt. for the annexation of the moon.

Lord Ripon

Roberts and the other commanders were fertile with expedients throughout the cold winter to keep the troops' morale high: skating and sliding, fresh snowballs for ammunition in mimic warfare attacking and defending forts, minstrel bands giving concerts, and a pantomime for which Roberts's ADC Neville Chamberlain wrote the topical songs. Things picked up with the arrival of supplies of champagne in early February. When spring brought milder weather, there were steeplechases, polo and cricket, canoeing with home-made craft and fishing, but always with a wary eye and a ready sentry. When Colour Sergeant Hector MacDonald of the Gordons was commissioned for his courageous service, the men of his company carried him shoulder high to the officers' quarters, their piper at their head. The officers of his Regiment presented him with a sword, the sergeants with a dirk.[1]

117

One event was less pleasant: the recall of Brigadier General Massy. Roberts had found him wanting in the advance to Kabul, and the events of 11 December clinched matters. He submitted his account of events and hoped that, although Massy should not be employed in the field, and certainly not again with him, another job might be found for him. Massy's own rather feeble defence pleaded that the country across which he had passed, ignoring Roberts's strict orders, was unsuitable to cavalry and guns. Haines, the Commander-in-Chief, found that events of 11 December 'shew [sic] Brigadier-General Massy to have been as wanting in judgment as in military appreciation of the circumstances in which he was placed', noting that he 'dismounted *thirty* lancers with carbines to stop the advance of *ten thousand* men'. His conduct led to loss of life and of the four guns, although Haines did not judge that this had led to the failure of Roberts's plan. He refused to agree to Roberts's plea for alternative employment, feeling that 'an officer who has failed so seriously in the field cannot be considered as fit for any responsible command of troops.'[2]

Massy was relieved and sent back to India, but he had powerful friends who influenced Cambridge, the Commander-in-Chief, he was eventually promoted Major General and given command in Ceylon. Roberts was doubtless keen to deflect blame for the reverse on 11 December 1879, but that Massy was unequal to a tight situation was certain. MacGregor had written to Greaves, the Adjutant General at Whitehall, to say that Massy was quite unfit to command anything in the field. Charles Gough wrote:

It is a bad business altogether, there is no doubt he is *incompetent*, not a single cavalry man speaks well of him, and he allows the most favourable opportunities to slip without taking advantage of them, still the matter will make so much noise and he has been so outrageously puffed in some of the papers, that these same people will assuredly take up the case and as *regards the loss of the ground on the 11th December* there will be a good deal to be said on both sides of the question.

Gough had a point: Massy was a bungler whom Roberts was well rid of, but the blame for the defeat on 11 December was not his alone. In showing clemency, Cambridge echoed Roberts's request. On 26 March, Cambridge wrote to Haines saying he was 'grieved beyond measure of his [Massy's] having made such a mess of his duties more than once', but hoped another post could be found. He did not know Massy personally and said that his views were based on Massy's 'good reputation as an officer'. George White would have snorted with contempt. On 30 April, Cambridge, having persuaded Haines to reinstate Massy to a brigade, admitted: 'I do not say that Brigadier General Massy has proved himself a first rate cavalry general,' but thought Roberts must share the blame of 11 December. Cambridge appears to have bowed to a storm in the press, raised by Massy's friends, and the whole episode caused Roberts considerable worry, his continued protestations that he cared not what the press said testifying to the opposite. In his papers is preserved an article from the *Civil & Military Gazette* of 21 May 1880, proof of the influence of Massy's supporters, claiming that 'an officer in high position' had said that if Cambridge 'could have his way Roberts would be shelved for good' and that a War Office official had stated, 'There was nothing to save Roberts [because the] facts were so strongly against him.' Added to the storm that had broken over his head following the Kabul executions, this made it an anxious time for a commander who, despite his under-estimation of Mohammed Jan and his political mistakes, had won a series of convincing victories and occupied the enemy's capital. That Massy was 'wanting in military instinct, prompt decision and quick action' cannot be gainsaid.[3]

As important as military conditions were political ones. On 26 December, Roberts issued a proclamation, giving amnesty to all those who submitted quickly except key leaders. The Military Court was re-established. In England public interest in the justice or injustice of the executions was suspended as everyone followed the fighting at Sherpur with bated breath, but a meeting of the Peace Society on 29 December called upon people to repudiate a system of terrorism, and Charles Spurgeon, celebrated Baptist preacher, made a similar attack four days later. A memorial signed by John Morley, Joseph Chamberlain, J.A. Froude, the Bishops of Oxford and Exeter, and the Duke of Westminster, among others, was sent to the Prime Minister calling for an end to the invasion of Afghanistan.

Both Roberts and Lytton were thoroughly disturbed. Durand reported that it was a trying time for the former, with telegrams from Calcutta, one from Colley:

> saying the hangings had been causing much excitement at home and that Roberts must be careful – another from Lyall about the deportation of prisoners, which was of a very cutting and disapproving character ... The telegram wound up with a strong warning to avoid undue severity in dealing with insurgents and treat them as belligerents not rebels. The little man was much upset by it all and talked of resigning if no longer supported.

Durand noted how the Liberals were taking up the question and the India Office requested a full explanation for use in Parliament. Roberts followed his earlier letters of defence by a detailed report of 27 January which reached the War Office on 12 March, listing in detail the eighty-seven men formally reported executed up to 26 December 1879. He claimed that the imposition of martial law benefited the Afghans by giving peace and order; it was necessary to control the natural Afghan fanaticism. By banning the carrying of arms on pain of death it protected British troops. His report reflected advice from Lytton, who suggested that he should refer to the necessity of safeguarding his force, and from the political officer Lepel Griffin. Lytton had sent Griffin to Kabul to find a way out of the political impasse.[4]

The report was received in London less than a fortnight before Parliament was dissolved. The last years of Disraeli's great ministry had not matched his earlier imperial success. Isandhlwana and the Kabul massacre seemed to prove his forward policy overseas a disaster. Gladstone launched his famous Midlothian attack on the Bulgarian massacres with his equally well-known pamphlet *The Bulgarian Horrors and the Question of the East* written in three days while he was in bed with lumbago. The atrocity was Gladstone's opportunity to re-enter politics and launch a moral crusade. The quarrel between 'Turks' and 'Bulgarians' introduced a venom into English politics and lay in large part behind Queen Victoria's almost pathological dislike of Gladstone. Afghan events confirmed radical mistrust of Disraeli, and determined the Liberals to make his foreign and imperial policy their main object of attack in the coming election. Supported by the immense wealth of his aristocratic colleague, Rosebery, Gladstone began his famous Midlothian campaign on 24 November 1879 and ended it a fortnight later. He reckoned he had addressed over 85,000 people and *The Times* printed about as many words of his speeches. His theme was the enunciation of 'the right principles of foreign policy', and Roberts's burning of Afghan villages was one of his targets. The economic slump and the fall in grain prices which hit farmers were also Disraeli's misfortune. Whether there really was a late nineteenth-century 'Great Depression' has been much debated by historians, but contemporaries certainly believed in one. Many characteristics of late Victorian Britain, including the imperialism and jingoism, stemmed from the belief that Britain was falling behind her rivals. The immediate beneficiaries in 1880 were Gladstone and his party – the Liberals won the general election and outnumbered the Conservatives in the new House of Commons by 353 seats to 238. The Liberal government did not act directly against Roberts for the executions, but the Viceroy was a major target of criticism. Lord Hartington, who was to be Secretary of State for India, described Lytton as 'the incarnation and embodiment of an Indian policy which is everything an Indian policy should not be'. Accordingly, when the result of the polls was known, that incarnation and embodiment resigned. The new government appointed Lord Ripon as Viceroy, a severe critic of Lytton's policy, drawn out of retirement by events at Kabul.[5]

Many of the soldiers in the field agreed with Roberts's measures. Two days after lunching with Roberts at Kabul, Charles Gough wrote to his wife:

There have been no atrocities, the executions that have taken place have been in retribution of the attack on the residency, or of people concerned in cutting up our wounded but I don't think any 'executions' have taken place except for the above. *If any prisoners* have been shot I can only say it was a mistake making them prisoners, they never spare, and reprisal becomes absolutely necessary among such brutes so as to strike terror into them. It is a *mercy* in the end and leads to less bloodshed. They are the most bloodthirsty villains going.

Donald Stewart was unusual thinking that shooting men, just because they resisted the British, was unjust and unwise, but he too shared a common view of the Afghans and their erstwhile Amir as treacherous. He believed an account from Sirdars of Kandahar claiming that Yakub could have saved the Embassy if he had shown a particle of pluck.[6]

Whether clemency rather than executions would have mollified the Afghans must be doubted; they remembered the British debacle of 1842 all too well. Roberts's troops controlled only the territory their guns covered. Lytton and Stewart feared that the native Indian army was being worn out through arduous picket and escort duties. With military impasse, a political settlement had to be found and even before the election Lytton sought to find a way. He instructed Lepel Griffin: 'I see no reason why you should not, as soon as you reach Kabul, set about the preparation of a way for us out of that rat-trap.' He stressed the need to settle matters before the harvest, to separate Afghanistan into three or more separate provinces and retain a permanent British garrison at Kandahar or close by. Sovereignty over an independent Kandahar was offered to a Barakzai prince, Sher Ali, whose father had been a Sirdar driven out in 1839. Sher Ali accepted after cautious negotiations and was installed as Wali or local ruler in mid-May 1880. Meanwhile, there was uncertainty about Herat. It was not to be made independent or brought under British control, for this would alienate Persia and drive her into the Russian camp. But in a reversal of previous policy the British said that if the Shah of Persia could occupy it they would not object. At the same time planning went ahead for the final military campaign. Stewart was to march from Kandahar to Kabul via Ghazni, traversing an area not hitherto crossed by the British. Roberts was to undertake operations in Kohistan and Bamian, and for this he would evacuate Sherpur for a smaller camp, and receive reinforcements and 3,800 camels. No sooner had the plan been approved than it began to fall apart because of transport difficulties: Roberts for example had 1,000 camels fewer than needed.[7]

There was fierce Afghan resistance to any movement, and the almost daily grind of resisting attacks on pickets, convoys and outposts imposed a heavy strain on the troops. The Political Officer at Kandahar, Oliver St John, came up with the solution:

Abdur Rahman. This son of Sher Ali's brother and rival, Afzal Khan, had been involved in the struggle for the Afghan amirship in the 1860s, trying to place his father on the throne of Kabul, but was defeated in 1868, driven into exile and in 1870 reached Tashkent, where General Kaufmann gave him permission to reside and obtained a pension of 25,000 per annum for him from the Tsar. He remained a pensioner of the Russians until at the end of 1879 they gave him financial aid and 200 breech-loading rifles, 2,000 rounds of ammunition and field equipment for 100 infantry and 100 cavalry. Thus accoutred he marched south to stake his claim. For Lytton supporting this 'ram caught in a thicket', as he biblically* termed him, was a leap in the dark, but he had been at his wit's end to find a satisfactory way to end the war. He still believed his policy had scored some successes – the Khyber and Bolan Passes in British hands, Baluchistan peaceful and friendly, Kandahar under Wali Sher Ali, and the Afghan state broken up. Once a friendly ruler was secure at Kabul, the troops could go home. Neither Lytton nor St John yet grasped that their new candidate was an extremely able politician and had had long years of exile in Samarkand to plan his tactics. Even before a conciliatory letter from Griffin reached him, he was in touch with Kohistan chiefs, claiming that he was ready to lead a holy war against the infidel British unless they listened to him.[8]

As arranged, at the end of March, Stewart handed over the command at Kandahar to Major General Primrose and set forth for Kabul with 7,249 soldiers, 7,272 camp followers and more than 11,000 animals. The march was overshadowed subsequently by the drama of Roberts's march in the reverse direction five months later. Whereas Stewart's took place during an election, Roberts's had the eyes of the Empire on it. Stewart was launching himself into the unknown and was forced to live off the country, with supplies short. He had experience having already taken a force 400 miles to Kandahar in the middle of winter through a dismal waste. This time empty villages and scorched earth en route showed the Afghans were spoiling for a fight. On 19 April, in the

---

*Genesis 23:13: 'And Abraham lifted up his eyes, and looked, and behold behind him a ram caught in a thicket of thorns; and Abraham went and took the ram, and offered him up for a burnt offering in the stead of his son.'

hills at Ahmed Khel, Stewart deployed for an expected attack. He had not long to wait. An enormous mass of Afghan soldiers and irregulars with standards formed on the hilltops, horsemen rode along the ridge with the intention of sweeping to the rear of Stewart's line to attack the baggage, and successive waves of swordsmen on foot, stretching right and left, rushed out, with cavalry on the flanks, seeming to envelop his column. The Afghan attack led by fanatical Ghazis, determined to sacrifice their own lives, threatened to overwhelm Stewart's force, the danger increased by his tactical error in ordering the 59th Regiment to a fresh position so that they were struck by the wave of Afghan swordsmen while still forming up and without bayonets fixed. Part of the cavalry stampeded in panic, rolled over the medical dressing station and came within a few yards of Stewart's headquarters. He and his staff drew their swords to defend themselves.

Superior discipline and firepower reasserted themselves. In an hour-long battle, Stewart's force drove off the attack, losing seventeen killed and 124 wounded. Losses were kept to a minimum by the discipline of the regiments, the 3rd Gurkhas suffering no casualties through forming company squares quickly and correctly. The Afghans left 1,200 bodies thickly strewn on the ground. Captain Elias, an eyewitness, wrote: 'Anyone with a semblance of a heart under his khaki jacket could not help feeling something akin to pity to see them advancing with their miserable weapons in the face of our guns and rifles, but their courage and their numbers made them formidable.' Stewart had not conducted the battle particularly well, in contrast to his management of the march, and in a country ideal for cavalry and horse artillery, gave no pursuit.[9]

He continued his march to Ghazni, where news of his victory ensured a respectful reception. Then came intelligence that Mushk-i-Alam and Mohammed Jan were raising forces to avenge Ahmed Khel. Stewart decided on quick action, and despatched Brigadier General Palliser with two cavalry and four infantry regiments, supported by artillery. Palliser found the enemy's vanguard entrenched in walled villages and informed his commander. Stewart brought forward the bulk of his forces and ordered an immediate attack on the enemy's left flank. The Afghans were routed with a loss to Stewart of only two dead and three wounded. Although the action was a small one, the moral effect was sufficient to disperse the gathered tribesmen without their offering further resistance, while Stewart continued his march in fine weather.[10]

Roberts had despatched from Kabul a force under Major General Ross to meet Stewart. Ross's column was attacked and his sappers' road-making operations hindered, but it reached Stewart's on 27 April. Stewart's column marched to the Logar Valley while their commander continued with Ross and his troops towards Kabul. On 1 May he rode ahead of his column and met Roberts who came out to see him 'looking very jolly and well'. He reached the capital on 2 May and took over command. 'Bobs, Griffin and all the swells came out to meet me this morning; very pleasant. Cabul looks very pretty just now, and everything is going right except as regards political affairs.' Although Roberts and Lepel Griffin had worked together amicably, Stewart was determined not to delegate political authority. As a tactician, Stewart may have been inferior to Roberts, but his political acumen at Kandahar had proved much superior, peace being kept at the city, aided by a good autumn crop. On 8 May, he sent Roberts and Baker on an expedition to gather supplies and secure communications. Roberts had written to his old friend: 'If there is one man in India I would and could serve under – it is you.' But he saw his subordination as a rebuke; moreover, the Liberal election victory hung over them. To his wife Stewart wrote that it had 'put a sad damper on all our spirits. We think it quite possible that there may be a complete change of policy. If the Liberals gain the day, everything that is being done here may be upset.'[11] But already Abdur Rahman was taking events out of their control. In mid-April, as Roberts informed Stewart, the aspiring Amir was advancing through Kohistan, gaining strength and appealing on the advice of his Afghan followers to the religious feelings of his countrymen. He played his cards well, called himself Amir, claimed that he had come to save his country, and head a religious war if necessary, but nonetheless felt no enmity for the British and would be glad to make friends with them if practicable. He sent circulars and letters to chiefs and sirdars, and his support grew. In his memoirs he wrote: 'I was unable to show my friendship publicly to the extent that was necessary: because my people were ignorant and fanatical.

If I showed any inclination towards the English, my people would call me an infidel for joining hands with infidels.'[12]

On the day of Stewart's arrival at Kabul news of the Liberal election victory was received. 'The result of the elections has called forth a good many d...s from the soldiers here,' wrote White. 'I fancy Sir F[rederick].R[oberts]. is about as much put out about it as anyone can be.' He had reason: Lytton noted that he was 'specially obnoxious to a powerful section of Liberal party and I fear he will be made victim of party feeling.' Lytton resigned – Roberts had lost his patron – and Ripon, a severe critic of Conservative policy in Afghanistan, was the new Viceroy. Stewart wondered about the fate of his old friend who had been a particular target of Radical criticism:

> There is no telling what may happen after Lord Lytton goes. It will be a great shame if they don't do something for Bobs ... There can be no doubt about his military capacity. He has done great service here, taking it at the estimate of those who are least friendly to him; and it will be an infamous shame if any petty feeling of jealousy is allowed to stand in his way.[13]

Early in June, Roberts, feeling that his policy was discredited and his protector Lytton about to sail from India, telegraphed Simla to ask permission to leave Kabul. 'I am not required here now. It is not possible to take an interest in the work and my health is not as good as it was. I am quite happy with General Stewart but my wish to leave is so strong I trust your Lordship will approve of my doing so.' Lytton replied sagely: 'I deeply sympathise, but as your sincere friend most strongly urge you not to leave your post till close of war ... I feel sure your premature retirement would be generally misinterpreted to your detriment.' Stewart was also keen to keep him: 'He [Roberts] is very true to me, and is of great use to me in many ways, and if there is to be fighting he will be my right hand.' To the new Viceroy he wrote on 11 June trying to reverse his unfavourable impression of Roberts's misdeeds at Kabul, insisting that he had blown up several of the fortified towers which made villages such strongholds as punishment, but inflicted only one burning. The destruction of a tower was often the only way of repressing

126

disorder.[14] Roberts was fortunate indeed in his friends; his ill-judged wish to resign his command, if carried out, would have altered his whole career. What would his future admirers have thought of his abandoning the army in mid-campaign?

That he felt under pressure from disapproving articles in the English press is shown by Lady Roberts's activity on his behalf. She had returned to England in early 1880 and had established 'my headquarters while at home' at Evercreech in Somerset, the home of her sister and brother-in-law, the Sherstons. From there she wrote to the young Lord Melgund thanking him for his letters to the press defending her husband, sending him maps marked with the cavalry charges near Kabul and enclosing copies of useful correspondence which might help him deal with hostile correspondents. Later in the year, from the seaside resort of Exmouth, where she had gone for 'for six weeks sea bathing & air for my chicks', she encouraged him to write against Captain Norman whose articles in *The Times* George White had so deprecated – 'nasty unfair letters' Lady Roberts called them. He had been writing to MacGregor behind Roberts's back, but MacGregor defended his chief.[15]

Lytton's wisdom in persuading Roberts was soon to be evident to his successor, but his Viceroyalty is generally judged a failure, despite its colourful opening in the Durbar and the spirited defence in later biographies by his daughter, Lady Betty Balfour, and grand-daughter, Lady Emily Lutyens. His Afghan policy left him grasping for a means to escape a difficult conflict. In 1878, to silence vociferous critics of the war, he passed the Vernacular Press Act singling out Indian language newspapers for censorship. This united educated Indians in opposition and appeared to contradict the Queen's post-Mutiny declaration that the races of her empire would enjoy equal rights. In fact, Lytton held enlightened views on race relations and determined not to compromise his principles. When Fuller, an English barrister at Agra, struck his groom who died of injuries, he was fined thirty rupees. Lytton decided to take official notice: 'If I could help it, the case should not be allowed to drop, until it dropped upon the head of Mr Fuller.' He published with full approval of council his letter to the Council of the North-West provinces, deploring Fuller's conduct, suspending the magistrate, and criticizing both the provincial government and the High Court. His statutory civil service attempted, with limited success, to throw open one-sixth of reserved official posts to Indians. His repeal of duties on Lancashire cotton imports against the advice of most of his council struck at the recently restarted Indian cotton mills of Bombay. The greatest blow to his rule was famine. The terrible famine of 1877–8 and official shortcomings were publicized by the editor of the *Madras Times*, William Digby, who used his influence to call for the alleviation of suffering. Largely owing to his representations a relief fund was opened at the Mansion House in London, £820,000 was subscribed, and the relief distributed through 120 local committees in India. Despite this the immediate effect was a tragic loss of life. Some good, however, came from the human disaster. Lytton's new famine code and procedures for monitoring drought and price levels proved effective in detecting and preventing potential famine. Roads built under programmes organized to combat the crisis improved India's infrastructure. A Royal Commission on Famine in India (1880) explored the conditions behind the original disaster and gave its approval to the new famine code, which served down to the end of the twentieth century. A sum of £1½ million was laid aside each year for future emergency. After 1876–8, no subsequent famine was to cause remotely so much devastation and loss of life, and between 1901 and 1943 India was safeguarded from famine entirely. The salt tax was rationalized and reduced. These achievements, however, were the work of other men, John and Richard Strachey and Allan Octavian Hume. Lytton's successor repealed his press law, but it was too late to reverse his Afghan policy entirely; the negotiations with Abdur Rahman continued at the point Lytton and his agents left them.[16]

The new Viceroy, Ripon, arrived at Simla on 8 June. He was one of the Liberals' foremost experts on India, having supported policies of conciliation after the Mutiny; he believed British rule must lead to self-government, and in the meantime wanted to prepare the way with political, administrative, and educational reforms. He corresponded with Florence Nightingale to implement new sanitary policies to fight disease. Although he disliked his predecessor's policies, he inherited that of bringing forward Abdur Rahman as Amir, maintaining the Wali, Sher Ali, at Kandahar, protecting the Khan of Khelat and preventing border tribes from falling under the power of Kabul. Ripon and

Hartington, Secretary of State for India, were both against the proposed division of Afghanistan. In a memorandum dated 9 May 1880 sent to Hartington before he left London, Ripon had laid down the principle points of his Afghan policy: evacuation of Kandahar as far as consistent with pledges to the Wali; retention of Sibi and Pishin on the North-West Frontier and linking them to India by railway; evacuation of Kabul and the establishment of a ruler there to be aided by grants of money and arms, but not troops; a native not British agent to be at Kabul; the ruler of Afghanistan to be allowed to take Herat if he could; and the policy of Afghanistan's disintegration to be repudiated. In the event these were carried out and substantially maintained until 1919.[17]

Abdur Rahman, astute as he was, realized that in the absence of other candidates acceptable to the British, and with the steady swing of tribal support, he was their best choice. Friendly greetings from local chiefs and joyful fusillades of rifle shots from tribesmen heralded his advance. Stewart told his wife on 5 July that Mushk-i-Alam and the former insurgent chiefs were ready to acknowledge any amir the British wished to recognize, but he knew it was because they saw Abdur Rahman as their man. He marched steadily towards Kabul, more and more chiefs voicing support, unwilling to accept the separation of Kandahar to which Ripon still felt committed by previous negotiations. Stewart was keen to evacuate the army before the morale of Indian regiments, too long far from home, suffered seriously. It was increasingly difficult to gather supplies and costs of the campaign had soared. On 27 June, Abdur Rahman seemed to accept Ripon's terms: 'You have resigned to me Afghanistan up to the limits which were settled of old by Treaty with my noble grandfather, the Amir Dost Mohammed Khan.'

He cleverly did not say which treaty. Ripon decided to agree and on 20 July, Stewart was ordered to send Abdur money and artillery, and signify that the British accepted him as de facto ruler of northern Afghanistan. At a durbar at Kabul on 22 July, he was declared Amir.[18]

On the last day of July, Griffin met him 16 miles north of Kabul and was struck by the new Amir's 'exceedingly intelligent face, brown eyes, a pleasant smile, and a frank, courteous manner. The impression that he left on me and the officers who were present at the interview was most favourable ... In conversation

[he] showed both good sense and sound political judgement. He kept thoroughly to the point under discussion and his remarks were characterized by shrewdness and ability.' Griffin told him he would receive a gift of ten lakhs of rupees and all the Afghan guns and equipment left at Sherpur and in the Bala Hissar. A formal treaty would await consolidation of his rule.[19]

Into these smooth negotiations, bad news burst like a whirlwind on 28 July.

Chapter 9

Fateful Decisions

As if sluices had been opened from some great dam, the raging torrents of screaming tribesmen poured forward, a rushing tempest of fury, surging on to desperate encounter.

Colonel Leigh Maxwell

A regular bad business ... and worse than anything in my time in India.

Colonel Charles MacGregor

A British brigade had been defeated at Maiwand near Kandahar with a loss of over a thousand men, more than 40 per cent of the force engaged. The victorious army, the Herati regiments which had mutinied at Kabul and killed Cavagnari and his escort, were led by Abdur Rahman's cousin and rival, Ayub, brother of the ex-Amir Yakub. At Simla, Ripon had been doubtful he would march: 'Ayub has cried wolf, wolf, so often, he will never come,' he said at council, but he had misquoted the fable, as the Commander-in-Chief, Haines, remarked after the meeting: 'Ayub is the wolf, we are the heedless shepherds ... Ayub *will* come, we shall have a disaster, and I shall be hanged for it.'[1] Ayub's declared aims were to drive the infidel British from Afghanistan and then wrest the throne from his cousin. A series of attacks on British outposts had heralded his advance, and towards the end of June 1880, with an 8,000-strong force of infantry and artillery, gathering support as he went, Ayub set

131

out for Kandahar as his first objective on the way to the throne. Scanty intelligence failed to show quite how formidable was his force and his modern artillery. His every action showed the qualities of a general and a politician; many Afghans looked on him as a leader of Muslims against the infidel and a true fighter for the Prophet.[2]

Major General Primrose, who had succeeded Stewart at Kandahar, had about 4,800 men of the Bombay Army. At this stage, British indecision reflected poor intelligence and divided counsels. The political advisor at Kandahar, St John, reported the Wali's views that troops should be despatched before the country rose in Ayub's favour, and recommended a brigade, over 2,000 men, be sent. The Commander-in-Chief at Calcutta, Haines, did not think the Kandahar force strong enough to detach one, so at first nothing was done. On 27 June, with Ayub's force halfway to Kandahar, St John repeated his recommendation. Although sensibly cautious, Haines, distracted as he was by news of the sudden death of his wife, does not appear to have been properly focused on events, and Ripon was fresh to the situation. As Ayub continued to advance and gather troops, Primrose requested reinforcements, but there was not time to send them and he had to make do with the available forces. He despatched 2,600 men under Brigadier Burrows, who had held desk jobs and had no experience of fighting since the Mutiny. The force was greatly outnumbered and the cavalry commanders were inexperienced. Burrows' first difficulty was dealing with a mutiny of the Wali's troops at the River Helmand on 14 July. He promptly crossed the river, disarmed the mutineers, captured their guns and recrossed the same day. The Wali's disarmed troops fled, some towards Kandahar, but many joined Ayub's force. Ripon became anxious and told Haines that he was prepared to take responsibility for an attack on Ayub. He called a meeting with Haines and his other military advisors, and proposed that Primrose be ordered to advance to strengthen Burrows, leaving only a small force in the citadel of Kandahar. Haines and Sir Edwin Johnson, the Military Member, strongly objected to the plan, and Ripon did not think he could overrule them. It was agreed that Haines should send a message to Primrose giving full liberty to attack Ayub if he considered himself strong enough, and stating it was of the greatest importance that Ayub's force should be dispersed and prevented reaching Ghazni. Primrose passed this on to Burrows, who in his later account said he interpreted it, not as a matter of choice, but as a definite order to strike a blow against Ayub. New information reaching Simla made clear that Ayub's force was much larger than expected, but the Council did not send further instructions. Primrose did not use his initiative and reinforce Burrows, who had not arranged cavalry patrols to scout the enemy nor made good use of intelligence gathered by St John. His movements were slowed by an enormous convoy of over 3,000 transport animals.[3]

Burrows marched on 27 July to intercept Ayub, who was moving towards Maiwand, but did not leave early enough. His plan appeared to have been to prevent Ayub reaching Ghazni by forcing him into battle, opening fire with his guns, then falling back to a less exposed position where his inferior numbers could better defend themselves. The armies encountered each other on the march on a flat plain ideal for artillery, with two ravines which provided cover for Ayub's troops to stage a surprise. The British-Indian force comprised 2,000 rifles, 500 sabres and 12 guns against an enemy of 8,000 regular troops, 32 guns and 3,000 mounted men supported by possibly as many as 15,000 tribesmen and religious warriors. Whereas the odds were heavy against Burrows, Ayub could scarcely believe his luck. Confronted with such a small force, he planned to surround the Anglo-Indian brigade with his unwieldy but vastly superior army, and after softening them up with a bombardment launch a simultaneous assault from all sides.

The British guns were outmatched from the start; indeed, the Afghan artillery was so superior in the initial exchange that some assumed they had Russian gunners. Burrows deployed his three infantry battalions in line, right to left, the 66th Foot, a veteran British battalion, Jacob's Rifles and the Bombay Grenadiers, both with good reputations, but with too many raw recruits and too few British officers known to their men. These young Indian soldiers fought on beyond normal expectations against vastly superior numbers, which began to lap around both flanks, particularly on the left of the Grenadiers where two companies of Jacob's, separated from their regimental comrades, were under an inexperienced 21-year-old subaltern. As the desperate

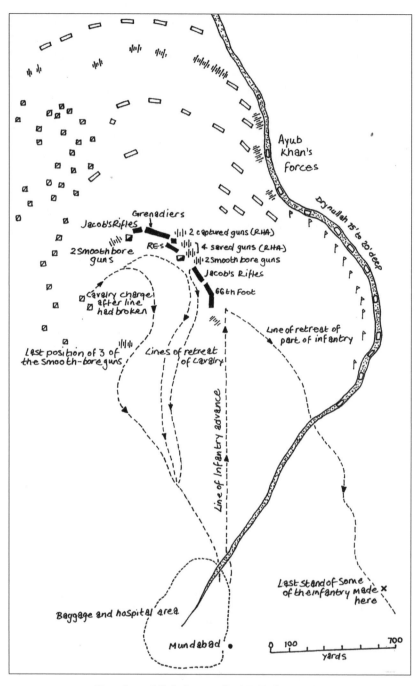

Battle of Maiwand, 27 July 1880

afternoon wore on and the Snider rifles became too hot to hold with endless firing, this subaltern was smashed into a bloody pulp by an Afghan cannonball, and a jemadar, the lowest rank of native officer, had to take charge. Burrows had kept no infantry in reserve, a gap which he tried to remedy in part by holding back the cavalry from the firing line; but they were exposed to enemy artillery, which took a toll of both men and morale. Major Hogg of the staff later wrote: 'It was quite clear to me soon after 1 pm that nothing but a miracle could save us.' The day was incredibly hot, the bare, rocky ground radiating heat, the men desperately thirsty.

After more than four hours' fighting the end came suddenly when the British smooth-bore battery, out of ammunition, withdrew to refill their limbers. Already Afghans were lapping round the Indian flanks, and, as the artillery fire ceased, a horde of Afghan soldiers and Ghazis rose from folds in the ground, and the two companies of Jacob's Rifles on the left gave way. One of the companies of the Grenadiers followed suit and began to press back. The Battalion, which had fought hard, was pushed into an awkward V-formation, and men were cut down, many unable to bring their rifles to play. The cavalry had been demoralized and crippled by the artillery, but prepared to charge. Unfortunately a blunder by the officer in command meant that half the force sheered off without charging home. Broken into small groups, the cavalry could not save the day. So confused was the situation that two majors found themselves carrying out a spirited two-man charge against most of Ayub's army, but managed to extricate themselves after hand-to-hand sabre fighting. The 66th continued to fire deadly volleys until a flight of sepoys from the two native regiments pushed them out of line. The British formation now broken, the force fell back, the infantry mostly to their right towards the village of Khig, the cavalry in the opposite direction. At Khig over one hundred officers and men of the 66th and some survivors of the Grenadiers made a series of desperate stands in gardens and orchards, young Ensign Honeywood, holding a colour high above his head, shouting, 'Men, what shall we do to save this?' before he was shot down. Surrounded by most of the Afghan army, they fought until only eleven men were left. These charged out of the garden with fixed bayonets to sell their lives dearly, to the

135

admiration of all that witnessed it, according to an artillery colonel of Ayub's army. There were other scenes of heroism. A party of the Bombay Grenadiers faithfully guarded the treasure chest of 13,000 rupees in silver through the retreat; Burrows gave up his horse to Major Iredell whose leg had been broken by a bullet; and the Wordi-Major (native adjutant) of the 3rd Sind Horse took up Burrows behind his saddle. The flight continued through the night, Ayub's force delayed by the stand of the 66th and plunder, but peasants came out of the villages to kill and steal. The Revd Alfred Cane recorded that he saw wounded men lying down and giving up all hope, and everyone begging for water. A mounted jemadar and his troop reached Kandahar before 2.00 a.m. on the 28th with news of the defeat, saying they were the only survivors and the whole force had been cut to pieces. The arrival of more fugitives and of a veterinary surgeon of the Royal Horse Artillery gave the lie to the story of annihilation. Brigadier Henry Brooke, the garrison's man of action, left with a relief force and met the survivors – gun carriages loaded with sick, wounded, dead and dying, horses themselves dying of thirst and fatigue, 'many poor fellows,' as Brooke wrote, clinging to the back of a horse or camel, knowing well the Afghan knives that waited if they fell off. Almost last of all, with the cavalry rearguard, came Burrows. He broke down completely when he saw his old Bombay Army compatriot, Brooke, and could not speak. His friend made him get off his horse, take a little whisky and water and a bit of biscuit, and then he became more composed. 'I had never seen the retreat of a panic-stricken military force before,' wrote Brooke, 'and I trust that I may never do so again, as it is too horrible for description, and this retreat excelled in terror any that I have ever heard of.'

Burrows' brigade lost 969 dead and 177 wounded, the proportion of dead showing the dangers of defeat in Afghanistan. The jemadar's report of the destruction of the whole force was unwisely telegraphed by Primrose to Bombay. Even more unwisely it was passed uncensored to London and read by Lord Hartington to the House of Commons that night. In fact, Ayub's force had paid heavily for their victory: 1,500 regulars lost and casualties among the Ghazis had been *beshumar* ('countless'), perhaps 3–4,000.[4]

While Brooke brought in the survivors, Major Adam and the senior medical officer collected all stores and equipment that they could find in the surrounding cantonments. There was indescribable confusion in the Kandahar citadel that day and night, the roads were blocked with laden camels, survivors staggered in thirsty and exhausted, and everyone talked endlessly of heart-rending scenes of defeat. Brigadier Brooke closed and barricaded all save one of the city gates. Broken walls were repaired, wire entanglements constructed around the perimeter, fields of fire cleared and the gates covered in sheet iron to prevent the Afghans burning them down with brushwood faggots soaked in oil, as had been done at Herat in 1842. Some 15,000 Afghans were expelled from the city to avoid treachery and to safeguard supplies, and a careful search revealed extra wells. Ayub's tribes-men began to appear on 5 August, but the main body of his force did not arrive until 6 August. Two days later his guns opened fire. The siege had begun.

British prestige alone demanded that the situation be retrieved; the Kandahar garrison had to be rescued. Ripon could not abandon Afghanistan and Abdur Rahman with his tail between his legs. Should the instrument of vengeance be troops at Quetta or those at Kabul? A march from Kabul to Kandahar through formerly hostile territory presented various risks and would weaken Stewart's force preparing to withdraw. Major General Phayre, commanding at Quetta, was nearest, and his ought to have been the force to relieve Kandahar, but his troops were strung out over the lines of communication and consisted only of Indian units from the Bombay Army, apart from a battery each of the Royal Artillery and Royal Horse Artillery, but none of the best infantry and cavalry. Few transport animals were ready, Baluchistan had been suffering drought for almost two years and forage was in particularly short supply. Phayre soon concluded that he could not hope to set out for Kandahar for at least fifteen days. In the event, he was unable to leave Quetta until 21 August, further complications having arisen from the mutiny of the troops of a British ally, the Khan of Khelat, which necessitated bringing up the 78th Highlanders from Karachi. So notorious were the delays that the wife of a British officer wrote to a friend: 'If [only] we could hear of Gen. Phayre's army making a start – a fortnight is past & still they have not been able to move – it is these delays which are so trying.'[5]

Both Haines and Stewart were at first uncertain whether to despatch a force from Kabul, although the latter made preparations. Roberts was in no doubt. On 30 July, after dining with Stewart, he wired Greaves, the Adjutant General at Simla:

> I strongly recommend that a force be sent to Kandahar. Stewart has organized a very complete one ... He proposes sending me in command ... You need have no fear about my division, it can take care of itself, and can reach Kandahar within the month. I will answer for the loyalty and good feeling of the native portion and would propose to inform them that, as soon as matters have been satisfactorily settled at Kandahar, they will go straight back to India.

The following day, Stewart reinforced this message by wiring the Viceroy that he proposed to despatch a column without wheeled artillery, which, thus unencumbered, 'can go anywhere, and can thrash any number of Afghans. I have made it purposely very strong, because it must depend on itself.' The retirement from Kabul could go ahead as planned. He wrote that day to his wife that Roberts was desperately keen to go, suggesting that he had already decided who would command the relief column. The same day, 30 July, at a Simla Council meeting, the decision was made that the column organized by Stewart was to be sent from Kabul under Roberts. The critical document was a reply from Haines to Ripon the following day:

> After your Excellency's Minute which came to me in circulation today, I no longer doubt that a force will be despatched from Kabul to Kandahar. I am also aware that if a force is to go it will be under the command of Lt Gen Sir F. Roberts; than this no better arrangement can be made; by virtue of his local rank in Afghanistan ... he will ... supersede Gen Primrose.

The decision was Ripon's; he was suspicious of Phayre and thought he would 'race for a peerage'. A force from Kabul would block Ayub if he intended to march for Ghazni and thence to

Kabul. Reinforcements from Quetta would not prevent this. Arriving at Kabul with a victorious army Ayub might easily defeat Abdur Rahman, thus replacing a neutral amir with an anti-British one.[6] By 3 August, the force was ready to march, but firm orders were not issued until the following day, although the quartermaster, Major Badcock, already had his.[7]

'This is a grand thing for Bobs,' Stewart reflected. 'If there is any fighting, he can't help being successful, and his success must bring him great credit.' The lucky Roberts had not gone home when he had thought of doing so. Stewart was generous in giving him the command, but judging by the Battle of Ahmed Khel, was not Roberts's equal as a field commander. George White wrote to his brother of Stewart: 'Now that I see more of his work I don't think he has much genius. He is an ambitious old Scotch man and makes few mistakes but he has not half the elements of a great general that Sir F. Roberts has.' White, judging his superiors as fighting generals, did not appreciate administrative and political gifts required for the task of evacuation, nor that Stewart would take responsibility if the march failed.[8]

Roberts was given the pick of the troops, almost exactly 10,000 men, 2,835 of them British: a cavalry brigade of four regiments under Hugh Gough and an infantry division of three brigades under Major General John Ross, the brigades commanded by MacPherson, Baker and MacGregor. They included excellent Sikh, Gurkha and Highland regiments, with eighteen pack guns, 7,800 followers and more than 8,000 ponies, mules and donkeys. As many soldiers of the Indian Army who had been at war for two years were looking forward to returning home, Roberts went among his regiments and did all he could to encourage them in this last effort. Lieutenant Colonel E.F. Chapman, his Chief of Staff, later observed:

It was not with eager desire that the honour of marching to Kandahar was sought for, and some commanding officers of experience judged rightly the tempers of their men when they represented for the General's consideration the claims of the regiments they commanded to be relieved as soon as possible from field service ... The enthusiasm which carried Sir Frederick Roberts' force with exceptional rapidity to Kandahar was an after-growth evolved by the enterprise

139

itself, and came as a response to the unfailing spirit which animated the leader himself.[9]

Not least he was able to promise them that they should not be left to garrison Kandahar, but should be sent back to India as soon as the fighting ended. He wired on 7 August that those men selected to march to Kandahar were as keen as possible. Anyone incapable of prolonged forced marches was weeded out. Haines reassured the Viceroy that 'Roberts' force is indeed a splendid one; whether as regards the quality of the troops composing it, or with reference to the officers selected for command or staff, it is unsurpassed. I don't see a single weak link in the chain of responsibility from Roberts downwards.'[10]

The young ADC, Lord Melgund, worried that although it was 'a splendid force with a magnificent leader', the simultaneous abandonment of Kabul absurdly left the force without a firm base, 'chucked down in the middle of Afghanistan on a most hazardous undertaking'. Nonetheless, he had implicit faith in Roberts and his men, but there were many Cassandras predicting the worst, and others set up the cry to bring Garnet Wolseley, 'our only general', from England.[11] One factor greatly favoured the march's success: Abdur Rahman's help. He had every interest in seeing the British defeat his rival Ayub. More important than the 200 camels and 300 ponies which he sent were the proclamation reassuring the people and the address to the venerable Mushk-i-Alam to exert himself as he had promised to assist the British. Mushk-i-Alam's change of heart was remarkable, a tribute to the astute politics of Abdur Rahman. The Mullah's eldest son, with the headman of each tribe, was deputed to precede the force, conciliating possibly hostile enemies and arranging supplies. Several of Abdur Rahman's officials attended the second briefing before Roberts's march and promised to provide everything necessary. Lepel Griffin judged that Mushk-i-Alam's co-operation had been instrumental, his son was assisting the march and that little hostility was felt now against the British 'except by the scum of the population of Kabul'. Chapman reported how much Abdur Rahman's aid contributed to the success of the march. Nightly camps were always pitched where fields of Indian corn existed, and the animals were well fed.

Regarding supplies we were especially fortunate; instead of our finding the country deserted, as it was in April, we owe it to Abdur Rahman's efforts, or to the withdrawal of Mushk-i-Alam's fanatical opposition, that the people remained to sell their grain and flour rather than suffer loss by having it taken during their absence from home ... a very fair market was daily established.[12]

Chapman, who had been Stewart's Chief of Staff for his march, contributed much to Roberts's success.

On the evening of 5 August, Stewart and his senior officers, and Roberts and his brigadiers attended a dinner in the sitting room of Lepel Griffin's political mess. Griffin spoke first: 'I wish to propose the success and speedy return with honour of Sir Frederick Roberts and the Kandahar army ... we have given you our last bottle of champagne.' He recited Tennyson's 'Ulysses': 'Come my friends 'tis not too late to seek a newer world.' Roberts replied graciously to Griffin's speech with one of his own. 'The last bottle of champagne' was a generous vintage of Moet and Roederer.[13]

On the day that Ayub's guns opened fire on Kandahar, 8 August, Roberts, 300 miles to the north, began his march. From the outset, with the fate of the garrison at Kandahar apparently hanging in the balance, speed was of the essence. Lieutenant Travers of the Gurkhas wrote: 'We are going to try and reach Kandahar by the 1 September and if we do it will be indeed something to talk about ever afterwards; as it is 27 marches and we must do it in 23 days including halts.'[14] Everywhere news of the march was eagerly awaited. Russian observers were convinced that 'the Mohammedan population' of India was 'greatly excited by the advantages which Ayub Khan has so far obtained over the English' and a British victory was essential. At Bombay the Commander-in-Chief, Lieutenant General Warre, surprised and indignant that the telegram incorrectly announcing Burrows's 'annihilation' had been posted at the Poona Club, had 'great faith in Roberts' to put things right and not to fight conventionally. Luckily, as one of Warre's correspondents wrote, 'the regulation drill book is nothing to a man like Roberts.'[15]

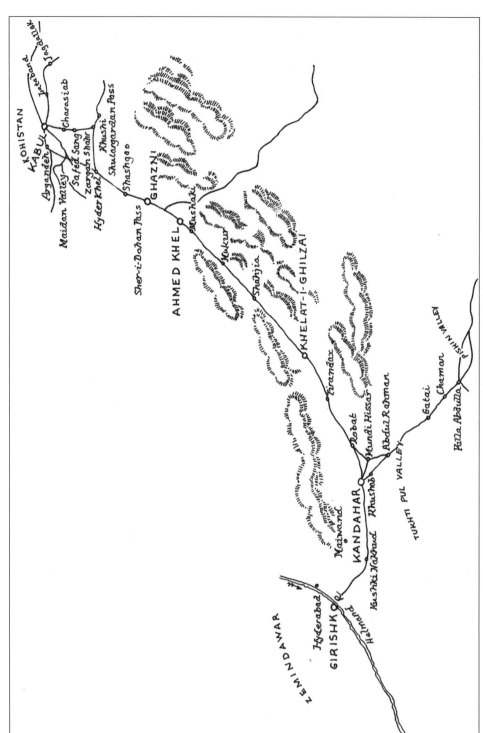

Kabul to Kandahar

Chapter 10

March to Victory

We are marching day after day through a half-desolate land, with no supports to fall back upon in case of disaster, and uncertain of what lay before us; with nothing but thin tents to shield us from a sun which laughed to scorn 100 degrees in the shade, and with a water-supply so uncertain that we never knew in the morning where our camping ground in the evening might be.

Howard Hensman

Heliograph message from Kandahar (27 August 1880):

Question: *'Who are you?'*

Reply: *'The advanced Guard of General Roberts's force – General Gough with two regiments of Cavalry.'*

When Lord Ripon gave leave to his Military Secretary, Major George White, hero of the fight at Charasia, to join Roberts's force on the march to Kandahar, it took him ninety-eight hours to cover the distance from Simla to Kabul. He was delighted to join what he described to the Viceroy as 'the finest force I have ever served with in India; I think I might safely say the finest Anglo-Indian force that ever marched.' The Gordons were looking very fit, and all troops, Indian and British, were soon eager for the work of wiping out Burrows' defeat. Roberts was delighted with the quality of his regiments and with the opportunity he had been given. The worry was that Ayub might escape without a battle, and White told Ripon that it would be

143

well to let Roberts strike the decisive blow without waiting for Phayre.[1] This reflected both force morale and Roberts's own thinking.

The column set off prepared to fight if need be, but the support of Abdur Rahman and Mushk-i-Alam meant that there was no resistance en route. Unlike Stewart, Roberts did not have to battle his way; the 300 miles were therefore a test of logistics and endurance, not of fighting qualities – those would be needed at Kandahar. The brigades moved out on 8 August and the following morning began the march in earnest. The march from Kabul to Kandahar naturally divided itself into three parts: 98 miles from Kabul to Ghazni; 134 miles from Ghazni to Khelat-i-Ghilzai; and thence to Kandahar, a further 88 miles. Ghazni was reached on the seventh day, the daily average being 14 miles, excellent work for troops not seasoned to marching steadily, in temperatures ranging from 84 to 92 Fahrenheit in the shade. This was the Logar Valley, with its varied beauty of cornfield, palm grove and poplar, inaccessible peaks and terrific crags, the foam of torrents flowing down mountainsides. Through the magnificent defile of the Sher-i-Dahan, the advance guard could see the whole column, 7 miles long, curving and trailing behind.[2] When possible they moved on a broad front, brigades and regiments leading by rotation. There was no news from Kandahar at Ghazni and therefore no halt. The steadfast march was resumed: 20 miles on the 16th, 27 miles on the 20th, the longest day. The method of marching, wrote the Chief of Staff, Chapman: 'called on all for exertion in overcoming the difficulties of the march, in bearing its extraordinary toil, and in aiding the accomplishment of the object in view'. The ground was a stony desert compared to the fields around Kabul, reported Lieutenant Robertson attached to the column; underfoot were sand and stone and choking dust, on either hand a barren wall of mountain, above the midday glare of the sun. Despite lack of shade and water, Khelat-i-Ghilzai was reached on the eighth day from Ghazni, a daily average of nearly 17 miles. The men were coated in dust and almost constantly thirsty. 'The worst torment that pursued us was our unquenchable thirst,' wrote Robertson. 'Tantalus dreams of ruby-coloured claret cup, or amber cider, used to haunt my imagination till I felt I must drink something or perish.'[3]

144

The troops set off each day in the early hours, at 4.00 a.m., and stopped for an alfresco breakfast at 8.00 a.m. – a slice of tinned bacon (for those who ate pig) between two cakes of the unleavened bread of India, washed down with cold tea. They halted ten minutes each hour, and usually came to camp in mid to late afternoon. The rearguard, who did not leave camp until 7.00 a.m., seldom ended their march before sundown. Those men who fell out on the march were placed on spare ponies, but were unmercifully 'chaffed' by their comrades. The weakest links in the force were the doolie-bearers and camp followers, who lacked the stamina of the sepoys, so the chief medical officer, Dr Hanbury, gave them a small meat ration. Those followers who attempted to creep away to sleep in a nullah were swept up by the rearguard cavalry.[4]

Chapman described the careful arrangements in a paper later given to the Royal United Services Institute in London. An officer of the Quartermaster General's department was specially entrusted with the duty of gaining intelligence through Afghan agents. Copies of maps prepared during Stewart's march had not reached Kabul from India in August, but tracings of original sheets were supplied to brigades and were copied to regiments so that the officers could have a general idea of the country. An extra tin of pea soup was issued to every two British soldiers, usually eaten before the march, extra rum to those who drank spirits, and extra meat to those not taking rum. Thirty days' supply of basic rations were taken, plus a few days of mutton on the hoof; the villagers proved willing to sell their houses for firewood. Quartermaster Major Badcock recorded that they came in freely and forage was 'in abundance', proof of Abdur Rahman's co-operation.[5]

Roberts and his staff had their work cut out for them with the long days, heat and dust, bitter cold at night, a column of 10,000 men and three-quarters that number of camp followers straggling along with impractical footwear, and many beasts of burden, the head of the column 7 miles ahead of the tail, and only the invaluable heliograph enabling them to keep in touch and save delays. Shortage of water was a constant problem, aggravated by the thick choking dust thrown up by the columns and temperatures soon rising over 100° Fahrenheit. The tail of the column arrived late after the day's march and some men fell out from exhaustion, having had little sleep. The work of the men was increased by night guards, and parties to collect firewood and cut forage for the animals; George White told the Viceroy: 'I was very tired every day, although I had a horse to ride on the march, and no fatigues nor working parties after it was over.' The troops, however, mostly remained in good form, encouraged by a tot of rum on arrival at camp, but the bulk of the followers and especially the doolie-bearers were in increasingly bad shape. Periodically a bitter wind swept across the Afghan plateau and through the passes, chilling these inadequately dressed followers. Behind the column Afghans hovered, looking for plunder or hoping to a send a hated unbeliever to eternal perdition. Rear-guard duty became more and more irksome, the camp followers becoming so weary and footsore that some hid themselves in ravines, making up their minds to die, and entreating when discovered to be left where they were. Every baggage animal that could possibly be spared was used to carry the worn-out followers. Roberts always rode forward after the breakfast halt, chose that night's camping ground, and then sometimes rested, but often rode back for miles to meet troops and cheer them by the news that camp was near. The order would then be given for bands to strike up, and the men would finish the march with renewed spirit. Roberts wrote in his diary for his wife:

> As soon as I am satisfied with the ground for our encamp-ment ... I then eat 2 or 3 hardboiled eggs, or a bit of cold chicken I carry with me and drink some cold tea. This quite refreshes me and if there is any shade obtainable ... I take a short snooze until the troops arrive. I always go out and see them march in. The men like it ... It shows them all that I take an interest in them, and that I don't take shelter or get rest before them.[6]

Two days beyond Ghazni, with 133 miles covered, he received a letter from an outpost commander reporting Kandahar closely invested. Four days later, on 21 August, he received a heliograph message of a disastrous sortie five days before against Ayub's force which resulted in severe losses.

After the return of the Maiwand Brigade, the Kandahar garrison had 450 sick and wounded men to care for, leaving 3,250 men to defend the walls, by no means a large force for a perimeter of 6,000 yards. The expulsion of the male Pathans of fighting age from the city made the task easier. Brooke, a man of spirit, had embarked on an active defence, leading sorties to destroy enclosures around the city which might provide cover for snipers. On the 12th, the defenders sallied out into a walled, loopholed orchard and suffered losses while inflicting even more. 'I think this will be the last of our excursions outside,' wrote the Revd Cane. 'It is getting a bit too hot for us.' Cane tried to cheer up those with long faces, but many remembered only too vividly the horrors of the retreat from Maiwand. Nonetheless, the siege was desultory and the investment incomplete, making possible sallies by Brooke and by the cavalry. Water could be brought in. There was plenty of food, but grain and hay for the animals was rationed. On 13 August, Ayub occupied closer villages north-east of the city and it was reported he was preparing scaling ladders. The chief Royal Engineer, Colonel Hills, prepared a plan for a sortie into Deh Kwaja, the closer and larger of the two nearest villages, to destroy enemy guns and loopholed walls. Brooke was inevitably chosen to lead the venture, but he was against the plan, believing advantages gained would not be commensurate with losses.

Early on the morning of 16 August, a hundred cavalrymen were sent out unseen round to the south-east of Deh Kwaja. Then, following a bombardment of half an hour, Brooke led 800 infantry supported by 100 cavalrymen directly into the village. The preliminary bombardment had warned every Afghan for miles about, who streamed to help the garrison of the threatened village, while the initial cavalry force, by cutting off Afghan retreat actually prevented them from running away. Instead, they fought resolutely from stronghold to stronghold. The columns came under heavy fire and many were hit. Primrose decided to recall them, but did so with a bugler sounding the retreat from the battlements of Kandahar, which also told the Afghans what was happening. As Brooke and his men fought their way desperately back towards Kandahar, Primrose and Hills watching on the walls engaged in angry mutual recriminations over the plan. Brooke refused to abandon Captain Cruikshank of the Royal Engineers who had been badly wounded while blowing up houses in the centre of the village, and for him the delay proved fatal. He fell dead, shot through the back from the walls they had just abandoned, and the men had to give way to a furious ghazi charge, abandoning the Brigadier's body and leaving Cruikshank to his fate. The losses were 108 dead and 116 wounded, too many for a garrison with extended defences. Revd Cane summed up the widely held view: '[The sortie] has weakened our garrison and dispirited our men ... General Brooke was a man we could ill spare & poor Cruickshank was one of those good, hardworking fellows one does not often meet with ... I hope General Roberts is not more than 10 days off. I have a fearful lot of sick & wounded to visit now.'

In fact, among the besiegers there was also disillusion and sinking morale by now, for Brooke's sortie had inflicted serious losses among Ayub's high-ranking friends and relatives in Deh Kwaja, who it was intended would play a part in his planned general assault. Indeed, the fighting spirit shown by Brooke's force caused Ayub to withdraw, leaving the siege very much an open affair. That Brooke was the life and soul of the garrison was shown by Primrose's supine lack of enterprise over the following days. Wrote Cane angrily:

> Here we are – not one of the enemy in sight & we remain doing nothing & waiting for 15,000 men to come & relieve us! ... Our generals seem to have lost their senses. The whole garrison is wild with indignation. We have about 1,000 cavalry eating their heads off & not one outside the gates. General Primrose is responsible. I always put him down as an old woman.

Then, on 26 August, Cane happily recorded the flash of a heliograph from Roberts's force.[7]

The last section of the march had been more easily completed than the first two. On 23 August, at Khelat-i-Ghilzai where there was ample water and forage, Roberts heard that the Kandahar garrison, although closely shut up, was no longer in immediate danger, and gave his men a day's rest. Lieutenant Robertson recorded his gratitude for a full night's rest instead of the three hours sleep he had been having nightly. The Bombay sepoys of the Khelat garrison told frightful stories of Ayub's numbers and invincibility, warning Roberts's Sikhs and Gurkhas that they

148

had but a week more to live. Roberts's answer was to take the garrison with him as he pushed on, two companies of the 66th, the 2nd Baluchis, and a hundred of the Sind Horse, 966 men in all.[8] The following day he received a letter from Kandahar informing him that Ayub had withdrawn his siege and shifted his camp. On the morning of the 27th, Gough was sent forward with two cavalry regiments, covering the 34 miles to Robat in ten hours while the main column advanced about halfway. Gough was accompanied by Captain Stratton, the principal signaller, who contacted Kandahar by heliograph. He then signalled Roberts that Ayub was well entrenched west of Kandahar and strengthening his position for the coming battle. On 28 August, the Political Officer, St John, and Major Adam, Primrose's Chief of Staff, rode out from Kandahar to discuss the situation. Roberts sent Badcock and Low, his quartermasters, to see to provisions. Major Leach was commissioned to prepare a detailed map of the country between Kandahar and Argandab, where the coming battle would most likely be fought. Meanwhile, Ayub sent an emissary to offer terms, claiming that he had been forced to fight at Maiwand by Burrows attacking him. Roberts was not impressed, and told him to give up his prisoners and surrender unconditionally to the authorities at Kandahar.

Despite his energy, Roberts himself felt knocked up by the heat and sun, and on the 27th was overcome by fever and was compelled to be carried in a doolie, a sick cart, 'a most ignominious mode of conveyance for a General on service'. In the journal letter he kept for his wife he first mentioned the illness only on the morning of 1 September as 'a very nasty fever ... quite the worst attack I have had for some years, and in the great heat regularly floored me.' With a sick list averaging 550 daily from poor food, blistered feet from the impractical boots and sandals, heat stroke and exhaustion – but only nine soldiers and eleven followers killed or missing, the latter probably murdered by tribesmen prowling at night – Roberts wanted a pause. The state of the soldiers' footwear can be judged from his telegram requesting boots for most of his soldiers and 'that several thousand pairs will be sent to Kandahar, and also shoes for the 92nd Highlanders and great coats, as only a hundred remained fit to be worn, and these were worn by rotation for night duties'.[9]

Meanwhile, Roberts divided the last 20 miles into two short marches in order that men and animals might arrive as fresh as possible, and on the morning of the 31st they marched into Kandahar, just over 313 miles from Kabul. The fever left him extremely weak and he was carried in a litter until 2 or 3 miles from Kandahar. Then he mounted his famous grey, Vonolel, to meet General Primrose and Brigadier Burrows, who came out to receive the column. There are conflicting accounts of the state of the garrison. It appears that only some officers and men crowded round the new arrivals, 'loud in their expressions of gratitude for our having come so quickly to their assistance'. Roberts was scathing in his memoirs about the morale of those besieged, and that they had not hoisted the Union Jack as a sign of defiance until the relieving force was close at hand. General Vaughan, correspondent of *The Times*, and Lieutenant Travers of the Gurkhas, wrote of the garrison's air of depression and that there was no greeting with bands and music. 'The appearance of the place was depressing in the extreme,' wrote George White. 'A few soldiers, white and black, stood on the walls; very few came out to meet us. No bands nor music & not a cheer.' 'Say what apologists may, the garrison had distinctly lost heart,' wrote Major Gerard of the cavalry later. 'One old brother officer of mine, who had been present at Maiwand, was especially outspoken on the subject.' Nor were the besieged confident at Roberts choosing to camp on the enemy's side of Kandahar. Did Roberts and the others exaggerate the poor morale of the garrison? Revd Cane thought the trouble was the garrison commanders, not the men: 'I always put [General Primrose] down as an old woman. I now find he is indolent, vacillating & without a single idea beyond extreme caution . . . I suppose that a division has scarcely ever before been under such an effete lot of commanders.'[10]

During his second halt, at Robat on the 29th, Roberts had received a letter from Major General Phayre which put out of the question all hope of co-operation by the forces advancing from Quetta, the leading brigade being still occupied in the passage of the Kojak Pass. Phayre's column had not set out from Quetta until 21 August, and had undergone severe privations. Behind the comments of observers who wrote with wry smiles of 'the race for the peerage' was the assumption that Roberts had the pick of the Indian Army to avenge Maiwand. Help from Phayre would have assisted materially in the battle, but on 3 September, two days after Roberts's decisive victory, he was still 26 miles away.[11]

Roberts, senior to Primrose, assumed command as Simla meant him to do. It was not in his nature to delay. He already had a good idea of the enemy's situation from Major Adam, and that afternoon Gough, with the 3rd Bengal Cavalry, infantry and two guns, accompanied by Chapman, conducted a close reconnaissance. He was pressed by the enemy and the whole of Roberts's force stood to arms as he fell back. He now had a full picture of enemy dispositions, supplemented by Roberts – 'seedy as I was' – struggling up a hill for a view. Gough's withdrawal was interpreted by Ayub's men as the defeat of a British assault, increasing their confidence that they could stand their ground. During the night piquets of MacGregor's 3rd Brigade came under attack, and at daybreak the men stood to arms. At 6.00 a.m. they were dismissed for breakfast and tents were struck, while Roberts summoned his senior officers and issued orders for the attack.

Ayub had skilfully posted his men behind a line of serrated ridges 3 miles distant in the Argandab Valley. The Baba Wali Kotal breached this, but so strong were Ayub's defences that an attack into this gap was an invitation to disaster, as Gough's reconnaissance had seen. Instead, the southern end of the ridge terminating in Pir Paimal Hill left another gap through which a force might attempt a turning movement, and Major Adam had recommended this route. The obstacles were fire from guns on Pir Paimal Hill and the stony villages with enclosed orchards and gardens providing strongpoints for defence. Roberts's plan was similar to those for the Peiwar Kotal and Charasia. He ordered Primrose's Bombay troops to make a feint against the Baba Wali pass while he launched the main attack round the southern end of Pir Paimal, intending then to sweep northwards along its western slopes to attack Ayub's camp. Gough would take the cavalry across the Argandab and by a wider march cut off the Afghans' likely route of retreat. Enemy strength was estimated at 4,800 regulars with thirty-two guns, and 8,000 irregulars and tribesmen. Haines had warned that Ayub's troops were better than any so far faced in Afghan battle, although the correspondent

Battle of Kandahar

Hensman thought their strength lay in the undrilled fanatical ghazis in their white costumes representing the purity of the devout, but only a third of the latter had rifles. The Afghan regulars carried Martinis, Sniders, Enfields and old-fashioned matchlocks or jezails. Some were dressed in the full kit of the 66th Regiment, taken from bodies at Maiwand.[12]

Roberts deployed nearly 11,000 men and thirty-two guns. MacPherson's and Baker's 1st and 2nd Brigades would carry out the main attack, with MacGregor's 3rd Brigade in support. Hanna, historian of the war, thought Roberts's plan of battle was both simple and sound, every major and minor unit supporting the rest.[13]

Whether by anticipation or chance, Ayub, who had proved himself a resourceful commander, reinforced the two villages of Abbassabad and Gundimullah during the night. His apparent victory the previous day had given his men great heart and morale was high. It was the same among Roberts's regiments. By 9.00 a.m. on 1 September, British and Indian troops had break-fasted and were in position, and Roberts took his place on Karez Hill. Brilliant sunshine shone out of a clear late summer sky. A tough battle was anticipated and Roberts allowed two days to achieve victory. Pir Paimal Hill immediately to his front, which concealed Ayub's camp on the Argandab, was 500 or 600 feet high, and bright with the standards of crowds of tribesmen along the skyline. Almost at its foot the large village of Gundimullah, whose flat-roofed houses, built upon a knoll, rose tier upon tier, was simply black with the heads of the enemy. Gundigan to its left was equally strongly held.

The British guns opened the ball, first the 40-pounders brought from Kandahar's walls, then the screw guns of Roberts's force, and the feint attack was made by the Bombay troops on the enemy's left flank opposite Baba Wali. It was a sensible gesture to use them, but their role was subsidiary: Roberts had marched his elite troops from Kabul for one purpose, to beat Ayub. Against the Afghan right, leading regiments of MacPherson's and Baker's brigades advanced, the Gordons in magnificent style. So clear was the air that cavalry onlookers could see their kilts waving. As a tremendous but ill-directed fire was opened upon them, George White dashed forward at their head. At Maiwand the Afghan artillery had had a static target. Now the

153

speed of advance and the counter-battery fire rendered the guns ineffectual. The 2nd Gurkhas who had been working their way round on the left sprang up and raced the Scotsmen into attack. The Seaforths and 2nd Sikhs of Baker's Brigade took a wider curve to storm to the village of Gundigan. The walled orchards and gardens, numerous enclosures and irrigation canals favoured defence, and the Afghans resisted fiercely. Gundimullah was taken in tough hand-to-hand fighting, and the dense network of walled enclosures and orchards around Gundigan was captured shortly afterward. Baker's force overcame fierce resistance, but the Seaforths lost their commander, Brownlow, mortally wounded by a shot in the throat.

MacPherson's Brigade, hugging the face of the Pir Paimal ridge, advanced against fierce resistance by a series of rushes. White, as always in the thick of the fighting, was astonished at the speed of the Gurkhas' and Highlanders' advance, the little Nepalese and the burly Scotsmen vying with one another. Brigadier MacPherson, 'cool as a cucumber' (in White's words), led from the front. At last, fearing encirclement now Pir Paimal was lost, the Afghans began to abandon their positions and make off through orchards and gardens fringing the east bank of the Argandab, a continuous black stream of fugitives followed by lighter figures in khaki firing into them at close quarters.

The first phase had been won. By 12.15 p.m. the brigades had rounded the southern end of the hills, seized Pir Paimal, and were ready for the final advance on the enemy camp. The 3rd Brigade was ordered forward to give added weight. Ayub's troops on the Baba Wali had so far been helpless spectators, but as MacPherson's men advanced on them, they resisted fiercely from a long boundary ditch, a small fort in rear of the ditch and a commanding knoll on the right held in great strength. In the centre were loopholed banks supported by guns. Here the Indians and British found the ghazis resisted every inch of ground, and the Afghan regulars were well supplied with captured British rifles. It was the moment for the final effort and fittingly White, having worked his men up to a pitch of enthusiasm, led the Gordon Highlanders, 2nd Gurkhas and 23rd Bengal Native Infantry over the defences at the point of the bayonet. He was the first to reach the enemy guns, but was closely followed by Sepoy Inderbir Lama who claimed one of the guns for the 2nd Gurkhas by putting his cap over the muzzle. The last enemy resistance on the Afghan right round three guns of Ayub's artillery was overcome by a charge of the 3rd Sikhs led by Lieutenant Colonel Money. Lieutenant Robertson noted how closely the different regiments worked together, the 2nd Sikhs and Gordons rallying one another when two companies of the former came under heavy fire, the 3rd Sikhs coming to the support of the 2nd when the danger was acute.

The Afghans were now in full retreat, and this was the point at which Gough's cavalry should have delivered the *coup de grâce*. His orders had taken him to the east bank of the Argandab and when he received instructions to return to the west to cut off retreating Afghans, he had to pick his way through orchards, gardens and deep irrigation canals. By the time the Brigade reached the west bank their horses were exhausted and the enemy was gone. In the early afternoon the Bombay Cavalry were ordered to advance through the Baba Wali Pass, and they pursued the enemy for some 15 miles, killing over 100 of them. Ironically, the Bombay horsemen who had not done well at Maiwand surpassed the Bengal Brigade.

Chapman wrote of the rapidity with which large numbers assembled for battle in Afghanistan were able to disperse in flight. Men who had been engaged in hand-to-hand combat disposed of their arms in the villages they passed through, and would meet their pursuers with melons or other fruit in their hands, adopting the role of peaceful inhabitants. Of the thousands with Ayub Khan, only a few horsemen and a small party of Herat infantry accompanied him in his flight. The Battle of Kandahar was, Chapman claimed, one of the rare instances in which a Muslim army had been so completely routed as to make but small effort to carry off its dead. Nearly 800 bodies were buried by the British during the following three days. Afghan dead probably numbered 1,200, the wounded another 1,200. British casualties amounted to forty killed and 228 wounded, including losses the previous day. Other than the failure of Gough's cavalry pursuit, the victory was complete. All of Ayub's artillery, including two guns lost by the British at Maiwand, was captured.[14] The Government of India later presented these two to Roberts. Ayub's large marquee with its fine carpets, the tents of his men and 'all the rude equipage of a half barbarous army had been abandoned – the meat in the cooking pots, the bread half kneaded in the earthen vessels, the bazaar with its *ghee* pots, dried fruits, flour and corn.'[15] The sick and wounded fell into British and Indian hands with all the baggage. Forty feet from Ayub's tent was found the murdered body of Lieutenant Maclaine, Royal Artillery, taken prisoner at Maiwand, his throat cut by his captors as they fled the British and Indian onslaught. Ayub had given orders that he should not be killed, but a ghazi passing in the retreat had seen and attacked him. Lieutenant Travers of the Gurkhas was furious about this and also about the failure after the battle to attend to some of the wounded: 'The General when he heard it was very angry. The Med[ical] arrangements were simply nil ... To think of men who had fought so well being thrown aside like dogs, and yet they were within 30 yds of a dressing station, it is too bad.'[16]

After the battle, the battalions formed up in their three brigades and Roberts rode to each to say a few words of congratulation, particularly praising the Gordons. 'No other troops could have done it,' he told them. Vaughan of *The Times* wrote: 'I can never forget the cheers which each regiment, Native as well as British, gave him, and I am sure they went straight to his heart. It was a proud day for the soldiers too.'[17] Roberts did not fail to commend to the Viceroy's favour his magnificent force, saying that no troops could have done better; that there was no doubt a feeling of disappointment when the order was first received to go to Kandahar, but 'the men soon plucked up and their enthusiasm and determination were all that could be wished'. He recommended an additional grant of batta (field allowance) and a special medal for the march and victory. 'These are rewards soldiers really valued.'[18] British observers were full of praise. 'I cannot do justice to the great military operation which Sir F. Roberts has undoubtedly accomplished,' said White. The Viceroy wrote to him: 'In my last letter to you I ventured in anticipation to say that your march would be famous in military history. It has more than fulfilled my expectations, and it seems to me to be one of the most remarkable exploits of the kind upon record.' Congratulations came from the highest quarter. 'The Queen Empress is anxious to express personally to Sir F. Roberts her high sense of the very great service he has rendered to his Sovereign & country by his grand march & brilliant victory

156

which came at a very critical time.' The Commander-in-Chief, Cambridge, sent his congratulations. Donald Stewart, with much reason to be proud of his unselfish contribution, told a friend at Simla: 'The perfect success of Roberts' operations brings the war to a close in a way that must be satisfactory to the Government and a carping Press.' Roberts himself wrote to his wife on 3 September: 'All anxiety is over, and our march has ended in a manner which I hardly hoped for in my wildest dreams.'[19]

In the chorus of praise, there was one dissenting voice,[20] and that one muffled. Throughout the 1879 and 1880 campaigns Roberts's Chief of Staff and then Brigade Commander, Charles MacGregor, had kept a diary extremely critical of Roberts. This intelligent, courageous, ambitious, opinionated and tactless officer, in his own words, 'a grim-faced Mephistopheles', and in the opinion of a fellow officer, not a friend to win hearts and influence people, wrote harsh criticisms of nearly all his fellow officers: Lockhart was 'flabby and uninteresting'; Bindon Blood 'an ass and a sycophant'; Hugh Gough 'is a big ass'; Stewart whom he liked at first was soon castigated, 'very stingy and canny, but he has not much go in him, and he is not by any means so straight as he ought to be'. Roberts's letters are full of praise for MacGregor, a leading advocate of the 'forward school'. Of Roberts, MacGregor wrote: 'He is fickle, like all Irishmen, lacks ballast, not much of a general, would be bowled over by a setback.' How much of this really stands up? MacGregor often proposed action counter to what was taken, and the success of Roberts's measures contradicted his predictions. He was against occupying Sherpur because it was too large. Of the march to Kandahar he wrote beforehand: 'I do not see how Bobs is to feed his force, if we go. We cannot carry large supplies with us, and as the whole country will be hostile, it will be very difficult to get enough. He is a very daring little devil, and will risk anything to get a peerage out of this.' By 3 August, when MacGregor found Stewart poring over Robert's memorandum, the decision to send a force from Kabul had been made. Roberts was not the only seeker of glory. MacGregor wrote: 'Oh! If I can only go, the eyes of all Europe, and India will be on us.' Roberts no doubt thought the same, and once the march began MacGregor noted that he was 'energetic and pushing'.

157

MacGregor claimed that the march was chaotic, 'that of a disorganised rabble', that Roberts was reckless and no organizer. 'Bobs has made a regular mess of it all.' It is worth noting that the day Roberts was persuaded to try MacGregor's 'dodge of marching in three columns' was the day of greatest disorganization, according to Lieutenant Travers. It may well be that the rearguard *was chaotic* trying to deal with the recalcitrant camp followers. The column stretching 7 miles was not amenable to rigid control. Stewart did not press his march at speed to save a garrison and took half again as long to cover the distance. When MacGregor recorded, 'Bobs has got a go of fever and is laid up', he hoped 'he will pick up, or we shall be left to the tender mercies of old Ross, and that will be awful. Bobs with all his faults is at all events, go a head [sic] and decided.' On 29 August, he added: 'It is a great misfortune [Roberts] being ill at this juncture, as there is no one else fit to take command.' When Roberts had briefed his senior officers for the attack on the morning of 1 September, MacGregor claimed it was a plan which he suggested, conveniently forgetting his earlier urging for passage down the Argandab to fall upon Ayub's rear. After the victory he crowed: 'It has been a brilliant success, and we have got all Ayub's guns.'[21]

George White who had been critical of Roberts's tactics at Kabul in December 1879 wrote to the Viceroy: 'Everywhere the contrast between Roberts' work at Sherpur and what has been done here cannot fail to strike the most casual observer. The absence of all enterprise and resource on the part of the officer in command is also conspicuous.' Buoyed up by the success he called Roberts's achievement 'the greatest military movement made by a British army in our day'. This was pardonable exaggeration, but it was a feat of arms to match those other Victorian triumphs: the soldiers' battle of Inkerman, and Wolseley's night march and surprise attack at Tel-el-Kebir. Some will attribute Ayub's failure to withdraw to the famed 'Roberts luck', White told Ripon, but remember Napoleon's dictum about lucky generals.[22]

The fighting over, Roberts faced the inevitable problem of supplies, especially as Phayre's force arrived at Kandahar on the 6th. To ease the shortage, the troops were progressively sent back to India, MacGregor's Brigade first. With it went Roberts, worn down by the mental and physical strains to which he had been subjected. A medical board recommended his immediate return to England. The findings of this board are remarkable in view of his just having brought off the greatest coup of his career.

This present illness [the board wrote] commenced from after he entered on the Cabul campaign of 1879–80. A continuous pain in his chest, a feeling of weariness and occasional passing of blood per anum ... tenderness or pressure ... sickness of the stomach, and a great disinclination for food ... have continued on and off since September, 1879, and in April last & during part of May an attack of fever which lasting some time further aggravated the primary disorder ... During the march from Cabul to Kandahar in August '80 Sir F. Roberts has had two attacks of fever, one about the middle of the month, slight, the other on the 28th by which he was completely prostrate for 4 days. On the latter occasion his liver was much deranged – he suffered from constant nausea, violent headache, pain in back and sleeplessness with total loss of appetite ... absolutely necessary that he should have complete rest both mentally & bodily and change of scene.

Roberts was ordered on leave 'as otherwise I [the chief medical officer] do not think his health can be restored'. He was possibly suffering from a duodenal ulcer.[23] On 15 October he handed over command to Phayre and left for Simla, where he saw Ripon and received a personal letter in the Queen's own hand, and then sailed for England, to his wife's undisguised pleasure. She had told Lord Melgund:

I felt quite sure you w[oul]d be glad to hear of Fred's success. To me it has been an immense relief after 4 weeks of the most intense anxiety and suspense. I am only anxious that he sh[oul]d get away. I have been very unhappy about him lately he has been so ill & for some time was unable to answer even a telegram himself.[24]

With Abdur Rahman established in Kabul, fierce debate raged as to whether Britain should hold Kandahar through the Wali

Sher Ali, but in November 1880 the Marquess of Hartington notified Ripon that Gladstone's government had rejected the argument of the 'forward school'. Britain's ally the Wali would be abandoned. Ripon was directed to arrange for evacuation and restoration of Kandahar to Abdur Rahman. Lyall was sent to persuade Sher Ali to abdicate; it took him five days. In April 1881, the British handed the town over.

Nearly a year after Roberts's march, at the end of July 1881, Ayub advanced again on Kandahar, defeated the Amir's troops and seized the city. A month later Abdur Rahman took the field himself, marched with 12,000 regulars and many tribesmen and on 22 September defeated Ayub. The battle was hard fought, but decided in the Amir's favour by the desertion of some of Ayub's troops. He fled to Persia where he continued to be a source of trouble until 1888, when he finally gave up the contest and accepted asylum in British India. He died at Lahore in April 1914.

The conclusion of the war led to Anglo-Afghan peace lasting thirty-nine years. Abdur consolidated his rule and accepted British diplomatic aid to secure his frontiers.

The cost of the 2nd Afghan War in both gold and men was heavier than expected. There was a financial blunder over the war, estimated in October 1880 at £17.5 million, including nearly £5 million for railways, although more accurate estimates raised the figure to £19.5 million. The British government contributed £5 million and India paid the rest, a heavy burden. The mistake cost the Viceroy's financial advisor, Sir John Strachey, his job; he resigned and returned to England. The Military Member, Edwin Johnson, whose department was directly responsible for the blunder also resigned. Total casualties are more difficult to calculate. The Indian Army lost an estimated 1,850 killed in action or died of wounds, and nearly 8,000 of disease. Afghan dead in major battles probably exceeded 5,000; deaths from wounds may have been lower because of better acclimatization.[25]

As MacGregor rode out of Kandahar in August 1880, he wrote of Roberts: 'What a lucky devil he is, two or three years ago he was a Colonel, now he will be a peer, a Lieutenant-General and Commander-in-Chief of one of the Presidencies.'[26] MacGregor was right about the second and third: the war had made Roberts's reputation. In the aftermath of Maiwand, English newspapers were calling for Sir Garnet Wolseley, 'England's only general', to be sent to the rescue; now they were saluting Roberts's march and victory, and he was received in England by cheering crowds.[27]

Roberts learnt from his difficulties with MacPherson of the *Standard* – in an age of greater literacy and increased newspaper readership, the help rather than the enmity of correspondents was necessary. Other senior officers, jealous of Roberts's success and growing fame, noted that he had the good luck to have a correspondent or two to commend his march to Kandahar. There was nothing of luck about it. Luther Vaughan of *The Times* wrote somewhat naively: 'I do not remember that during my ten months' stay at Kabul with Roberts' army, or on the subsequent march to Kandahar, anything in the nature of a censorship of the Press existed.' He admitted that it might have been different with more correspondents, but only Vaughan and Howard Hensman went with the column. Roberts showed them kindness and great courtesy. 'Amongst my most cherished memorials of the period are the notes he from time to time wrote me approving my letters and telegrams,' wrote Vaughan, 'and the manner in which I placed matters before the English public. Nor can I ever forget his kindness in mentioning me as if I had been officially attached to his army.'

As Vaughan observed, the fame of Roberts's march owed much to the peculiar circumstances – an army of 10,000 men setting off into the Afghan hills, being lost to view, and then found again having won a victory that ended a war and wiped out a previous disgrace.[28] Colonel Hanna claimed when he wrote his history of the Afghan War that the battle at Futtehabad on 2 April 1879, in which Brigadier Charles Gough drew the Afghans from their positions by a clever ruse, was 'the most successful engagement of the war'. Roberts himself praised Stewart's march in the reverse direction, from Kandahar to Kabul. The public, however, best remembered the dashing attack on Peiwar Kotal, the successful defence of Sherpur against odds, and the march to victory at Kandahar.[29]

Chapter 11

Epilogue

Then ere's to Bobs Bahadur – little Bobs, Bobs, Bobs,
Pocket Wellinton.

Rudyard Kipling, 'Bobs'

I have always regarded [Roberts] as a scheming little Indian who
has acquired a great reputation he would never have had but for
the necessity of setting someone up to counteract my influence in the
Army.

Sir Garnet Wolseley

Ripon was greatly pleased with the success of Roberts's march
to Kandahar, a triumph despite cries of doom from those who
felt that launching Roberts without a base seemed 'to be to send
him to his destruction'. He had been prepared to overrule
Haines, feeling that 'the chances of success [were] good enough
to set aside the usually accepted principles of theoretical warfare.' He published relevant papers in two volumes under the
title *Kandahar Correspondence* with an appendix of letters from
officers on his staff including White.[1] Ripon's General Order
dated Simla, 12 October 1880 gave everyone, including the
Viceroy himself, a pat on the back, especially Roberts and his
column: 'The enterprise could not have been prudently entrusted
to a leader less able or to troops less efficient than Sir Frederick
Roberts and the soldiers so worthy of his leading.'[2] Roberts was
not to fight a major war again for nearly two decades, although
he narrowly missed action in South Africa in 1881 and was on

the periphery of a guerrilla campaign in Burma. He could be justly proud of his handling of the march and battle. He had faced the toughest Afghan troops in a strong position and had deployed his men ably. The quality of his force and its superior firepower, however, virtually guaranteed victory, unless he had blundered badly.

When he boarded ship for England he was dangerously thin and suffering from 'constant nausea, violent headache, pain in the back and sleeplessness with a total lack of appetite'.[3] He was also the happiest man in India – gone were worries about the radical press, Massy and his friends, and the reaction of the Duke of Cambridge, who even then was writing to Haines to say that all Europe was complimenting Roberts's operations 'which they conceive have been conducted with the greatest vigour & sound judgement'.[4] In England, he was lionized as the Empire's newest hero. His last leave had been twelve years before when he had been an obscure artillery major. Now he was famous. Despite terrible weather at Dover, a large crowd waited to see him disembark. He and Nora were the Queen's guests at Windsor, Victoria being impressed with his 'very keen, eagle eye';[5] he was presented with swords of honour by Eton and the City of London; Oxford conferred an honorary degree. A special medal was struck and came to be called the Roberts Star, awarded to all those who made the march from Kabul to Kandahar including his grey, Vonolel. Nonetheless, he was soon bitterly disappointed with the rewards for the Afghan War compared with those for other Victorian campaigns. He and Stewart were made baronets and each given £12,500, but Wolseley had received twice that and promotion for the Ashanti campaign which, in the unkind words of the United Service Gazette of 4 June 1881, had resulted in 'the capture of an umbrella'.[6] He and Wolseley were soon to become rivals, not just in the public eye, but in the imperial strategy they espoused, each zealously backed by a circle, or 'ring', of admirers.

Lack of commensurate reward for Roberts was ungrateful, for he had retrieved Britain's reputation, but reflected Liberal feelings towards a Conservative war which they had been only too glad to finish. Radicals in Parliament had not forgotten the hangings at Kabul the previous year and opposed the vote of thanks to him on the ground of 'atrocities'. Childers as Secretary

163

of State for War said that the charges were without foundation. Lord Hartington added, 'rarely, if ever, had a war been conducted with such strict regard to the principles of humanity and honour, and with such a total absence of excess of any kind,' a reply that would have brought wry smiles to the faces of MacGregor, White and Durand. The vote in Parliament on 'Kabul to Kandahar' was carried by 165 votes to 76. Roberts told Lytton that he would not be a party man; he had taken Kabul under the Conservatives and relieved Kandahar under the Liberals; but lack of reward rankled, and to the Governor of Madras he wrote that he had 'never anticipated that, after an arduous campaign which lasted 2 years, and which was brought to a successful conclusion by the decisive action at Kandahar, my services would be weighed in the somewhat fickle scale of politics'.[7]

The Kabul executions did not dog Roberts's future career. There had been no television cameras in Afghanistan in 1879, and only one of the beautifully produced black-and-white photographs by J. Burke now in the National Army Museum shows the gallows; it is captioned 'The Gate & the Gallows where several of the murderers of Sir L. Cavagnari and party were executed'. Ripon had been a fierce critic of Roberts while in England, but once in the Viceroy's seat, he had employed the best fighting soldier available to defeat Ayub Khan. Roberts did not mention the executions in his autobiography. Biographies of George White and Mortimer Durand quote their letters in bowdlerized form: Durand wrote White's on Roberts's recommendation and could hardly damn him; Sir Percy Sykes, Durand's biographer, composed his with Roberts's elder daughter looking over his shoulder. MacGregor, a fierce critic in the privacy of his journal, edited the official history of the 2nd Afghan War, but the section on the hangings is taken verbatim from Howard Hensman's dispatches. Hensman defended Roberts throughout. The official history was shortly suppressed, not by Roberts with a guilty conscience, for he had no need to worry, but by the Government of India who did not wish it read during their diplomatic wooing of Abdur Rahman in the 1880s. Indian Army men said that the Afghans got their deserts for the treacherous massacre of Cavagnari and his men and the disfiguring of the corpses of British and Indian soldiers. Brigadier Charles Gough spoke for others when he wrote: 'They are the most bloodthirsty villains going, such is the case with *all* Orientals, War with them means Death & Destruction to their Enemy.'[8]

Roberts's fame as 'our only t'other general' in Mr Punch's words led in time to a rift with Wolseley and the famous clash of the 'rings' – 'Ashanti' and 'Indian'. Roberts entered the lists against Wolseley in a speech on the question of long- and short-service enlistments. Short-service enlistments were a feature of the Cardwell reforms. Edward Cardwell, Secretary of State for War in Gladstone's first government, had instituted a famous series of reforms which did much to establish the nature of late Victorian Britain's Army in the wake of Prussia's smashing victories over Austria and France. Cardwell's measures were striking but incomplete. He moved the reluctant Commander-in-Chief, the Duke of Cambridge, from his separate offices in the Horse Guards to the War Office in Pall Mall, emphasizing the constitutional supremacy of the secretary of state over the Commander-in-Chief. The Army Enlistment Act of 1870 provided for service of six years with the colours and six with the reserve with the option of only three years service with the colours for recruits to home regiments; it attempted to create a reserve of 60,000 men to be mobilized in a great European war, but provide six years' long service for men garrisoning India and the rest of the Empire. Without, however, an increase in pay and expensive improvements in service conditions, changes which a parsimonious Gladstonian administration was unlikely to agree to, recruitment remained a problem. A second reform, the 'linked-battalion' system, had to wait until 1881 and another reforming Secretary of State, Hugh Childers, to take the final step of forming two-battalion regiments, one battalion at home, one for overseas service. Purchase of commissions, which seemed to epitomize control of the Army by a narrow and incompetent landed elite of nobility and gentry, stood in the way of reform and a professional army. There was a violent Parliamentary struggle over abolition and the House of Lords threw out the bill. Cardwell turned the diehards' flank in July 1871 by inducing the Queen to end purchase by royal warrant. The abolition neither altered the social composition of the officer corps nor infused the Army with a new professional spirit; it could not do so unless officers' salaries were increased and promotion made dependent upon merit in action and passing examinations. Both Wolseley and

Roberts found accelerated promotion for their ablest followers difficult in the face of the dominance of seniority. Cambridge and his allies continued to resist change, and the War Office became a byword for compromise and dithering. A proper assessment of Britain's strategic needs had to wait until the Stanhope Memorandum of 1891, soon to be rendered obsolete by events.[9]

For service in India, not young recruits but seasoned men were needed. Therefore, Roberts was not alone in being unhappy with short service and its effect on *esprit de corps*. On 14 February 1881 he was guest of honour at the Mansion House, London, with the Duke of Cambridge in the chair. In his speech Roberts protested against short service: 'What is it that has enabled a comparatively small number of British troops, over and over again, to face tremendous odds, and win battles against vastly superior numbers? The glorious annals of our regiments give the answer – discipline, *esprit de corps*, and powers of endurance – the three essentials which are absolutely wanting in the young soldier.' Roberts argued for Britain having two armies – a home army and a foreign service army, the latter 'always be in the most perfect state of efficiency, ready to take the field in our distant possessions on the shortest possible notice'.

Among the listeners at the Mansion House, Lord Melgund praised the speech as 'the best I ever heard … The speech has been received with rapture by nearly every soldier.' The Duke of Cambridge echoed this, writing to Haines: 'we have had a great speech by Sir Frederick Roberts at the Mansion House dinner last Monday [which] has had a great impression … certainly the public have taken the subject up very warmly & I am not sorry they should have done so whatever may come of it.'[10] Cambridge was an opponent of short service and pleased that a younger general shared his views. Roberts's words had a lasting impact and in 1903 his admirers were still quoting them.[11] Wolseley, a partisan of Cardwell's reforms, took the opposite view. He replied to Roberts in the March 1881 issue of *The Nineteenth Century* in intemperate language, castigating the critics of short service as chronic grumblers and whining pessimists. He argued that armies and navies were by their very nature conservative, opposed to the Liberal government's reforms. The rivalry between Roberts and Wolseley was based, not just on differences over terms of enlistment, but on differing strategies and competition for top army jobs. Wolseley wished to make the home army, with the mobility which sea power conferred upon it, the basis of imperial defence; Roberts advocated a continental policy in which the Indian army played the key role. Their 'rings' competed in the last years of the nineteenth century in 'a deadly game of musical chairs' for the key commands in Ireland and India, at Aldershot and the War Office.[12]

Roberts's career flourished in India where he was Commander-in-Chief first at Madras and then at Calcutta and Simla. His influence was far reaching, partly because of excellent relations with Viceroys Dufferin and Lansdowne, and with Military Members of their council, Major Generals George Chesney and Henry Brackenbury, the latter a follower of Wolseley, won over to the 'Indians'. Roberts continued to develop links with newspapermen, notably with Hensman, now Simla correspondent of the Allahabad *Pioneer,* reputed to know all the army secrets ('Roberts made him, and he made Roberts,' it was alleged).[13]

While Roberts was Commander-in-Chief, MacGregor took over the Intelligence Department, which he dramatically improved in efficiency. He prepared plans to mobilize an army corps quickly in the event of sudden emergency. In 1884 his comprehensive and exhaustive treatise, *The Defence of India: a Strategical Study,* was privately published, but its characteristically outspoken and alarmist views on British strategy in the event of Russian attack led to its suppression by the imperial authorities. When MacGregor was appointed to command the Punjab Frontier Force, his health broke down and a few days after his promotion to major general, he died of peritonitis at the age of forty-six.[14] After his death, Roberts became main spokesman of the 'forward school', arguing for readiness on the North-West Frontier against possible Russian invasion. His advocacy of the 'martial races' of northern India, and especially the Gurkhas, those bullet-headed, broad-chested, loyal paladins of empire, had an effect which has continued today. He was popular with soldiers both Indian and British, noted for his care for young recruits, but tough on those two idols of the enlisted man, drink and sex. He was Commander-in-Chief for an unusually long time, nearly eight years, and he engineered the appointment of George White as his successor, over the heads of senior men. Roberts was not alone in pushing for his appointment, however, as he had the support of Lansdowne, then Viceroy, and Sir Henry Brackenbury, the Military Member. White was a convert to Roberts's 'forward policy', and had made his reputation in Burma in 1885–7 by excellent leadership and administration. He had always 'liked the little man' and was immensely grateful when he gained him his major generalship in 1889. There was also someone else to be thanked. To his wife White wrote: 'Don't neglect to call upon Lady Roberts and remember to go out of your way to be grateful to Sir Fred. His kindness & interest in me has been something that I have not been accustomed to and I have enlisted more thoroughly than ever under his standard. Find her out and call upon her.'[15]

In 1893 Colonel Henry Hanna was busy on his history of the 2nd Afghan War. He had been denied promotion by Roberts when the latter was Commander-in-Chief, and to frustrated ambition he added disagreement over relations with Afghanistan and the frontier tribes. Despite successful advances made in Baluchistan by Robert Sandeman and George White, and British consolidation of Quetta, Hanna was a convinced opponent of the 'forward policy'. He claimed that since the war one tribe after another had come to view the Indian government with growing mistrust and that this was the fault of the government's policy, a policy inspired by Roberts. His building of strategic railways and stationing troops on the frontier against possible Russian incursion was disastrous, thought Hanna, who was determined that his history of the 2nd Afghan War would show this.

He wrote to Brigadier Charles Gough, who was still sore at Roberts for his telegrams in December 1879 asking him to march through snow and Afghans to Sherpur. Repeating his charge that Roberts ruled at Kabul with a harsh and not always just hand, Hanna continued, 'In my opinion Gen[era]l Roberts is in all public matters the most dangerous & unscrupulous man I have ever known. He would not hesitate to sacrifice any man to save his own reputation, or to pander to his personal ambition.' Hanna hoped to draw Gough on the question of whether he had been in a race with Roberts to reach Kabul after Cavagnari's murder in 1879, just as he maintained that there had been 'a race for the peerage' to Kandahar the following year. Gough, whose victory at Futtehabad on 2 April 1879 Hanna was to praise as 'the most successful engagement of the war', did not agree. He reminded Hanna that Roberts's reputation for self-advertisement was well known, but he would not engage in public denigration of the victor of Kandahar, whose reputation then stood high on the eve of his leaving India.

Hanna did not let the matter drop. Two years later the North-West Frontier was in the news again, as the ruler of the border state of Chitral was murdered, Afghan tribesmen invaded from the north and a British garrison was surrounded Beau-Geste-style in the loop-holed fort. Hanna published an angry pamphlet entitled *Lord Roberts in War*, full of interesting insights into the 2nd Afghan War designed to prove that Roberts's success at the Peiwar Kotal had been luck, that Massy and MacPherson had saved him in the Chardeh Valley, that he had selfishly called Charles Gough to his succour at Sherpur and had not properly thanked him in his despatch. Alone of Roberts's deeds in Afghanistan, the march to Kandahar escaped criticism. 'I have no wish to depreciate Lord Roberts' one great achievement,' wrote Hanna, mixing praise with damnation. 'The advance on Kandahar was a splendid soldiers' march, fully testing the endurance and spirit of the veteran troops who took part in it; and the battle of Kandahar was the battle of a good tactician.'[16]

Another two years passed, and in 1897 the embittered Hanna was back to his theme, emphasizing in a letter to Gough how the writing of his history had enabled him to form strong views on the North-West Frontier, contrary to those of Roberts, needless to say. He was, however, trumped in true literary style by the intended object of his criticism. The year was Queen Victoria's Diamond Jubilee, a festival of rejoicing, both domestic and imperial. In January, with impeccable timing, there appeared in the London bookshops an exciting new account of army life in Britain's Indian Empire, written by none other than Roberts himself. *Forty-One Years in India: From Subaltern to Commander-in-Chief* was a runaway best-seller. On 9 January, five days after the book's appearance, one reviewer commented: 'There has only been one thing to do in London this week – to go to India with Lord Roberts. No autobiography has been so run after for years, and novel-reading is in abeyance.' In just over a year twenty-eight editions were published; eventually there were thirty-five and the book was translated into Braille, German, Italian and Urdu. 'Few young officers will rise from the story of [Roberts's]

169

life,' *The Times* stated, 'without feeling that they would like to serve under such a chief.' Roberts's protégés agreed whole-heartedly. Colonel Sir Henry Rawlinson, who had served on Roberts's staff, congratulated him on *The Times* review. Colonel Sir Reginald Pole-Carew, veteran of Kabul and Kandahar, told Roberts he was giving away copies and growing in popularity. The book became standard reading for young men thinking of an Indian career. The young Winston Churchill's mother sent him a copy. The descriptions of India, the tribulations of army life there in the 1850s and 1860s, daring deeds on the Afghan frontier, the support of Lady Roberts, the cheerful and encouraging spirit of the writing – these all contributed to the image of Frederick Roberts as a *chevalier sans peur et sans reproche*, and set the seal on the image of 'Bobs Bahadur', 'Bobs the hero', the five-foot-four-inch pocket Wellington.[17]

That a talent for spectacular, well-publicized victories, contacts in many high places and an ability to woo the press outweighed diplomatic and administrative capacity is shown by the subsequent careers of the two British heroes of the war, Roberts and Stewart. Following the 2nd Afghan War, Stewart was first Military Member of the Viceroy's council, and then succeeded Haines as Commander-in-Chief of the Indian Army. Understandably he kept a keen eye on the North-West Frontier, and approved Abdur Rahman's victory over Ayub in August 1881. 'I have always considered the Amir to be by far the astutest politician and statesman in Afghanistan,' he wrote, 'but I did not credit him with energy and high military qualities. So far, however, the Afghan policy of the present government has been a success, and every one must rejoice that it is so, whether they approve or disapprove of it.' He believed that although the Amir could not injure friends who had sheltered him and treated him generously during years of exile – i.e. the Russians – Abdur would realize that Russia was an aggressive power in central Asia in a way that Britain was not. That was in October 1883. The following year, Russia's capture of Merv about 150 miles from the Afghan border raised British fears. The Liberals accused the Conservative government of obsessive anxiety, 'mervousness' as the Duke of Argyll called it, but the attack of the Russian general Komaroff on Afghan troops at Pandjeh seemed to show they were right. The crisis occurred when Abdur was visiting the Viceroy,

Dufferin, and meeting again British commanders of the war that brought him to power. Abdur's cool nerve and Dufferin's tact avoided the crisis deepening. Russia kept Pandjeh, exchanged for other territory. Stewart gave evidence of the Amir's clever calculation when in March 1885 the latter produced a Martini-Henry rifle which his country had been manufacturing. A British officer asked about ammunition, whereupon, recorded Stewart: 'The Amir, with an intelligent and significant look on his face, said: "I did not attempt to manufacture the arms until I succeeded in making the ammunition."'[18]

As Commander-in-Chief, Stewart, like Roberts after him, favoured camps of exercise – i.e. extended manoeuvres – on the model of their patron Napier. The armies of Bengal, Bombay and Madras combined in January 1884 at Bangalore, with benefit to all three in their fighting readiness. 'Roberts is full of enthusiasm and inspires every one around him with a like spirit,' noted Stewart. 'All are anxious to learn, and the experience gained here must be beneficial, especially to the senior officers and staff.'[19]

Stewart was the last man to write himself up, or to care for praise. 'His one idea was that a man should do his duty,' wrote his friend and admirer Revd Warneford. 'He was blamed I know by many for not having made more mention of his march, and of his battles.' He did ensure, however, that when the time came to relinquish his command, his old friend put forward his bid to succeed him. On 17 July 1885, he wrote to Roberts: 'Though I am very busy with my home letters I must write one line to urge you to put all your irons into the fire *without delay* if you want to succeed me.'[20] Roberts's appointment followed at the end of that month, but appears primarily to have been due to Lord Randolph Churchill, Secretary of State for India. He had been impressed with Roberts on an Indian tour and also by his forecasting the poor conduct of what seemed a very smart regiment, the 17th Bombay Native Infantry, which broke and fled at Tofrek in the Sudan fighting against the Dervishes. Roberts had reminded Churchill of his prediction in a letter of 15 April 1885.[21] Stewart returned to England and joined the Council of India, old India men who advised the Secretary of State. On his death in North Africa in March 1900, while the Boer War was its height, *The Times* recorded: 'While Lord Roberts of Kandahar is prosecuting a difficult campaign in South Africa with characteristic ability and energy, the great Indian soldier who sent him on his famous march from Kabul has passed away quietly in Algiers.'[22]

Roberts's career might have ended after his return from India in 1893 and his taking over the Irish command in 1895, a backwater leading to retirement. By that time, however, war with the Boers in South Africa appeared certain. Roberts, urged among others by Rawlinson, wrote to the former Viceroy, Lansdowne, now Secretary of State for War, offering his services. Instead, the former Adjutant General and commander at Aldershot, Redvers Buller, was sent out in command. Early British defeats in South Africa dismayed the Empire, the British government and Buller, who was unable to cope with supreme responsibility. Roberts was despatched to redeem British arms once again, this time in partnership with Major General Sir Herbert Kitchener as his Chief of Staff. Just before he sailed, he and Lady Roberts received news of the death of their son Freddie, mortally wounded trying to rescue guns captured by the Boers at Colenso. He was posthumously awarded the Victoria Cross.

Within nine weeks of his arrival at Cape Town and four weeks of opening his campaign, he turned the tide of war: Kimberley and Ladysmith were relieved and a force of 4,000 Boers under Cronje were surrounded at Paardeberg and captured. After a pause to bring up supplies, Roberts continued his advance in overwhelming strength, capturing Bloemfontein, capital of the Orange Free State, Johannesberg, heart of the Rand, and Pretoria, capital of the Transvaal. Following a final battle at Diamond Hill, Boer forces dispersed. Roberts had defeated but not destroyed the enemy and the commandos continued to fight on. The last of Britain's Victorian colonial wars turned into the first of the people's wars of the twentieth century, and the methods of the future – farm burning, hostages and concentration camps – were started by Roberts and then introduced full scale by Kitchener, who succeeded him and finally ended the war in May 1902.

Roberts's annexation of the Transvaal was followed by a Conservative victory in the 'Khaki election', and he returned to England at the start of 1901 to claim his rewards: the Garter, £100,000, and the top job he had coveted, Commander-in-Chief of the British Army in succession to his rival, Wolseley. Installed in the War Office he wrote encouragingly to Kitchener, who was chasing Boer commandos, pressed Kitchener's claim for the Indian command and finally sent out Colonel Ian Hamilton as Chief of Staff. Despatched to co-ordinate operations in the western Transvaal, Hamilton was able to pull off a victory on the stony hillside at Rooiwal which helped convince Boer leaders to seek peace.

Meanwhile, as Commander-in-Chief, Roberts found that he had little of the scope offered in India. Some useful reform was achieved: a new rifle, the magazine-fed Lee-Enfield, and the 18-pounder field gun were brought into service. Roberts took a close interest in the Staff College, where his protégés Rawlinson and Sir Henry Wilson both proved outstanding commandants.

One of the reforms he initiated proved his own undoing. With his lengthy experience on the Indian Army staff, he was keen to create an army operations staff, and set Lieutenant Colonel Gerald Ellison to work. The Committee established simultaneously under Viscount Esher to reform the War Office took over Ellison's work and finished it, the difference being that they abolished Roberts's post of Commander-in-Chief and gave the operations staff the name 'General Staff', rather than 'Quartermaster General's Staff', as Roberts would have had it following Indian Army practice. Ellison wrote, 'The credit of creating a General Staff belongs to the Esher Committee, but to Lord Roberts is due the initiative which gave us a staff system in 1914 so widely at variance with what had obtained in the Boer War.'[23]

Roberts's removal was tactlessly handled, but he never harboured bad feelings. Esher continued to be impressed with the energy and vision of a man over seventy years old. In January 1910, he found him ageing a little, 'but wonderfully open-minded and virile for so old a man. He is full of modern ultra radical ideas about the army and tactical fighting.'[24]

In old age Roberts's family became even more important to him, his elder daughter supporting her father at public events. For him and Lady Roberts, the young officers they gathered round them – the 'Roberts kindergarten' in the words of the Canadian historian Nicholas d'Ombrain – were in part a substitute for their dead son, Freddie.[25] They both missed India, Lady Roberts reminiscing:

What happy days those were – it is good to have them to look back again ... the fact is the happy life of those

173

Indian days full too of large interests quite unfits one for the toleration of the narrow conventional life of English society where most people's object seems to be push themselves into notoriety of some kind and no one seems to have time for or need of real friends.[26]

On 23 December 1907, at a dinner for veterans celebrating the fiftieth anniversary of the Mutiny, with Roberts presiding, Curzon, former Indian Viceroy and guest of honour, finished a toast to those present 'with the name of the hero of 1857, who was still their hero in 1907, endeared to the nation by half a century of service and sacrifice not one whit less glorious than that of his youth'.[27] That hero's last years were spent campaigning in vain for compulsory service and working, behind the scenes, to prevent the Army being employed to coerce the Ulster Protestants in the summer of 1914 after the passing of the Home Rule Bill. The Irish crisis was temporarily forgotten on the outbreak of the First World War. Appointed Colonel of Overseas Forces in Britain, Roberts decided to visit his beloved Indian regiments on the Western Front in November 1914, accompanied by his elder daughter. For two days, in great spirits, 'like a boy going on his holidays', he visited old comrades at headquarters and wounded soldiers in hospitals, stopping to speak to every Indian soldier he met. On 13 November, he climbed to the top of the Scherpenberg next to Kemmel Hill near Messines for a distant view of the trenches; the day was cold and wet and windy, and he caught a chill. It quickly turned to pneumonia, he fell very ill, and after a brief rally died at 8.00 p.m. the next day, 14 November. He was deeply mourned and seen as a splendid example, not only by former protégés, but by the whole Empire. '[O]ne of the saddest days of my life,' wrote Sir Henry Rawlinson. 'I went in to pay my last respects to my dear chief. I could not believe that he was dead.' Field Marshal Sir John French's telegram to Lady Roberts summed up the Army's view: 'Your grief is shared by us who mourn the loss of a much-loved chief ... It seems a fitter ending to the life of so great a soldier that he should have passed away in the midst of the troops he loved so well and within the sound of the guns.' The Scottish Rifles (the Cameronians) marching to the front, swinging along to snatches of popular song, lapsed into gloomy silence when they heard that 'Bobs, the idol of the army' was dead. The Sunday night edition of *The Times* of 15 November headed its front page: 'Sudden Death of Lord Roberts'. 'A profound shock of sorrow will be felt by the nation at the announcement of the death of Field Marshal Lord Roberts ... One of the most famous and best beloved of British soldiers passed away in an hour of national trial, to prepare for which he had exerted himself with unsparing devotion.'[28]

Frederick Roberts was a contradictory character, a mixture of cheerful kindness and ruthless ambition, a selfish careerist who warm-heartedly advanced many others who had served him, a soldier on the frontiers of empire yet a devoted father and husband, who valued home life above all else, the ruthless slaughterer of Afghans who wept uncontrollably when he heard of the courage of his mortally wounded son. In his astute wooing of the press, he strikes a modern note. By the end of his career, however, he had achieved an imperial apotheosis. He seemed to epitomize British ideals at a time when courage, duty, the Empire and the family were revered. His small stature and famous nickname endeared him to many. His reward was to be laid to rest close to the tombs of Nelson and Wellington, buried in a state ceremony at St Paul's Cathedral, his pall bearers being admirals of the fleet, field marshals and generals, the congregation a huge uniformed throng including representatives of his many regiments. Kipling, friend of Roberts for many years and poet of empire, wrote in tribute. None of this would have been possible without the march to Kandahar, which retrieved his reputation from possible disgrace after the hangings at Kabul.

If Roberts's career seemed to his family and friends the proud fulfilment of his many ambitions, the fate of Afghanistan is a sad contrast. At the conclusion of the 2nd Afghan War Abdur consolidated his rule and accepted British diplomatic aid to secure his frontiers against Russia. His reign until 1901 was harsh but efficient. He crushed internal rebellion with cruelty, put robbers in cages and left them to die, while unjust tradesmen had their ears nailed to their shop entrance. Relations with India were peaceful. Nevertheless, there was scarcely a moment when the British were free from worry about Russian designs. The 2nd Afghan War coincided with the final Russian victory at Gek Tepe over Turkoman tribes between the Caspian and the northern Afghan border, so for practical purposes the Russian border was contiguous with Afghanistan's. The Pandjeh crisis of 1885, when the Russians routed an Afghan force on the border, brought Russia and Britain to the verge of war. The Russians realized what a powerful diplomatic lever British fears about Afghanistan placed in their hands. Nicholas II boasted in 1899 that he could immobilize British policy throughout the world by mobilizing Russian forces in Turkestan. With the major tribes on the Indo-Afghan frontier between the Khyber and the Bolan Passes, there was no peace, despite the Durand Line of 1893 dividing the Pashtuns between India and Afghanistan. Mortimer Durand persuaded Abdur Rahman to accept the line in return for an increase of his subsidy from twelve to eighteen lakhs. Meanwhile the British attempted to assert their authority over the tribes on their side of the line. The Chitral campaign of 1895 led to the general Pashtun uprising of 1897 which needed a force of 35,000 under General Sir William Lockhart to quell it. Abdur Rahman and his people remained neutral.

Afghanistan's unhappy role as buffer between Great (and Super) Powers continued into the twentieth and twenty-first centuries, periods of instability and Islamic Jihad alternating with attempts at progress. In 1919, Abdur Rahman's grandson Amanullah declared a Holy War against India. In the 3rd Afghan War, the Indian Army deployed Rolls-Royce armoured cars and Handley Page bombers, and the war ended with a bloody Afghan repulse.[29] Nineteenth-century British fears that Russia would control Afghanistan seemed to have come true when Babrak Kamal came to power in 1979 supported by the Russians, who appeared to have won the last round of Kipling's 'Great Game'.* The invasion of Afghanistan by the Red Army in support of Kamal followed. Tanks and helicopter gunships were no more successful at suppressing the warlike Afghans than the Indian Army had been, especially when the Mujahedin were equipped by the CIA with Stinger ground-to-air missiles. Gorbachov's withdrawal was part of a series of policies which lead to the end of the Cold War and the break-up of the Soviet Union, an event

* The phrase was originated by Captain Arthur Conolly, British agent murdered in 1842 by the Shah of Bokhara, and popularized by *Kim*.

of world history far more important than Lytton's invasion, and Roberts's and Stewart's short-lived rule at Kabul.

Even this did not end fighting in Afghanistan. American and British forces invaded in October 2001 in the wake of the destruction of the World Trade Center in New York, supporting a Northern Afghan alliance in overthrowing the Taliban. These modern equivalent of the ghazis, who had fearlessly faced Roberts's and Stewart's armies in 1880, have proved equally resilient. Western casualties continue to mount in what is proving an unpopular foreign war. The shades of Disraeli, Salisbury and Ripon must be pondering our rulers' inability to learn from history. Can they find 'a ram caught in a thicket', a new Abdur Rahman, to lead them out of the impasse?

Notes

Abbreviations

BL, Add. Mss.   Additional Manuscripts in the British Library.

Bobs   Roberts papers 7101-23 and 5504 at the National Army Museum. Papers catalogued under 7101-23 have been simplified so that, for example, 7101-23-139 is simply noted as 'Bobs 139'. Those under 5504 have been left complete.

DNB and *ODNB*   *Dictionary of National Biography.*

41 Yrs   Roberts, Field Marshal Lord, *Forty-one Years in India: from Subaltern to Commander-in-Chief*, 2 vols, London, 1897.

Hanna   Hanna, Colonel H.B., *The Second Afghan War 1878–79–80: Its Conduct and its Consequences*, 3 vols, London, 1899–1910.

IOL, Mss Eur.   European manuscripts in the India Office Library (British Library).

JSAHR   *Journal for the Society of Army Historical Research.*

Kandahar Correspondence   *Kandahar Correspondence: Sirdar Ayub Khan's Invasion of Southern Afghanistan, Defeat of General Burrows' Brigade, and military operations in consequence*, India Office Library, Miscellaneous

	Public Documents, 2 vols and appendix of correspondence with Members of Viceroy's Staff attached to Forces for the Relief of Kandahar, Simla and Calcutta, 1880–1.
MacGregor	MacGregor, Major General Sir C.M., *The Second Afghan War: Compiled and Collated by and under the orders of . . . MacGregor, QMG in India*, 5 parts, Simla and Calcutta, 1885–6. (Official Indian Army history of the 2nd Afghan War.)
NAM	National Army Museum.
NLS	National Library of Scotland.
Robson	Robson, Brian, *The Road to Kabul: The Second Afghan War 1878–1881*. London, 1986.
Trousdale	William Trousdale (ed.), *War in Afghanistan 1879–1880: the Personal Diary of Major-General Sir Charles Metcalfe MacGregor*, Detroit, 1985.
WO	War Office papers at the National Archives, Kew (formerly the Public Record Office).

Introduction

1. Events at Simla: BL, Add. Mss. 43, 574, Ripon papers, ff. 141 et seq.
2. Robson, B. (ed.), 'The Kandahar Letters of the Reverend Alfred Cane,' *JSAHR*, vol. LXIX (1991), pp. 211–12.
3. Consequences of Maiwand and plans to send Wolseley, *Kandahar Correspondence*, I, pp. 53 & 74c-d; Elsmie, G.R., *Field Marshal Sir Donald Stewart*, London, 1903, pp. 373–4; NAM Warre papers 8112/54-702 & 713, 30 July & 4 August 1880; 'that gloomy telegram', NAM Haines papers 8108/9-29, No. 52, 31 July 1880.
4. Wolff, L., *The Life of the First Marquess of Ripon*, 2 vols, London, 1921, II, pp. 26–32.
5. Elsmie, *Stewart*, p. 375.
6. Roberts to Greaves and decisions by Stewart and Ripon, *Kandahar Correspondence*, I, pp. 68, 83–4 & 99, and Elsmie, *Stewart*, pp. 372–6.
7. The Second World War book referring to the march was Johnson, Major S.H.F., *Britain's Soldiers*, Britain in Pictures Series, Collins, 1944. Modern references are from the *Daily Telegraph* website and, of all places, that of the American Rhododendron Society: 'Lord Roberts' is a species of rhododendron. Ripon's quote in Wolff, *Ripon*, II, pp. 32–3.

179

8. Modern controversies, see e.g. Strachan, H., *The Politics of the British Army*, Oxford and New York, 1997, and Streets, H., *Martial Races: The Military, Race and Masculinity in British Imperial Culture 1857–1914*, Manchester and New York, 2004; for hostile views of Phayre see NAM, Haines papers 8101-9/30, nos 46, 47, 49, 50.
9. 'Cutting Roberts down to size'; see Hanna, Colonel H.B., *The Second Afghan War*, London, 1899–1910 and *ibid.*, *Lord Roberts in War*, London, 1895, and for modern accounts notably Trousdale, W., *War in Afghanistan 1879–80*, Detroit, 1985 and Pakenham, T., *The Boer War*, London, 1979.

Chapter 1

1. Sources for Afghan background include inter alia Hopkirk, P., *The Great Game: on Secret Service in High Asia*, London, 1990; Macrory, P., *Signal Catastrophe*, London, 1963; Heathcote, T.A., *The Afghan Wars 1839–1919*, London, 1980; Meyer, K. and Brysac, S., *Tournament of Shadows: the Race for Empire in Central Asia*, Washington, DC, 1999.
2. Moorhouse, G., *India Britannica*, London, 1983, pp. 161–4 for modernizing.
3. Roberts family and his background see Bayley, W.J., 'The Roberts Family of Waterford', *Journal of the Waterford and South-East of Ireland Archaeological Society*, ii (1895), pp. 98–103; grandmother a Rajput: Moorhouse, *India Britannica*, p. 184; his half-brother: Dalrymple, W., *The Last Mughal: the Fall of a Dynasty, Delhi, 1857*, London, 2006, pp. 291–2; Saksena, R.B., *European & Indo-European Poets of Urdu & Persian*, Lucknow, 1941, pp. 128–53. In 1911 Eurasians were officially dubbed 'Anglo-Indians'. His blindness in one eye was not widely known and was revealed to a wider public by the *Daily Express* of 28 October 1930. See NAM, Ellison papers 8704-35-711.
4. Parents' ambitions: *The Times*, 30 September 1932, p. 13, 'Field Marshal Lord Roberts – Field Marshal and Reformer – Some Personal Memories' by Brigadier General H.F.E. Lewin and from the preface of *Letters written during the Indian Mutiny by Fred. Roberts. Afterwards Field-Marshal Earl Roberts.* With a preface by his daughter Countess Roberts, London, 1924. His letter is quoted on p. xviii.
5. Bobs 5504-64, item No. 9, final Addiscombe report; 41 Yrs, I, p. 1; Adams, R.J.Q., 'Field Marshal Earl Roberts: Army and Empire', in J.A. Thompson and Arthur Meija, *Edwardian Conservatism*, London, 1988, p. 41.
6. Roberts's early career in India; 41 Yrs and James, D., *Field Marshal Lord Roberts*, London, 1954, pp. 15–16. Information about artillery service on the frontier from Will Townend and Tony Young of the

Royal Artillery Historical Society; loose formations, see Moreman, T.R., *The Army in India and the Development of Frontier Warfare, 1849–1947*, London, 1998, pp. 13–15.

7. Rapid rise in QMG's department, Bobs 225, 'Some turning points of my career'.
8. For Mutiny background see inter alia Hibbert, C., *The Great Mutiny: India 1857*, London, 1978, pp. 1–78; David, S., *The Indian Mutiny 1857*, London, 2002, pp. 1–77; James, L., *Raj: the Making of British India*, London, 1998, pp. 221–38; Spear, P., *Penguin History of India*, vol. II, London, 1990, pp. 139–41; Sen, S.N., *Eighteen Fifty-Seven*, Calcutta, 1957.
9. Incompetent British leaders: Roberts, *Indian Mutiny Letters*, pp. 2–15; Hibbert, *The Great Mutiny*, pp. 120–1.
10. Nicholson: 41 Yrs, I, pp. 59–60; Roberts, *Indian Mutiny Letters*, p. 7; Fortescue, Sir J., *A History of the British Army*, 13 vols, 1899–1930, xii, p. 474 and Allen, C., *Soldier Sahibs: the Men who Made the North-West Frontier*, London, 2001, pp. 44–7, 53–6 and 163–7.
11. David, *Indian Mutiny*, pp. 143–4 and Allen, *Soldier Sahibs*, p. 276.
12. Allen, *Soldier Sahibs*, p. 290; 41 Yrs, I, pp. 129–30.
13. Porter, B., *The Lion's Share: a Short History of British Imperialism 1850–1995*, London and New York, 1996, p. 43.
14. Roberts, *Indian Mutiny Letters*, pp. 24–5.
15. Allen, *Soldier Sahibs*, pp. 323–7 and Roberts, *Indian Mutiny Letters*, pp. 58–61.
16. Roberts, *Indian Mutiny Letters*, pp. 59–60; 41 Yrs, I, pp. 258–9.
17. Forbes-Mitchell, W., *The Relief of Lucknow*, London, 1962, originally published 1893, pp. 36–7.
18. Roberts, *Indian Mutiny Letters*, pp. 29 & 120–1: Hope-Grant's despatch in Bobs 5504-64, No. 15, 8 February 1858; Colonel Wemyss Fielden in Kipling, R., *Something of Myself*, London, 1937, pp. 193–4.
19. Jones, Captain O., *Recollections of a Winter Campaign in India 1857–8*, London, 1859.

Chapter 2

1. 41 Yrs, I, pp. 25–6.
2. Jones, *Recollections of a Winter Campaign*, p. 145.
3. Roberts, *Indian Mutiny Letters*, p. 119.
4. Details of courtship, early marriage and C-in-C's words: Lady Roberts's obituary, *The Times*, 22 December 1920, p. 13; 41 Yrs, I, pp. 459–60, 471 & 473–4.
5. Burne, Major General Sir O.T., *Memories*, London, 1907, pp. 48 & 50.
6. 41 Yrs, I, p. 489 & II, pp. 26–7; James, *Field Marshal Lord Roberts*, p. 63.

7. Saksena, *European & Indo-European Poets*, pp. 128–53; from Dalrymple, *Last Mughal*, pp. 291–2 one could easily think his role much more active; Abraham Roberts's biographer, Lieutenant Colonel I. Edwards-Stewart, does not mention the illegitimate children in *A John Company General: the Life of Lt. General Sir Abraham Roberts*, Bognor Regis, 1983. Tony Heathcote kindly pointed out the reference in Dalrymple to me.

8. 41 Yrs, II, pp. 387–8; Gilmour, D., *The Ruling Caste: Imperial Lives in the Victorian Raj*, London, 2006; Spear, *Penguin History of India*, II, pp. 145–55; Fergusson, N., *Empire: How Britain Made the Modern World*, London, 2003, pp. 168–88 & 215–18; Porter, *Lion's Share*, pp. 37–48.

9. Army reforms: Spiers, E.M., *Army and Society 1815–1914*, London, 1980, pp. 135–40; Heathcote, T.A., *The Military in British India*, Manchester, 1995, pp. 119–23; MacMunn, Major G.F., *The Armies of India*, London, 1911, Chapter iv.

10. 41 Yrs, I, p. 454; Bobs 225, 'Some turning points'; Robson, B., 'Roberts', *ODNB*.

11. James, *Lord Roberts*, p. 61.

12. Elsmie, *Stewart*, pp. 15 & 186; 41 Yrs, II, pp. 29–30.

13. Robson, B. (ed.), *Roberts in India: The Military Papers of Field Marshal Lord Roberts 1876–1893*, Stroud, 1993, p. 7, letter of 21 May 1874; Bobs 49, R to Napier, 11 June 1874 and Bobs 49, Napier to R, 21 January 1879; James, *Lord Roberts*, p. 68 mentions a difficult relationship at first; but the letters exchanged with Napier in Bobs 49 speak clearly of their mutual admiration; 41 Yrs, II, p. 71; IOL, Mss Eur. F234,3, vol. III, R to Grant Duff, 11 August 1883.

14. Elsmie, *Stewart*, pp. 186–7.

15. Mayo's assassination: *ibid.*, pp. 191–4.

16. Heathcote, *Afghan Wars*, pp. 88–9.; James, *Roberts*, pp. 77–8; Preston, A., 'Sir Charles MacGregor and the Defence of India, 1857–1887', *The Historical Journal*, XII, I (1969), p. 70; Sykes, *Durand*, pp. 81–6.

Chapter 3

1. Blake, R., *Disraeli*, London, 1966, pp. 760 & 765; E.J. Feuchtwanger, *Democracy and Empire: Britain 1865–1914*, London, 1989, pp. 129–31; Porter, *The Lion's Share*, chapter III.

2. Mary Lutyens, *The Lyttons in India: an Account of Lord Lytton's Viceroyalty 1876–1880*, London, 1979, pp. 96–7 & 155; Gopal, S., *British Policy in India 1858–1905*, Cambridge, 1965, p. 66; Blake, *Disraeli*, p. 656; Washbrook, D., 'Lytton', *ODNB*.

3. Bobs 225 'Some turning points'; Robson, *Roberts in India*, p. 1; *ibid.*, p. 423n1 notes that the paper is not extant; Balfour, Lady B., *The*

History of Lord Lytton's Indian Administration 1876 to 1880, London, 1899, p. 51.

4. Blood, General Sir B., *Fourscore Years and Ten*, London, 1933, pp. 140ff; Cohn, Bernard S., 'Representing Authority in Victorian India', in Eric Hosbawm and Terence Ranger, *The Invention of Tradition*, Cambridge, 1983, pp. 186–7; Roberts, A., *Salisbury: Victorian Titan*, London, 1999, p. 215; Lytton, Robert, 1st Earl, *Personal and Literary Letters*, 2 vols, London, 1906, II, pp. 48–9.

5. Balfour, *Lytton's Indian Administration*, pp. 114 & 189–239; Moon, Sir P., *The British Conquest and Dominion of India*, London, 1989, pp. 841–4.

6. Rait, R.S., *The Life of Field Marshal Sir Frederick Paul Haines*, London, 1911, p. 212.

7. Preston, 'Sir Charles MacGregor and the Defence of India, pp. 70–2; Preston, 'Wolseley, the Khartoum Relief Expedition and the Defence of India', p. 260.

8. Robson, *Roberts in India*, p. 3; 41 Yrs, II, pp. 100–2.

9. 41 Yrs, ii, p. 107.

10. Preston, 'Sir Charles MacGregor', pp. 64–5 & 67. Trousdale deals mainly with the war, trivializes MacGregor's writings and dwells at length on his (and Roberts's) defects of character. 41 Yrs, ii, pp. 103 et seq. for forward school's arguments; p. 105n similar circumstances preceding both 1st and 2nd Afghan Wars, i.e. Russian officers at Kabul.

11. Hanna, I, pp. 183–93; James, *Raj*, pp. 372–3.

12. Balfour, *Lord Lytton's Indian Administration*, pp. 39–40 and 51; NAM, 9011-42-13, No. 18, Spenser Wilkinson papers, Wm Nicholson to Wilkinson, 15 September 1893.

13. MacGregor, II, pp. 108–9.

14. Roberts, P.E., *History of British India under the Company and the Crown*, Oxford, 1977, p. 434.

15. Blake, *Disraeli*, pp. 575 et seq.

16. G.W. Forrest, *The Life of Field Marshal Sir Neville Chamberlain*, Edinburgh and London, 1909, pp. 476–7.

17. Robson (ed.), *Roberts in India*, pp. 47–8; Forrest, *Sir Neville Chamberlain*, pp. 480–2 & 484–5; Cavagnari had hoped to precipitate matters by a coup de main, seizing Ali Masjid by surprise attack. See Beckett, I.F.W., *The Victorians at War*, London, 2003, pp. 113–20.

18. That Lytton's was the chief responsibility is admitted by nearly all authorities. His justification is in IOL L/P & S 20/MEMO5/5, Memorandum by Sir O.T. Burne. MEMO5/1.

19. Blake, *Disraeli*, pp. 662–3.

20. Forrest, *Sir Neville Chamberlain*, p. 485.

21. Roberts, *History of British India*, p. 441; IOL, Mss Eur. C336, Notes by Sir Torick Ameer Ali, p. 15; Northbrook's responsibility: Preston, 'Sir Charles MacGregor', pp. 70–2; Hanna's views, I, pp. 278–9 and *Lord Roberts in War*, pp. 10–11.
22. IOL Mss Eur. D1227/1, f.6, Melgund to mother, 22 January 1879.
23. Bobs 92-18.
24. Lytton, *Personal & Literary Letters*, II, p. 133.
25. Bobs 92-18; Robson, pp. 71–3 & 80.

Chapter 4
1. Lutyens, *Lyttons in India*, p. 140; Hanna, I, pp. 320–53; Elsmie, *Stewart*, p. 214; Robson, p. 69.
2. Heathcote, *Afghan Wars*, pp. 103–4; Anglesey, Marquess of, *A History of the British Cavalry, 1816–1919*, 5 vols, London, 1973–1986, III, p. 159; Sandes, E.W.C., *The Military Engineer in India*, 2 vols, Chatham, 1933–5, I, p. 379; IOL, Mss Eur. F108/101(a), P6/9, 13 March 1879.
3. IOL, L/MIL/5/678 No. 2538 including despatch 5 December 1878 for Roberts's quote; L/MIL/5/679, No.4749, information from Russian sources; Soboleff, Major General L.N., *The Anglo-Afghan Struggle*, translated by Major Gowan, Calcutta, 1885, p. 40; Robson, pp. 18–21 & 66–7; Durand, Sir M., *The Life of Field Marshal Sir George White, V.C.*, 2 vols, London, 1915, p. 162; Gerard, Lieutenant General Sir M.G., *Leaves from the Diary of a Soldier and Sportsman 1865–1885*, London, 1903, pp. 229–30 & 310–11 including 'bullets from Dum-Dum'.
4. Heathcote, *Afghan Wars*, pp. 105–6; Elsmie, *Stewart*, pp. 215–18.
5. Hanna, I, pp. 330–2.
6. *Ibid.*, I, pp. 279 & 336; Heathcote, *Afghan Wars*, p. 104: Robson, p. 80.
7. MacGregor, II, p. 157.
8. Sykes, *Sir Mortimer Durand*, p. 89.
9. The battle: IOL, L/MIL/5/678, No. 2538 incl. Roberts's despatch 5 December 1878; MacGregor, II, pp. 158–68; Hanna, II, pp. 80–5; Robson, pp. 80–6; Heathcote, *The Afghan Wars*, pp. 106–10 with a good illustration; Hanna, *Lord Roberts in War*, pp. 17–19; Roberts's success: C.G. Robertson, *Kurum, Kabul & Kandahar*, Edinburgh, 1881, pp. 41–2; Robson, p. 115n; Rait, *Haines*, p. 254; NAM, Haines papers 8108/9-44, No. 23. For doubts see No. 21.
10. Bobs, 147-2, Colley to Roberts, 8 December 1878.
11. Hanna, II, pp. 97–8 and n1.
12. Bobs 92-18 diary for 1878 for 'I am glad it is all over'; IOL, Mss Eur. C212/2, ff.8–9; 41 Yrs, II, pp. 149–56.
13. Hanna, II, p. 201, n1.

14. *Ibid.*, II, pp. 144 et seq.; Robson, p. 157.
15. MacGregor, II, pp. 178–80; Colquhoun, Major J.A.S., *With the Kurram Field Force 1878–9*, London, 1881, pp. 204–5.; IOL 17/14/35, 'Papers relating to proceedings of Major General Roberts', report of Major Collis, 20 March 1879; IOL, L/P & S/MEMO 2, copy of report of Major General Roberts in the Khost Valley; Hanna, II, pp. 205–29.
16. Hanna, II, pp. 205–29; Robson, pp. 92–4 ; Bobs 160, R. to Major General Martin Dillon, 7 February 1879. Hanna, *Lord Roberts in War*, pp. 22–3, argues that the raid was unnecessary and leaves a slur on his reputation. The last would be true if anyone remembered it; the former is easier seen in retrospect.
17. Robson (ed.), *Roberts in India*, pp. 81–3 & 85–7; IOL L/MIL/17/14/35, 'Return to an Address of ... the Commons, dated 16 June 1879 ... relating to the Proceedings ... in the Khost Valley'.
18. Vaughan, General Sir J.L., *My Service in the Indian Army – and After*, London, 1904, pp. 181–2 & 191. See the hostile assessment by Hanna, II, p. 314n.
19. Hanna, II, pp. 133 et seq.; Heathcote, *Afghan Wars*, p. 112.
20. Blake, *Disraeli*, pp. 666–72.
21. Vaughan, *Service in the Indian Army*, p. 196.
22. Hanna, II, p. 345; Heathcote, *Afghan Wars*, pp. 112–13; Robson, pp. 111–13.
23. Heathcote, *Afghan Wars*, p. 114.
24. Robson, p. 214.

Chapter 5
1. 41 Yrs, II, pp. 177–9; IOL, L/MIL/5/681, No. 7119a, 20 July 1879; NLS, Minto letters, Lady R to Minto, 27 October 1879.
2. Forrest, *Neville Chamberlain*, p. 494; Ensor, R.C.K., *England 1870–1914*, Oxford, 1960 (originally published 1936), p. 63n2.
3. Lutyens, *Lyttons in India*, p. 158.
4. MacGregor, II, pp. 281–7 incl. account of Risaldar-Major Kakshband Khan; Younghusband, Colonel G.J., *The Story of the Guides*, London, 1908, pp. 97–116; IOL, Mss Eur. C212/2, ff. 16 & 17.
5. IOL, Mss Eur. C405, Duke, p. 405; see also IOL/P & S 20/MEMO5/6, report of commission investigating.
6. Heathcote, *Afghan Wars*, pp. 117–18; Lutyens, *Lyttons in India*, p. 159; Hanna, III, p. 42.
7. P. Fredericks, *The Sepoy and the Cossack*, London, 1972, p. 210.
8. Blake, *Disraeli*, p. 674.
9. MacGregor, II, pp. 3–5; Hanna, III, p. 44; Durand, *Sir George White*, I, p. 166.

10. NAM, Gough papers, 8304-32-222, 22 March 1880, italics original; MacGregor, III, pp. 4–5; NLS, Minto papers, Lady Roberts to Melgund, 27 October 1879 & 24 March 1880; Sykes, P., *Sir Mortimer Durand*, London, 1926, p. 89.
11. 41 Yrs, II, pp. 186–7.
12. Robson, *Roberts in India*, pp. 119–22.
13. *Ibid.*, pp. 123–4; Heathcote, *Afghan Wars*, p. 119.
14. Sykes, *Sir Mortimer Durand*, p. 62; Bobs 92-19; IOL, Mss Eur. F108/101(a), P.6/33, 15 September 1879; F108/97(a), 24 November 1879; Durand, *Sir George White*, p. 162.
15. Colquhoun, *With the Kurram Field Force*, pp. 327–8 & 339.
16. IOL, L/P & S/MEMO 3; Soboleff, *Anglo-Afghan Struggle*, pp. 50–1.
17. NAM 7804-16-8 and 9, 18 & 20 September 1879; MacGregor, III, pp. 5–7; Hensman, Howard, *The Afghan War*, London, 1881, p. 5; Fredericks, *Sepoy and Cossack*, p. 211; 'bare bones and sores' is from Sykes, *Durand*, p. 90. See Russian praise: Soboleff, *Anglo-Afghan Struggle*, pp. 55 & 58.
18. Vaughan, *My Service*, p. 212.
19. Hanna, III, pp. 45–6; 'I think all this blackmail' is in Sir C.M. MacGregor, *The Life and Opinions*, edited by Lady MacGregor, 2 vols, Edinburgh, 1888, II, p. 107.
20. IOL, Mss Eur. C405; Duke, J., *Recollections of the Cabul Campaign 1879 and 1880*, London, 1882, p. 113; Robson, *Roberts in India*, p. 125; Hanna, III, p. 56; Trousdale, pp. 91–2.
21. Bobs 92-19; Trousdale, p. 99; Robson, *Roberts in India*, p. 125.
22. Trousdale, pp. 104–5; Robson, pp. 123–6.
23. Robson, *Roberts in India*, pp. 122–4, letters of 12 & 13 September 1879.
24. Sykes, *Sir Mortimer Durand*, p. 95.
25. Robson, *Roberts in India*, pp. 129–133, telegrams of 13 & 21 October 1879.
26. 41 Yrs, II, pp. 202–6.
27. *The Second Afghan War*. Abridged and re-edited in the Intelligence Branch of the QMG's department, Simla by Lieutenant F.G. Cardew, Calcutta, 1897, I, pp. 204–5.
28. IOL, Mss Eur F108/98(a), P3/57, White to brother, 15 November 1879, and F108/1, mss copy, letter of Major Hammond, 3 December 1879 for 'Major White then led'.
29. Soboleff, *Anglo-Afghan Struggle*, p. 58.
30. Battle of Charasia: IOL, L/MIL/5/681, Nos. 7959 & 7961 encl. R's despatches 20 and 22 November 1879; MacGregor, III, pp. 29–33; IOL, Mss Eur. F108/101(a) 6/36a, White to his wife; Hanna, III, pp. 77–9; Robson, pp. 128–9. White was recommended for the VC

thrice, being turned down firstly because he was 'only doing his duty'. See Durand, *Sir George White*, I, pp. 247, 263, 267 & 275.

31. IOL, Mss Eur. F108/101(a), P6/36, letter of 15–17 October 1879; SOAS Library, PP MS 55/31, Durand to sister, No. 19, 26 October 1879.

32. IOL, L/MIL/5/681, No. 7959. Major General Greaves AG to Colonel Johnson, Sec Mil Department, 5 November, enclosing R's despatch of 20 October 1879 and L/MIL/683 no. 12, 513, copy of Roberts's despatch 22 November 1879.

Chapter 6

1. Robertson, *Kurum, Kabul & Kandahar*, p. 100; also photos of J. Burke in Khan, Omar, *From Kashmir to Kabul: the Photographs of John Burke and William Baker 1860–1900*, Ahmedabad, India, 2002.

2. Hensman, *Afghan War*, pp. 51–6, also quoted in MacGregor, III, p. 43; Mss Eur. C403, Duke pp. 160–3; Trousdale, p. 104; IOL/P & S20/MEMO5/6 report of commission; IOL, Mss Eur. F108/101 (a), F6/36, White to wife, 15 October 1879; Sykes, *Sir Mortimer Durand*, p. 98.

3. SOAS Library, Durand Papers MS PP 55/21, diary, 13 October 1879; Sykes, *Sir Mortimer Durand*, pp. 96–7.

4. Mss Eur. C405, p. 188; MacGregor, III, pp. 51–2. Durand and MacGregor are the sources of the cat story, not mentioned by others. Trousdale, p. 106 and SOAS Library, PP MS 55/21, 13 October 1879.

5. IOL, Mss Eur. C212/2 ff.31 and 43. 'A dispensary at Cabul', 18 March 1880; Hensman, *Afghan War*, pp. 298–9 & 302; and MacGregor, III, pp. 73–4.

6. Trousdale, p. 108.

7. Robson, pp. 136–7; Vaughan, *My Service in the Indian Army*, pp. 143 and 212–13.

8. Bobs 82-19.

9. Robson, pp. 138–40.

10. SOAS Library, PP 55/31, no. 19, 25 October 1879 and M21, diary, 18 & 30 October; Robson, *Roberts in India*, pp. 138–43 for MacGregor's report.

11. Allen, *Soldier Sahibs*, pp. 167, 173–5, 286–8, 321, 326 & 337–8.

12. Trousdale, pp. 82–3; SOAS Library PP MS 55/21, diary, 18 October 1879; Robson, *Roberts in India*, pp. 119–22.

13. Trousdale, pp. 111–14 & 149–50; SOAS Library, PP MS 55/31, No. 19, 18 & 25 October 1879: 'Even MacGregor, whose feelings towards the Afghans are strong, is shocked at what goes on, and has got off some

condemned prisoners.'; Soboleff, *Anglo-Afghan Struggle*, pp. 92–3; IOL/P & S 20/MEMO5/6, investigation of committee reporting Kotwal carried out Amir's orders to throw bodies into ditch.

14. Hanna, III, p. 140 citing the view of Hensman; 'Hanging is too good for them': Mss Eur. D1227/1, 2 March 1879; 'cold-blooded murder like this': Mss Eur. C405, Duke, p. 251.

15. SOAS Library, PP MS 55/21, diary, 20 November 1879; Trousdale, pp. 108, 114 & 133; IOL, Mss Eur. F108/98(a), P3/57, 15 November 1879; MacGregor, III, pp. 60–1, 70–3 & Appendix A.

16. Hanna, III, pp. 149–50; F. Harrison, *Martial Law in Kabul*, London, 1880, reprinted from *Fortnightly Review* of 1879; quote from Ripon's diary on p. 95 is from A. Denholm, *Lord Ripon 1827–1909: a Political Biography*, London, 1982, pp. 126–30; Blake, *Disraeli*, p. 700; MacGregor, III, Appendix A; White's comment is in IOL, Mss Eur F108/98(a), P3/64, 13 April 1880.

17. Anglesey, *British Cavalry*, III, p. 227.

Chapter 7

1. SOAS Library, Durand Papers, MS PP 55/31, No. 19, 25 October 1879.

2. IOL, Mss Eur F108/101(a), P/69 & P/40, 16 & 23 November 1879.

3. IOL, L/MIL/5/682, No. 8392 incl R's telegrams; Heathcote, *Afghan Wars*, p. 126; Soboleff, *Anglo-Afghan Struggle*, pp. 201–2; Hanna, II, pp. 158–9; IOL, Mss Eur. C405, Duke, pp. 212–15.

4. IOL, Mss Eur. F108/97(a) & 98(a), P2/56(a) & P3/58, both 2 December 1879.

5. Trousdale, p. 132.

6. IOL, L/MIL/5/683, No. 12518, R's dispatch, 7 March 1880; Trousdale, pp. 101, 122–3 & Note 135; Heathcote, *Afghan Wars*, p. 127; SOAS Library, PP MS 55/21, 19 December 1879; Sykes, *Durand*, pp. 104–5; Hanna, *Roberts in War*, p. 41 argues that had Massy not ordered his guns to fire, a terrible disaster would have ensued. Massy by his own account admitted that the guns came into action without his knowledge or orders; a good example of Hanna's prejudice against Roberts.

7. Bobs 92-19.

8. IOL, Mss Eur. C405, Joshua Duke, p. 262, manuscript note by Roberts in pencil.

9. Robson, *The Road to Kabul*, pp. 158–9.

10. *Ibid.*, pp. 148–59; Hanna, III, pp. 175 et seq.; IOL, Eur MSS C405, Duke, pp. 231–71; IOL, L/MIL/5/682, Nos. 8375, 8376, 8380, 8384, 8385, 8387; Heathcote, *Afghan Wars*, pp. 127–32.

11. Mss Eur. C405, Duke, p. 271, inscription in pencil.
12. SOAS Library, Durand Papers, MS PP 55/21, long entry 19 December 1879. Sykes biography omits. For Roberts's cheerfulness see G. Younghusband, *A Soldier's Memories*, pp. 227–8.
13. IOL, Mss Eur. C405, Duke, p. 280.
14. Rait, *Haines*, pp. 276–7.
15. Gardyne, Lieutenant Colonel C.G. and Gardyne, Lieutenant Colonel A.D.G., *The Life of a Regiment: The History of the Gordon Highlanders from 1816–1898*, London, 1929, pp. 133–5; SOAS Library, PP MS 55/21, Durand diary, 30 December 1879; MacGregor, III, pp. 119–27; IOL, L/MIL/5/683, No. 8392; WO106/63, appendix III; Soboleff, *Anglo-Afghan Struggle*, p. 75; *ibid.*, p. 86 is clearly too low, a figure gleaned from the press.
16. NAM Gough papers, 8304-32-215.
17. Soboleff, *Anglo-Afghan Struggle*, p. 86.
18. Roberts's diary: Bobs 92-19; IOL, L/MIL/5/683, no. 8392.
19. Hensman, *Afghan Wars*, p. 277.
20. *Ibid.*, p. 282.
21. Gardyne and Gardyne, *The Life of a Regiment*, p. 135; Diver, Maud, 'Bobs Bahadur', *The Cornhill Magazine*, vol. xxxviii (January-June 1915), pp. 27–9; IOL Mss Eur F108/101 (a), P6/43.

Chapter 8

1. Gardyne and Gardyne, *The Life of a Regiment*, pp. 135–6; IOL, Mss Eur. F108/101(a), P6/39, 8 February 1880.
2. Massy's removal: IOL, L/MIL/5/681, No. 1959, R's report 20 October 1879; L/MIL/5/683, No. 12513, Adjutant General Greaves to R, 9 February 1880 and Roberts to Greaves, 21 February 1880 enclosing Massy's defence; NAM, Gough papers 8304-32-220, 29 February 1880, italics original; Robson, *Roberts in India*, docs. 111–12, 117–18, 134 & 146; see also MacGregor's views, Trousdale, pp. 122–3 and NAM, Haines papers 8108/9/-40-4, Greaves to Haines, 2 March 1880. That Roberts had prepared the ground with his own letters is undoubted, as Robson shows; that this indicates he was wrong and Massy his rival as Trousdale claims is nonsense.
3. NAM, Haines papers, 8108/9-46-10, 13, 18, Cambridge to Haines, 5 & 26 March, 30 April 1880; Bobs 160, to Major General Martin Dillon, 23 February, 15 May & 9 June 1880; Robson, *Roberts in India*, p. 170; Soboleff, *Anglo-Afghan Struggle*, pp. 60–1: 'We consider it necessary to state that ... the English cavalry did not show any aptitude for good work.'

4. MacGregor, III, appendix A; SOAS Library, Durand PP MS 55/21, 10 January 1880; Robson, *Roberts in India*, p. 432, n9 & n10.
5. Blake, *Disraeli*, pp. 597–607, 670–5, 697–8 & 711–2; Feuchtwanger, *Democracy and Empire*, pp. 108–11; Roberts, *History of British India*, p. 447; Denholm, Anthony, *Lord Ripon 1827–1909: A Political Biography*, London, 1982, pp. 128–9.
6. NAM, Gough papers 8304-32-221, 5 March 1880; Elsmie, *Stewart*, p. 296; Heathcote, *Afghan Wars*, pp. 122–3 offers defence.
7. Robson, pp. 177–8; Robson, *Roberts in India*, p. 182.
8. MacGregor, IV, pp. 96–7; Robson, pp. 180–7; Heathcote, *Afghan Wars*, pp. 132–7. 'A ram caught in a thicket': Lytton, *Personal and Literary Letters*, ii, p. 202.
9. Heathcote, *Afghan Wars*, pp. 137–41; Elsmie, *Stewart*, pp. 331–3; IOL, L/MIL/5/683, No. 11,834 enclosing Stewart's dispatch, 5 May 1880; IOL/P& S20/MEMO 3.
10. Maxwell, L., *My God! Maiwand*, London, 1979, pp. 56–7.
11. Elsmie, *Stewart*, pp. 321, 324 & 344.
12. Roberts, *History of British India*, p. 447.
13. IOL, Mss Eur. 108/98(b), P3/64, 13 April 1880; Robson, *Roberts in India*, p. 186; Elsmie, *Stewart*, p. 350, quoting letter to wife, 27 May 1880. The argument that Stewart's march was forgotten, Roberts's remembered, is specious. It got Stewart the Commander-in-Chiefship and was still argued in *The Times* nearly half a century later. *The Times*, 19 January 1929, p. 8, letter from 'J.E.D'.
14. James, *Lord Roberts*, pp. 146–7; Heathcote, *Afghan Wars*, p. 144; Elsmie, *Stewart*, p. 360.
15. NLS, Melgund-Minto papers, Lady R to M, 24 March, 19 May & 24 August 1880; Trousdale, p. 204: 'Did about as good a stroke of business as I have done for some time. Wrote a draft letter to Norman bucking up Bobs.' Lady R's brother-in-law J.D. Sherston wrote to *The Times* in April 1880 on Roberts's behalf.
16. Balfour, *Lord Lytton's Indian Administration*; Lutyens, *Lyttons in India*; Gopal, *British Policy in India*, pp. 115–27; Moon, *British Conquest and Dominion of India*, pp. 836–62; D. Washbrook, 'Lytton', *ODNB*. Charles Allen pointed out to me that recent economic historians have condemned Lytton's policies. He is the particular villain of Mike Davis's *Late Victorian Holocausts: El Nino Famines and the Making of the Third World*, London, 2001.
17. Wolf, *Ripon*, II, p. 20; see also, Denholm, *Lord Ripon*.
18. Balfour, *Lord Lytton's Indian Administration*, pp. 409 et seq.; Wolf, *Ripon*, II, pp. 21–4; Roberts, *History of British India*, pp. 446–9.
19. Robson, pp. 204–11; Elsmie, *Stewart*, pp. 365–6.

Chapter 9

1. Rait, *Haines*, p. 297n1.
2. Soboleff, *Anglo-Afghan Struggle*, pp. 264–8.
3. BL, Add Mss 43,574, Ripon papers, ff.141 et seq.; Wolf, *Ripon*, ii, pp. 28–9; Maxwell, *My God! Maiwand*, pp. 85–9 & 92–3.
4. MacGregor, V, pp. 331–5; Maxwell, *My God! Maiwand*; Heathcote, *Afghan Wars*; Robson, 'Maiwand, 27 July 1880,' *JSAHR*, vol. 51 (1973), pp. 194–221 and *ibid.*, 'The Kandahar Letters of the Rev. A. Cane,' *JSAHR*, LXIX (1991), p. 206; *The Times*, 23 March 1883, G.W. Forrest's account drawn from narratives of survivors; Anglesey, *British Cavalry*, III, pp. 252–63, for casualties.
5. IOL, Eus Mss F108/113, PP1/8, Lady Brooke to Mrs White, 13 August 1880.
6. *Kandahar Correspondence*, I. pp. 68, 74–74A, 223, Nos 197, 203 & 223; Elsmie, *Stewart*, pp. 375–6; Robson, pp. 210–11; Rait, *Haines*, pp. 306–9; Haines papers 8108/9-30, Nos 2 & 3, both Haines to Ripon, 1 August 1880; MacGregor in his diary records Stewart looking at a Roberts memorandum on 3 August which he did not like; by then the decision had been made. Trousdale, p. 220. White's subsequent summary in IOL, Mss Eur. 108/2 dated Simla, 18 October 1880 is pertinent: 'Roberts, a commander well known for his dash and administrative ability as a soldier, had volunteered to lead ten thousand men across Afghanistan from Kabul to Kandahar. This plan, warmly supported by the bolder spirits, awed the timid and shocked the men of rule. That General Roberts should be launched alone to struggle unsupported and without a base against the combinations which were sure to be organised against him seemed to the latter to be to send him to his destruction. There were others, however, who judged the emergency great enough, and the chances of success good enough, to set aside the usually accepted principles of theoretical warfare. Lord Ripon took upon himself the responsibility for Roberts's march.'
7. Hensman, *Afghan War*, p. 444; NAM Badcock 2005-12-9-2 (1880 diary).
8. Robson, pp. 211–12; IOL, Mss Eur. F108/98(a), P3/75, 19 October 1880; Elsmie, *Stewart*, pp. 375–7 & 385–7.
9. *Kandahar Correspondence*, I, p. 124.
10. *Ibid.*, I, p. 135.
11. IOL, Mss Eur. 1227/2, 9 August 1880.
12. *Kandahar Correspondence*, I, pp. 114, 125 & especially Chapman's account, pp. 228a-230.

13. IOL, Mss Eur. C212/2, f. 62; Ashe, Major W., *Personal Records of the Kandahar Campaign*, London, 1881, pp. 127–9 gives an imaginative account, demolished by Lepel Griffin's letter to *The Times*, 21 October 1881, p. 6 as 'melodramatic trash, only fit for a South London music-hall'.
14. Travers, 'Kabul to Kandahar 1880', *JSAHR*, vol. 59 (1981), p. 216.
15. IOL, Mss Eur. D625/14, 'Abstract', 28 August 1880; NAM Warre papers, 8112/54-625 & 713, 3 September & 4 August 1880.

Chapter 10

1. Kandahar Correspondence: Appendix, item No. 2, pp. 2–3.
2. A. Forbes, *Afghan Wars 1839–1842 & 1878–1880*, London, 1892, pp. 307–9; Diver, M., *Kabul to Kandahar*, London, 1935, pp. 171–2.
3. Robertson, *Kurum, Kabul and Kandahar*, pp. 199–201.
4. Vaughan, *My Service in the Indian Army*, p. 230; Hensman, *Afghan War*, pp. 476 & 485.
5. Chapman, Lieutenant Colonel E.F., 'The March from Kabul to Kandahar in August, and the Battle of the 1st September 1880,' *Journal of the Royal United Services Institute*, xxv (1882), pp. 282–315; NAM, Badcock 2005-12-9-2, 1880 diary, entries 3 August–1 September 1880, not all legible.
6. *Kandahar Correspondence*, appendix, pp. 7–11, No. 5; Roberts quote: James, *Lord Roberts*, p. 159.
7. Robson, 'Kandahar Letters of Rev Cane', pp. 216–18; Maxwell, *My God! Maiwand*, pp. 210–15.
8. Kandahar Correspondence: appendix, pp. 7–11, no. 5.
9. Trousdale, p. 237 n235; 41 Yrs, II, p. 354; *Kandahar Correspondence*, pp. 182–3 & 198a; James, *Field Marshal Lord Roberts*, pp. 159 & 160.
10. Vaughan, *My Service in the Indian Army*, p. 236; Travers, E., 'Kabul to Kandahar, 1880: Extracts from the diary of Lieutenant E.A. Travers, 2nd PWO Goorkhas', *JSAHR*, vol. 60 (1982), p. 39; IOL, Mss Eur F108/101(c) & (d), P6/73, 6 September 1880; Hensman, *Afghan War*, p. 504; Robson, pp. 256–7; 41 Yrs, ii, p. 356; Robson, 'Kandahar Letters of Reverend A. Cane', p. 217; Gerard, *Leaves from the Diary*, p. 302.
11. MacGregor, VI, p. 29n; Cadell, Sir P., *The Bombay Army*, London, 1938, p. 244; Robson, pp. 251–3; Beckett, *The Victorians at War*, p. 50; WO106/63, Appendix XII.
12. NAM, Haines 8108/9-30, No. 11; Hensman, *Afghan War*, p. 522; Robertson, *Kuram, Kabul and Kandahar*, pp. 209–11; 'Only a third had rifles': MacGregor, V, p. 43.
13. Hanna, III, pp. 504 & 515; Hanna, *Lord Roberts in War*, p. 55.

14. *Kandahar Correspondence*, I, pp. 210 et seq., and especially No. 394, pp. 212–212a; MacGregor, V, pp. 135–41; Chapman, 'Kabul to Kandahar'; Vaughan, *My Service in the Indian Army*, pp. 286–93; Robson, pp. 259–60; IOL, Mss Eur. F108/101(b) & (c), P6/73, 6 September 1880, White to his wife; Gerard, *Leaves from the Diary*, pp. 304–6; Robertson, *Kurum, Kabul and Kandahar*, p. 215.
15. Hensman, *Afghan War*, p. 521.
16. Travers, 'Kabul to Kandahar', *JSAHR*, 60 (1980), p. 38; Vaughan, *My Service in the Indian Army*, p. 240.
17. Vaughan, *My Service in the Indian Army*, p. 240.
18. *Kandahar Correspondence*, I, p. 220b, No. 613a.
19. Wolf, *Ripon*, II, pp. 32–3; *Kandahar Correspondence*, I, p. 208; Elsmie, *Stewart*, p. 388; Trousdale, pp. 239–40; James, *Lord Roberts*, p. 160.
20. 'One dissenting voice' ignores the snide comments of Wolseyites, Brigadier Baker Russell telling Wolseley it was 'a most ill managed scramble.' This is refuted by of all people the critical Hanna, see *Lord Roberts in War*, p. 55, 'the battle of Kandahar was the battle of a good tactician ... General Roberts kept his troops well in hand, every division, brigade and regiment mutually supporting each other.'
21. Trousdale, pp. 63, 125, 129, 154, 159, 217, 221, 233, 236–7 & 239–40; on trying three columns, Travers, 'Kabul to Kandahar', p. 223. MacGregor agrees that three columns was a muddle, but blames MacPherson. His views on Roberts's executions at Kabul stand up much better than those on his leadership.
22. *Kandahar Correspondence*, appendix, pp. 9–10, No. 5.
23. Bobs 5504 item No. 38, results of a medical board of officers, Kandahar, 8 September 1880. 'Possible duodenal ulcer': *ibid.*, item Nos 39 and 40, orders from Adjutant General.
24. NLS, Melgund-Minto papers, 19 September 1880.
25. Hanna, III, p. 564 ; Robson, p. 277 and appendix 6 on p. 297 for the estimate of 1,850 dead in battle. Hanna, III, p. 564 thinks a figure of about 50,000 for overall losses on both sides not exaggerated.
26. Trousdale, p. 144.
27. Various newspapers in Bobs 139, vol. 1.
28. Vaughan, *My Service in the Indian Army*, pp. 224 & 229.
29. Bobs 139, vol. 8, *The Manchester Guardian*, 17 June 1893; Hanna, II, p. 291; Farwell, B., *Seekers of Glory: Eminent Victorian Soldiers*, New York, 1986, p. 174.

Chapter 11

1. *Kandahar Correspondence*, I, p. 356, Sir G. White's memo No. 915. Also in Mss Eur F108/2, typescript memo, 18 September 1880.

2. IOL, L/MIL/5/684, No.14, 429.
3. Bobs 5504, item No. 38, 8 September 1880.
4. NAM, Haines papers 8108-9-46-37, 23 September 1880.
5. Hibbert, C., *Queen Victoria in her Letters & Journals*, London, 1984, p. 265.
6. James, *Lord Roberts*, pp. 175–6.
7. *Ibid.*, p. 173; IOL, Mss Eur F243, 3, vol. III, 25 December 1882.
8. Durand, *White*, I, preface; Sykes, *Durand*, preface, pp. 11–12, 336, 341–2; Durand stood for Parliament in 1906 favouring Roberts's national service; NAM 1969-03-8-40 photograph, for which I am grateful to Dr A. Massey and P. Dodd; MacGregor, III, pp. 60–70 & 73; B. Robson, 'The Strange Case of the Missing Official History', *Soldiers of the Queen*, 76 (March 1994), pp. 3–6; NAM, Gough papers 8304-32-221, 5 March 1880; see also Younghusband, *Story of the Guides*, pp. 115–16.
9. Spiers, E., *The Late Victorian Army 1868–1902*, Manchester, 1992, pp. 2–24; Barnett, Corelli, *Britain and Her Army 1509–1974*, London, 1974, pp. 304–10. Sir J. Fortescue's classic *History of the British Army* ends with a brief nod at Cardwell.
10. James, *Lord Roberts*, pp. 170–1; NAM, Haines papers 8108/9-47-7, 18 February 1881.
11. Churchill College, Cambridge, Amery papers, AMEL2/5/2, Gen Beckett to Amery, 30 March 1903.
12. Hamilton, Ian, *Listening for the Drums*, London, 1944; Strachan, *Politics of the British Army*, pp. 95–6; Beckett, I.F.W., 'Wolseley and the Ring,' *Soldiers of the Queen* 69 (June 1992), pp. 14–25; 'musical chairs': Preston, 'Wolseley, the Khartoum Relief Expedition and the Defence of India', p. 272.
13. Carrington, C., *Rudyard Kipling*, London, 1955, pp. 82–3.
14. MacGregor's death: *Life & Opinions*, II, p. 397.
15. IOL, Mss Eur F108/101(i), P6/312, 30 October 1899 & 101(e), P6/180, 8 January 1887.
16. NAM, Gough papers, 8304-32-350 to 357; Hanna, I, preface & III, pp. 550–8; Hanna, *Lord Roberts in War*.
17. Bobs 139, vol. 10 for reviews of 41Yrs; for Rawlinson and Pole-Carew letters, *ibid.* 61/6 & 59/23; W. Churchill's mother: Churchill, Randolph, *Winston Churchill: Companion Volume I*, Part 2, 1896–1900, London, 1967, p. 744.
18. Elsmie, *Stewart*, pp. 406–23.
19. *Ibid.*, p. 411.
20. Robson, *Roberts in India*, p. 325.
21. *Ibid.*, pp. 232, 317 & 324–5.

22. *The Times*, 27 March 1900, p. 9. Also Chapman, Lieutenant Colonel E.F., 'Two years under Field Marshal Sir Donald Stewart in Afghanistan 1878–80', originally published in *Blackwoods Magazine*, Edinburgh, 1902, pp. 255–63.

23. Much of the latter part of this chapter is covered in my article in Beckett, I.F.W., *The Victorians at War: New Perspectives* (Special Publication of the Society for Army Historical Research, No. 16, 2007), pp. 59–74; letter from Lieutenant General G. Ellison to *The Times*, 3 October 1932, p. 10, and Ellison, 'Lord Roberts and the General Staff,' *The Nineteenth Century and After* (December, 1932), pp. 722–32.

24. Brett, M.V. (ed.), *Journal and Letters of Reginald Viscount Esher*, 4 vols, London, 1934–8), I, p. 432.

25. d'Ombrain, N., *War Machinery and High Policy: Defence administration in peacetime Britain 1902–1914*, Oxford, 1975, pp. 141 et seq.

26. IOL, Mss Eur. D951/3, f.223 Lady R to Sir O.T. Burne.

27. *The Times*, 24 December 1907, p. 6.

28. Roberts's daughter's account, Bobs 205; Sir John French's words, *The Illustrated War News*, Part 15, 18 November 1914; Rawlinson, Major General Sir F. Maurice, *The Life of General Lord Rawlinson of Trent*, London, 1928, p. 116; Scottish Rifles: Imperial War Museum, the 1912–1922 Memoirs of Captain M.D. Kennedy.

29. Spear, *Oxford History of India*, p. 256; Sykes, *Durand*, pp. 218–23; Robson, pp. 277–8.

Select Bibliography

Manuscript and Other Sources

British Library: India Office Library
Mss Eur. A208, Roberts to 'Lady Dorothy'.
Mss Eur. A164, two letters from Roberts to Sir Donald Stewart.
Mss Eur. C212, three albums of newspaper cuttings 2nd Afghan War.
Mss Eur. C262, journal of Hugh Bixby Luard.
Mss Eur. C336/10, notes by Sir Torick Ameer Ali on Roberts, Lockwood Kipling and the 2nd Afghan War.
Mss Eur. C405, 'Recollections of the Cabul Campaign, 1879 and 1880' by Colonel Joshua Duke (1847–1920), Indian Medical Service 1868–1902, 1914–1917; privately printed version 1882, annotated by Field Marshal Sir Frederick Sleigh, 1st Earl Roberts of Kandahar, then Commander-in-Chief, Madras Army.
Mss Eur. D567, 'The Afghan War 1879–1880', papers of Henry Durand Baker.
Mss Eur. D625, Colonel Sir William Lockyer Mereweather.
Mss Eur. D1227, typescripts of Lord Minto's letters and journals from the 2nd Afghan War.
Mss Eur. F108, the papers of Field Marshal Sir George White.
Mss Eur. F206/312, Macnabb papers.
Mss Eur. F234/10, letters from Viscount Wolseley, Earl Roberts, Marquess of Lansdowne to Sir M. Grant Duff
Mss Eur. F234/99, confidential papers, Madras 1881–6.
IOR/L/L/2, Lady Roberts's home estate, Murree, Rawalpindi: deeds granting estate to government of India for hospitals.
L/MIL/17/5/1613, Short Report on the Important Questions dealt with during the tenure of Command of the Army in India by General Lord Roberts 1885–1893, Simla, 1893.

L/MIL/5/678-688, military correspondence, 2nd Afghan War.
L/MIL/17/14/35, 'Papers relating to Major General Roberts in the Khost Valley'.
L/P & S20/MEMO2, MEMO3 and MEMO5. 'Papers relative to Afghanistan'.

British Library: Additional Manuscripts
Add Mss 43,607, 43,608 and 43,574, Ripon papers: items relating to the 2nd Afghan War.

National Army Museum
NAM 2005-12 Badcock papers.
NAM 7804-76 Baker papers.
NAM 8704-35 Ellison papers.
NAM 8304-32 Charles Gough papers.
NAM 8108-9 Haines papers.
NAM 5504 & 7101-23 Roberts papers.
NAM 8112-54 Warre papers.

National Archives (formerly the Public Record Office)
WO106/163, The Campaign in Afghanistan 1879–80.
WO106/167, Badcock's report on supplies at Kabul and on Kandahar march 1879–80.
WO 138/53, Field Marshal Lord Roberts's service record.
WO158/1, Lord Roberts's death and funeral.

National Library of Scotland
Minto papers, letters from Lord and Lady Roberts.

Library of the School of Oriental and African Studies (SOAS)
PP SS 55, papers of Sir Henry Mortimer Durand.

Primary Printed Sources, Contemporary Accounts and Works Containing Documents
Ashe, Major Waller (ed.), *Personal Records of the Kandahar Campaign, by Officers Engaged therein.* London, 1881. (But see letter to *The Times* by Lepel Griffin, 21 October 1881, p. 6.)
Barrow, General Sir George de S., *The Fire of Life*, London, 1942.
Birdwood, Field Marshal Lord, *Khaki and Gown* London and Melborne, 1941.
Blood, General Sir Bindon, *Four Score Years and Ten*, London, 1933.

Brett, Maurice V. (ed.), *Journal and Letters of Reginald Viscount Esher*, 4 vols, London, 1934–8.

Burne, Major General Sir Owen Tudor, GCIE KCSI, *Memories*, London, 1907.

Candler, Edmund, *The Sepoy*, London, 1919.

Cardew, Lieutenant F.G., *The Second Afghan War*, abridged and re-edited in the Intelligence Branch of the QMG's Department, Simla by Lieutenant F.G. Cardew, 2 vols, Calcutta, 1897.

Chapman, Lieutenant Colonel E.F., 'The March from Kabul to Kandahar in August, and the Battle of the 1st September, 1880', *Journal of the Royal United Services Institute*, vol. xxv (1882), pp. 282–315.

——, 'Two years under Field Marshal Sir Donald Stewart in Afghanistan 1878–80,' original publication in *Blackwoods Magazine*, Edinburgh, 1902, pp. 255–63.

Colquhoun, Major J.A.S, *With the Kurram Field Force 1878–79*, London, 1881.

Duke, Joshua, *Recollections of the Kabul Campaign, 1879 & 1880*, London, 1883. (Roberts's own copy with inscription by author, 1 June 1883, and 'Presented to Joint Services Staff College by The Countess Roberts of Kandahar, Pretoria and Waterford'.)

Durand, Sir Mortimer, *The Life of Field Marshal Sir George White, V.C.*, 2 vols, Edinburgh and London, 1915.

Elsmie, G.R., *Field Marshal Sir Donald Stewart: An Account of his Life, Mainly in his own Words*, London, 1903.

Gerard, Lieutenant General Sir Montagu Gilbert, *Leaves from the Diary of a Soldier and Sportsman*, London, 1903.

Hamilton, Ian, *Listening for the Drums*, London, 1944.

——, *The Commander*, edited by Major Anthony Farrar-Hockley, London, 1957.

——, *A Staff Officer's Scrapbook*, London, 1912.

Harrison, Frederic, *Martial Law in Kabul*. Reprinted from the *Fortnightly Review*, with additions, London, 1880 (originally December 1879).

Hensman, Howard, *The Afghan War*, London, 1881.

Jones, Captain Oliver, RN, *Recollections of a Winter Campaign in India in 1857–8*, London, 1859.

Kandahar Correspondence: Sirdar Ayub Khan's Invasion of Southern Afghanistan, Defeat of General Burrows' Brigade, and military operations in consequence, 2 vols and Appendix, Simla and Calcutta, 1880–1.

Kipling, Rudyard, *Something of Myself*, London, 1937.

Lawrence, Walter, *The India We Served*, London, 1928.

Lytton, Robert, 1st Earl, *Personal and Literary Letters*, edited by Lady Betty Balfour, 2 vols, London, 1906.

MacGregor, Major General Sir C.M., *The Second Afghan War: Compiled and Collated by and under the orders of ... MacGregor, QMG in India,* 5 parts, Simla and Calcutta, 1885–6.

MacGregor, Sir Charles Metcalfe, *The Life and Opinions of Sir C.M. MacGregor,* edited by Lady MacGregor, 2 vols, Edinburgh, 1888.

Rait, Robert S., *The Life of Field Marshal Sir Frederick Paul Haines,* London, 1911.

Roberts, Field Marshal Lord, *Forty-one Years in India: from Subaltern to Commander-in-Chief,* 2 vols, London, 1897.

Roberts, Fred., *Letters written during the Indian Mutiny by Fred. Roberts. Afterwards Field Marshal Earl Roberts,* with a preface by his daughter Countess Roberts, London, 1924.

Robertson, Charles Grey, *Kurum, Kabul & Kandahar: Being a brief record of Impressions in three Campaigns under General Roberts,* Edinburgh, 1881.

Robson, Brian (ed.), 'The Kandahar Letters of the Reverend Alfred Cane,' JSAHR, vol. LXIX (1991), pp. 146–60, 206–20.

——, ed., *Roberts in India: The Military Papers of Field Marshal Lord Roberts 1876–1893,* Army Records Society, Stroud, Glos., 1993.

Soboleff, Major General A.N., *The Anglo-Afghan Struggle,* translated and condensed from the Russian by Major W.E. Cowan, Calcutta, 1885.

Spenser Wilkinson, Henry, *Thirty-Five Years 1874–1909,* London, 1933.

Travers, Eaton, 'Kabul to Kandahar, 1880: Extracts from the diary of Lieutenant E.A. Travers, 2nd PWO Goorkhas', edited by Major General J.LO. Chapple and Colonel D.R. Wood, *JSAHR,* vol. 59 (1981), pp. 207–28; vol. 60 (1982), pp. 35–43.

Trousdale, William, *War in Afghanistan 1879–80: The Personal Diary of Major General Sir Charles Metcalfe MacGregor,* Detroit, 1985.

Vaughan, General Sir J. Luther, *My Service in the Indian Army – And After,* London, 1904.

Younghusband, Major General Sir George, *A Soldier's Memories in Peace and War,* London, 1917.

Secondary Sources

Adams, R.J.Q., 'Field Marshal Earl Roberts: Army and Empire,' in J.A. Thompson and Meija, Arthur, *Edwardian Conservatism: Five Studies in Adaptation,* London, 1988.

Allen, Charles, *Soldier Sahibs: The Men Who Made the North-West Frontier,* London, 2001.

Anglesey, Marquess of, *A History of the British Cavalry, 1816–1919,* 5 vols, London, 1973–1986.

Anon., 'Field Marshal Earl Roberts', *Journal of the Royal Artillery*, vol. clii (1915–1916), pp. 1–12.

Balfour, Lady Betty, *The History of Lord Lytton's Indian Administration, 1876 to 1880*. London, 1899.

Ballhatchet, Kenneth, *Race, Sex and Class under the Raj: Imperial Attitudes and Policies and their Critics, 1793–1905*, London, 1980.

Barnett, Corelli, *Britain and Her Army 1509–1970*, London, 1974.

Bayley, William J., 'The Roberts Family of Waterford,' *Journal of the Waterford and South-East of Ireland Archaeological Society*, vol. 2 (1895), pp. 98–103.

Beckett, Ian F.W., 'Women and Patronage in the Late Victorian Army,' *History*, vol. 85 (2000), pp. 463–80.

——, 'Wolseley and the Ring,' *Soldiers of the Queen: The Journal of the Victorian Military Society*, issue No. 69 (June 1992), pp. 14–25.

——, *The Victorians at War*, London, 2003.

Blake, Robert, *Disraeli*, London, 1966.

Butler, Sir William, *The Life of Sir George Pomeroy-Colley*, London, 1899.

Cadell, Sir Patrick, *The Bombay Army*, London, 1938.

Cannadine, David, *Ornamentalism: How the British Saw their Empire*, London, 2001.

Carrington, Charles, *Rudyard Kipling*, London, 1955.

Chandler, David (ed.), *The Oxford Illustrated History of the British Army*, London and Oxford, 1994.

Cohen, Stephen P., *The Indian Army: its contribution to the Development of a Nation*, Delhi, 1990.

Cohn, Bernard S., 'Representing Authority in Victorian India', in Eric Hosbawm and Terence Ranger, *The Invention of Tradition*, Cambridge, 1983.

Dalrymple, William, *The Last Mughal: the Fall of a Dynasty, Delhi, 1857*, London, 2006.

David, Saul, *The Indian Mutiny 1857*, London, 2002.

Denholm, Anthony, *Lord Ripon 1827–1909: A Political Biography*, London, 1982.

Dictionary of National Biography, Oxford University Press, 1975 (and various dates previous).

Diver, Maud, 'Bobs Bahadur', *The Cornhill Magazine*, vol. xxxviii (Jan–June 1915), pp. 25–37.

——, *Kabul to Kandahar*, London, 1935.

Edwards-Stewart, Lieutenant Colonel Ivor, *A John Company General: the Life of Lt. General Sir Abraham Roberts*, Bognor Regis, 1983.

Ensor, R.C.K., *England 1870–1914*, Oxford, 1960 (original publication 1936).

Farwell, Byron, *Seekers of Glory: Eminent Victorian Soldiers*, Harmonds-worth and New York, 1986.

——, *Queen Victoria's Little Wars*, London, 1972.

Ferguson, Niall, *Empire: How Britain made the Modern World*, London, 2003.

Feuchtwanger, E.J., *Democracy and Empire: Britain 1865–1914*, London, 1989.

Forbes, Archibald, *The Afghan Wars 1839–1842 and 1878–1880*, London, 1892.

Forrest, G.W., *The Life of Field Marshal Sir Neville Chamberlain*, Edinburgh and London, 1909.

Fortescue, Sir John, *A History of the British Army*, 13 vols, London, 1899–1930.

Fredericks, Pierce, *The Sepoy and the Cossack*, London, 1972.

Gardyne, Lieutenant Colonel C.G. and Gardyne, Lieutenant Colonel A.D.G., *The Life of a Regiment: The History of the Gordon Highlanders*, vols 2 & 3, London, 1929 & 1939.

Gilmour, David, *The Ruling Caste: Imperial Lives in the Victorian Raj*, London, 2006.

Gopal, S., *British Policy in India 1858–1905*, Cambridge, 1965.

Guy, Alan H. and Boyden, Peter B., *Soldiers of the Raj: the Indian Army 1600–1947*, London, 1997.

Hanna, Colonel H.B., *The Second Afghan War 1878-79-80: Its Conduct and its Consequences*, 3 vols, London, 1899–1910.

——, *Lord Roberts in War*, London, 1895.

Hannah, W.H., *Bobs: Kipling's General: The Life of Field Marshal Earl Roberts of Kandahar, V.C.*, London, 1972.

Heathcote, T.A., *The Afghan Wars 1839–1919*, London, 1980.

——, *The Military in British India: The development of British land forces in South Asia, 1600–1947*, Manchester and New York, 1995.

Hibbert, Christopher, *The Great Mutiny: India 1857*, London, 1978.

Hopkirk, Peter, *The Great Game: on Secret Service in High Asia*, London, 1990.

Hyam, Ronald, *Empire and Sexuality: the British Experience*, Manchester, 1991.

James, David, *Field Marshal Lord Roberts*, London, 1954.

James, Lawrence, *Raj: The Making and Unmaking of British India*, London, 1998.

Johnson, R.A., ' "Russians at the Gates of India?" Planning the Defence of India, 1885–1900,' *The Journal of Military History*, XLVII (July 2003), pp. 697–744.

Kakar, Hasan Kawum, *Government and Society in Afghanistan: the Reign of Amir Abd al-Rahman Khan*, Austin, Texas and London, 1979.

Keegan, Sir John, 'Better at fighting: how the "martial races" of the Raj still monopolize service in the Indian Army,' *Times Literary Supplement*, 24 September, 1995.

Khan, Omar, *From Kashmir to Kabul: the Photographs of John Burke and William Baker 1860–1900*, Ahmedabad, India, 2002.

Lutyens, Mary, *The Lyttons in India: an Account of Lord Lytton's Viceroyalty 1876–1880*, London, 1979.

MacMunn, Major G.F., *The Armies of India. With a foreword by Field Marshal Earl Roberts*, London, 1911.

Maxwell, Leigh, *My God! Maiwand*, London, 1979.

Menezes, Lieutenant General S.L., *Fidelity and Honour: The Indian Army from the Seventeenth to the Twenty-First Century*, New Delhi, 1993.

Meyer, Karl and Brysac, Shareen, *Tournament of Shadows: The Great Game and the Race for Empire in Asia*, Washington DC, 1999.

Moon, Sir Penderel, *The British Conquest and Dominion of India*, London, 1989.

Moore, Julian, 'Kipling and Lord Roberts', posted on the Internet by the Kipling Society, 11 April, 2006.

Moorehouse, Geoffrey, *India Britannica*, London, 1983.

Moreman, T.R., *The Army in India and the Development of Frontier Warfare, 1849–1947*, London, 1998.

Omissi, David, *The Sepoy and the Raj: the Indian Army 1860–1940*, London, 1994.

Porter, Bernard, *The Lion's Share: a Short History of British Imperialism 1850–1995*, 3rd edition, London, 1996.

Preston, Adrian, 'Wolseley, the Khartoum Relief Expedition and the Defence of India, 1885–1900', *Journal of Imperial and Commonwealth History*, VI (1978), pp. 254–80.

——, 'Sir Charles MacGregor and the Defence of India, 1857–1887', *The Historical Journal*, XII, I (1969), pp. 58–77.

Roberts, Andrew, *Salisbury, Victorian Titan*, London, 1999.

Roberts, P.E., *History of British India under the Company and the Crown*, Oxford, 1977 (first published 1921).

Robson, Brian, *The Road to Kabul: The Second Afghan War 1878–1881*, London, 1986.

——, 'Maiwand, 27th July 1880', *JSAHR*, LI (1973), pp. 194–221.

——, 'The Eden Commission and the Reform of the Indian Army – 1879–1895,' *JSAHR*, LX (1982), pp. 4–13.

——, 'The Strange Case of the Missing Official History', *Soldiers of the Queen*, vol. 76 (March 1994), pp. 3–6.

Saksena, Ram Babu, *European & Indo-European Poets of Urdu & Persian*, Lucknow, 1941.

Sandes, Lieutenant Colonel E.W.C., *The Military Engineer in India*, 2 vols, The Institution of Royal Engineers, Chatham, 1933–5.

Spear, Percival, *The Oxford History of Modern India 1740–1947*, Oxford, 1965.

Spiers, Edward M., *The Late Victorian Army 1868–1902*, Manchester, 1992.

——, *Army and Society 1815–1914*, London, 1980.

Stearn, Roger T., 'War correspondents and colonial war, c.1870–1900', in John M. Mackenzie, *Popular Imperialism and the Military 1850–1950*, Manchester, 1992.

Strachan, Hew, *The Politics of the British Army*, Oxford and New York, 1997.

Streets, Heather, *Martial Races: the Military, Masculinity and Race in British Imperial Culture 1857–1914*, Manchester, 2004.

——, 'Military Influence in late Victorian and Edwardian Popular Media: the Case of Frederick Roberts', *Journal of Victorian Culture*, VIII, part ii (2003), pp. 231–56.

Sykes, Percy, *Sir Mortimer Durand*, London, 1926.

Watteville, H. de, *Lord Roberts*, London and Glasgow, 1938.

Wolf, Lucien, *The Life of the First Marquess of Ripon*, 2 vols, London, 1921.

Younghusband, Colonel G. J., *The Story of the Guides*, London, 1908.

Index